Self Transformation

Self Transformation

Selected lectures by
Rudolf Steiner

RUDOLF STEINER PRESS

Compiled and edited by Stefan Leber

Rudolf Steiner Press
Hillside House, The Square
Forest Row, RH18 5ES

Published by Rudolf Steiner Press 1995
Reprinted 2003

Originally published in German under the title *Wege der Übung* by
Verlag Freies Geistesleben, Stuttgart, in 1980

A catalogue record for this book is available from the British Library

ISBN 1 85584 019 7

Cover by Andrew Morgan
Typeset by Imprint Publicity Service, Crawley Down, Sussex
Printed and bound in Great Britain by Cromwell Press Limited,
Trowbridge, Wiltshire

Contents

Prefatory Note   1

Introduction *by Stefan Leber*   2

I   The Path of Knowledge and its Stages:
     The Rosicrucian Spiritual Path
     Berlin, 20 October 1906   24

II   Three Paths of Practice
     Stuttgart, 2 September 1906   40

III Oriental and Christian Training
     Stuttgart, 3 September 1906   51

IV   Rosicrucian Training and Mysteries of the Earth
     Stuttgart, 4 September 1906   63

V   The Ancient Yoga Civilization and
     the Michael Civilization of the Future
     Dornach, 30 November 1919   77

VI   The Way of Inner Development
     Berlin, 7 December 1905   95

VII Practical Training in Thinking
     Karlsruhe, 18 January 1909   117

VIII Occult Science and Occult Development
     London, 1 May 1913   136

IX   The Three Decisions on the Path of Imaginative
     Cognition
     Berlin, 2 March 1915   155

X   Beyond the Sphere of Scientific Knowledge
    Vienna, 1 June 1922   177

XI Anthroposophy and Psychology
    Vienna, 2 June 1922   199

XII Sense-free Perception
    Vienna, 26 September 1923   218

    Sources of the lectures   241

    Notes   242

Prefatory Note

The lectures by Rudolf Steiner collected in this volume are all concerned with one common theme – with methods whereby full spiritual consciousness can be developed through a schooling and exercising of soul-life. We are given both the contents of such a practice as well as methods for engaging in it. We are also made aware – and herein lies, perhaps, a justification for this collection alongside the fundamental writings of Rudolf Steiner – how radically the anthroposophical understanding of the path of spiritual development differs from other ancient and traditional teachings.

The lectures chosen for inclusion here were given between 1905 and 1923. Since this selection is based, as indicated, upon the drawing out of a common theme, the actual circumstances obtaining at the time of each lecture and the specific needs that Rudolf Steiner was addressing in them – social and biographical needs or needs of a particular time and place – necessarily lose their prominence. Such circumstances can be gleaned from the Complete Edition of the works of Rudolf Steiner, much of it now translated into English, which is essential for any further and deeper study. References to related works can be found at the end of the volume.

Stefan Leber

Introduction: The Distinctive Historical Position of Anthroposophically Broadened Knowledge

by Stefan Leber

Contemporary paths of study: boundary and expansion

IN ALL ages there have been teachings given directly from expanded human consciousness that decisively influenced and formed the culture of the day, yet remained largely unknown. Such a consciousness reaching beyond the current level of culture and commonly held opinions of the day, is what forms a source of inspiration and guidance for the development of both individuals and whole societies. Whether we are considering a Delphic Oracle, the vision of Old Testament prophets, the clairvoyance of a seeress or the revelations of saints, there is no doubt about their seminal influence upon history nor the inner merit of such testimony. Doubt, criticism, questions and objections can, however, arise when enquiry is made into the way such prophecies arose. The Pythian Oracle, the prophesying of Jeremiah, the Voluspa: each of these appeared in a form that was unique and unrepeatable, and was also – in the final instance – incomprehensible, surrounded by an aura of secrecy, of mystery, of the 'occult'. The sense of such revelations may be obvious, their usefulness to the individual and to the community may be clear and immediate, yet their source remains hidden from all outer investigation, from any explanation of its why and wherefore.

Is this not deeply unsettling? Obviously not so for earlier civilizations; but it is an enigma for a questioning, critical contemporary consciousness that wishes to understand the form as well as the content of such revelation, for this contemporary unease is no longer satisfied by knowing only the content. In believing in its creation, it demands to know a method that as well as providing indisputably useful results also has something to say as to how and under what circumstances these can continue to be achieved. Indeed, our changed consciousness requires a still more rigorous approach: it demands that, in as far as conditions remain constant, the application of a specific method must achieve, on every occasion, the same result. For if a process of achieving knowledge is under my disciplined control the results of this process become available to all, rather than remaining inaccessible to common understanding, as revelations which must simply be believed. Knowledge thus becomes open and explicable, and becomes – while nevertheless still requiring a decided human effort – common property, accessible to everyone.

This need arose at the beginning of our modern age and expressed itself in varying degrees, finding fulfilment in the process of scientific research, which established itself with astonishing speed. Applied to the visible world, it means that:

1. the phenomenon under study is exactly circumscribed and observed; that is, it is subject to 'pure' and therefore controllable conditions;

2. the resulting observations are subjected to appropriately rigorous, controllable mental laws which only – so it is believed – can be provided by the inner consistency and necessity of mathematics.

If this method of research is correctly handled, then the whole – to be succinct, we can say scientific – process remains under the control of human, critical consciousness. Likewise, its results can be 'produced' and a world of new objects and materials can be created at will – and this fact is taken as tangible proof of the correctness of the path being followed.

This method of knowledge has, although it is confined to the world of physical objects, an inestimable advantage: every step of its process is easily surveyed, is certain and measurable – nothing is left unaccounted for. Therefore it marches on triumphantly, diffusing itself without hindrance through

universities and schools, reaching even as far as the nursery
and early childhood. It becomes part of our common culture
and provides a basis for prosperity and economic growth,
which are the footprints left by a dissemination of knowledge
and understanding on a scale hitherto unknown.

At the same time, though, the certainty of this method has
its grave limitations. If we wish to be truthful, we must
recognize how incapable it is of giving any insight into the
most basic questions of human existence. One cannot, for
instance, explain how consciousness arises if one simply
observes physiological processes. Degrees and stages of consciousness are an inner soul-experience of every human
being, about which science has little to say if it respects its own
limitations. The limitations to knowledge appear even more
constricting when we consider the threshold experiences of
human life – birth and death – and try to gain clear ideas about
what, in a spiritual sense, precedes the one and succeeds the
other. If one does not wish either simply to take refuge in a
new, materialistic belief system or resort to a traditional
received wisdom that lives in uneasy partnership with our
rational, 'enlightened' capacities, then we must sense an
urgent need to enlarge the narrow scientific method. Such a
broadening cannot, however, consist in the return to a
standpoint which science has rightly and usefully overcome
but rather in an enlarging of the boundaries of its method,
thus opening up new territory to its research.

The human being has the capacity for 'transcendence' –
that is, although his consciousness is limited and enclosed, he
is still capable of further growth and learning, he is not fixed
and finalized. Therefore he can 'go beyond himself', he can
transcend his present state of consciousness. If his capacity
for transcendence, though, is hindered by a limited method of
research, if he must, instead, reach his goal on the wings of an
obscure longing, then he may search for help in the traditions
of his own and also of other cultures. At present we can
experience, at the same time that a broadening of scientific

method is in fact taking place, a return to ancient pre-rational, transcendental ways of thought. There is currently in the West and Central Europe a 'renaissance' of, and receptiveness to, Indian yoga and African tribal religion.

Rudolf Steiner's impulse, on the other hand, which belongs fully to our time and to the future, aims to broaden knowledge in a way which is both necessary and overdue. He does not reach back to methods which have existed for thousands of years, but grasps with both hands the special achievements of science and carries them on to new shores. His impulse is radically original, however thematically related to others it might appear.

Wherein lies the special achievement of science? It is in the mastery of controlled observation and in clear consequent thinking. The isolation of individual phenomena from their living context, and their subjection to 'pure' and therefore controllable conditions, is fully justified for a chemical or physical analysis. As an example, let us take the phenomenon of falling objects, which make their way towards the earth's centre until they come into sudden contact with its surface. As long as certain interference-factors are allowed to play into this, no two occurrences of this phenomenon will be comparable; in which case one can come to no conclusion about the laws underlying an object's fall. Only when conditions are created that exclude haphazard interference can the law common to every occurrence be grasped. Lumps of lead and goose-feathers are then found to fall at the same speed. It is only the carefully prepared observation which can demonstrate a 'free' fall and even then only approximately, since perfect experimental conditions are in fact unattainable. A deduction based on clear thought is needed to create the general law whose truth and self-accord can be grasped as ideal content, whose workings – in whatever modified form – can be traced in natural phenomena.

This procedure is productive and successful. However, it becomes questionable when one wishes to grasp subtler or more complex phenomena, as, for example, the movement of the human arm. With the same object-orientated method it is possible to investigate and clarify the processes of strain, pull, pressure, circulation, metabolism, fatigue, motion, anatomy and physiology. However, it is not possible to grasp in this way the will and the intention giving rise to these, impelling and directing them. To do so, it is necessary to develop and extend the method of research. The field of observation, as communicated to us through our senses, retains its full importance, but is enlarged by applying an additional technique: I refer the phenomenon back to myself. By so doing, perception remains precise and its field is at the same time extended, instead of being diminished in favour of some vague depths of feeling. This process will be referred to in what follows – where it will be described in more detail – as the process of self-knowledge. First of all, though, I would like to discuss the other element of scientific research – thinking.

The significance of thinking

In Homer's *Iliad*, we hear how Achilles is so overcome by rage against Agamemnon that he becomes incapable of doing anything. The whole army of Achaeans sense Achilles' depth of feeling which hangs above their tents like an oppressive mist, so that no one dares to leave their tent for several days. Of a similar dimension are the feelings, ascribed to Krimhild in the *Nibelungen* epic, of hatred towards Hagen after he has murdered her husband Siegfried. For more than 20 years she is overcome daily by the pain, until her devouring hatred is finally assuaged by the downfall of the Nibelungen; and she herself dies. Compared with such 'giants of emotion' our own powers of feeling are fairly meagre, even though, of course, we are familiar with depths and differentiation, as well as with petty-mindedness and meanness. What human beings have gained in our modern age, however, is the illumined soul-capacity of thinking to set beside the power of emotion. This capacity, which the cunning Odysseus possessed – unlike anyone else in the camp of the Greeks – is what brings at least some degree of clarity into our observations, sets boundaries, illuminates. It has come to be that faculty of soul which holds the rudder and steers us safely through the storms of passion and feeling. In fact, 'Our life of thinking is an emancipation of the soul from itself, whereas in our life of feeling and sensation we remain within ourselves.' (R. Steiner, *The Threshold of the Spiritual World*, chapter 1). This capacity of thinking – which also underpins all science – is a reliable point of departure for the soul's further and higher evolution. 'The soul has a natural trust in thinking and feels that without this trust life would lose all certainty. The soul-life becomes unhealthy when it begins to lose its faith in thinking. If thinking cannot help one to find clarity about something, one must allow oneself the consolation that all would become clear if it were only possible to develop sufficient power and acuity of thought. There is no need to be too unsettled by one's own inability to shed light on something through thinking; it would, however, be unthinkable that thinking itself might be incapable of finding a solution if one could enter as fully into its workings as would be necessary to gain insight. Such a disposition of soul towards thinking underlies all mankind's striving for knowledge.' (*Ibid.*)

If one becomes aware of the nature of thinking, one experiences, firstly, its illumined clarity; secondly, that the thinker is himself actively involved in the formation of its content; and thirdly, that the content thus gained can be communicated to others – because it has both an objective and a shared quality. Only thinking has a dual nature in that it bears a subjective, individual character as it arises – that is, it is dependent upon a thinker's subjectivity – and yet on the other hand the ideas thus produced reflect an objective, common validity. The concept that I create or 'think' is not only meaningful for me but is equally so for all people, for it grasps and reproduces a spiritual correspondence – of which we cannot become aware simply through our senses – which forms, indwells and permeates phenomena. Therefore the completed thought-process has huge significance. Through it I take hold of a portion of reality, of true existence.

It is precisely because of this dual nature of thinking – the subjective act of thinking and its objective result (concept or thought-content) – that the knowledge thus gained always retains a controlled lucidity, which is inherent in the nature of thinking itself. Such lucidity is not characteristic of communications which are simply 'revealed'. From the outcome, the result of a thought process, it is possible to discover and retrace the path that thinking took, whereas this is quite out of the question in the case of revelation, which is received as a gift, which simply 'comes over one'. In the case of a thought process, I can 'arbitrarily' determine its individual stages and hence control them. They are then – unlike the contents of revelation – subject only to inner laws and therefore partake of freedom. For I am on the one hand free to determine the steps taken and on the other hand free to accompany and retrace these steps, in the process of which I may perhaps discover alternative or additional results. Of course, I can accept or reject knowledge given by means of revelation, but I am quite excluded from retracing or accompanying the stages which gave rise to it.

As a 'philosopher of freedom', it was Rudolf Steiner's concern to demonstrate that thinking – both in the determination of its content and in the activity of accompanying and retracing – could lay claim to freedom. This is in complete accord with the convictions of modern science, which is concerned with phenomena accessible to the senses. But as long as one remains true to these convictions, it does not matter whether the process of thinking finds its starting point in a sense perception or in a content which I determine myself. What is important is the process of thought itself. In concentration exercises and in meditation the place of outer sense perceptions is taken, at first, by an encompassable content of thought or knowledge upon which the light of thinking activity is shone. What creates this light and also controls the direction of thought is my own 'I'. Such a process is completely self-determined and therefore an expression of individual freedom. But there is not only a subjective thinker involved in this activity; in the thought content is present a universal essence which belongs both to myself and to 'the world which exists independently of me' (R.Steiner, *ibid.*).

'Such a repeated concentration upon a fully permeated thought focuses and concentrates faculties within the soul which are to some extent usually dispersed in ordinary life. These concentrated faculties become the organs of perception for the spiritual world and its reality ... first of all one works one's way through to a thought which can be encompassed with the means provided by ordinary life and understanding. Then one repeatedly enters into this thought, grows at one with it. The strengthening of the soul comes about by living with such a thought.' (*Ibid.*)

So it can come as no surprise that for the anthroposophical or Christian-Rosicrucian path of knowledge and schooling (as described in these lectures) thinking alone can be a sure guide. Unlike other very prevalent methods of self-development, which start from an abandonment both of ordinary everyday experience and of thinking, this approach sets out from mankind's present achievements, yet broadens, deepens and transforms them. 'The human being's ordinary thinking is usually very disordered' – therefore thinking must be clarified and disciplined. How can that come about? By occupying oneself with the theory of knowledge. That is already the first step towards concentrating inner faculties in order to develop a capacity for perceiving realms of knowledge beyond the senses.

'One thing alone remains constant through all the universe, and that is logical thinking ... the laws of thinking are in all ... [higher] worlds the same ... for this reason the student of Rosicrucianism must first learn this thinking so that he does

not wander from a safe and certain path.' (See the lecture of
22.2.1907, GA97.)

The study of works permeated by thinking – such as those
of spiritual science – expands the capacity for thinking;
spiritual science offers 'material' that is not taken from the
visible world of phenomena, but from a world beyond the
senses. Precisely this material can allow us to experience the
spiritual thought-form, the inner interwoven context and
consistency of spiritual phenomena; it can allow us to create
them inwardly in a way that strengthens consciousness and
develops organs of sense-free perception.

The perceived world and self-knowledge

Once our modern consciousness has grown strong and certain
by developing a capacity for precise and reliable observation,
then this achievement should contribute to, and be retained
within, a broadened perception and understanding. It is of
course true that modern science has, initially, recognized only
the quantitative attributes of observed phenomena, those that
can be weighed or measured; whereas the qualities which bring
joy to human beings, such as the constantly changing moods and
hues of light and colour in the course of a day, are relegated to
the domain of subjectivity, of mere pleasure. Currently then, the
human being lives on the one hand as naive, subjective observer
experiencing phenomena with joy or antipathy; on the other
hand as strict and methodical scientist within a circumscribed
world of perception.

Only when perceptions that have been excluded from a
restricted procedure are reintegrated into the process of
knowledge can the human being again consciously inhabit his
senses. How can that be done? According to Rudolf Steiner,
through self-knowledge – at first glance an astonishing sug-
gestion. What is meant by it?

Whoever set foot in the sacred enclosure at Delphi and
climbed the holy road to the temple of Apollo came face to

face with the inscription upon its east pediment: 'O Man Know Thyself' – the greeting of the god of light. And so as to make quite clear what the required response to the god should be, the reply was also inscribed: 'Thou Art'. This means, though, that the human being replies in recognition of the fact that existence is a quality or character of the gods, whereas he, the greeter, belongs to a finite and circumscribed domain until he can share in eternity by means of self-knowledge.

This form of self-knowledge is different from what is commonly meant by it: not a return to oneself or a 'going inwards', but an opening out to the world. This is not to dispute that I can observe in myself, and therefore attempt to change unjustified prejudice, irritability, anger, hatred and all that is unbalanced or unresolved; I can perceive these as well as I can observe some of the ways in which I interact with the world around me. But this is only a limited understanding of the nature of self-knowledge, taking into consideration only one aspect, the state of my soul, but not my greater Self, my 'I'.

This greater Self is hidden from direct observation: when am I 'I'? In that action in which I thought that I fulfilled myself? Peer Gynt, who grew from a dreamy, vigorous peasant boy to a successful, world-wise and subsequently ruined businessman, believed that he had always been himself. Yet, at the end of his life he has to ask himself – in the face of reproaches from the Button-maker at the crossroads – if he is in fact himself, and is unable to find an answer. Earlier he had sought to find the core of an onion and found only parings. Where is the core of himself, the 'I' at the centre of the onion-skins of his actions, his feelings, his despair? Ibsen lets Peer Gynt meet a figure who has been known to him from childhood, Solveig, whose name means 'path of the sun'. Gynt is upheld in her love. He finds in her his true kernel – in other words, it is outside himself, in another.

It is apparent that the 'I' does live within us, in our deeds, emotions, ideas, intentions and memories, without however being fully absorbed in them. It imparts to the transitory, finite nature of our soul-life something of real existence. The self which I observe in myself and also call 'I' is nothing other than my commonplace, run-of-the-mill 'I', the shadow-image of that other, higher 'I' that I search for through self-knowledge. 'The Self is not to be found by looking into oneself but by looking outwards. There one finds the Self that formed the eye and created the sun ... You must learn to recognize your Self in what is outside and around you. Gazing only inwards leads to a hardening of oneself, to a higher egotism ... Self-knowledge may only be practised when the student of the white path unites it with self-effacement ... Everywhere in the outer world are the elements of our Self ... That is why the student of Rosicrucianism lays such value on a calm and objective observation of the outer world. If you wish to recognize your Self, look into the mirror of the world and its beings. What lies within your soul will speak far more clearly to you from the eyes of your fellow human being than when you grow hard within yourself and sink down into your own soul.' (See the first lecture of 20.10.1906.)

That power within us which does not wholly enter, with all its being, into the expressions of our soul, nor fully realize itself, is also present in the wider world. That spirit in us, our higher 'I', which works upon our soul-life and leaves the traces of its footprints in our biography without ever being fully present itself, is present in the world as the spiritual ground of all phenomena, as the power of creation. Just as my personal biography expresses itself in the many 'layers of onion peel' of my experiences and actions, so the world's 'I' manifests in the kingdoms of nature: the forms of mineral, plant and animal worlds reveal the gestures of a spiritual principle which also lives in me as a human being. If, in my perceptions of the world, I search for those gestures which express the spiritual, then I can experience something of the creative world-spirit of the (world) 'I', which, since it is also the higher 'I', at the same time tells me of myself. So the exercising of sensory perception is the point of departure for a broadening of understanding and knowledge.

'A higher self-knowledge only begins when we start to realize that our daily self by no means contains our higher Self, which is outside us in the world with stone and animal, above us in the stars, sun and moon; the same being that dwells in us is also everywhere around us. When someone says that he wishes to develop his higher Self by withdrawing from the world and wishes to have nothing to do with material existence, then he completely fails to see that the Self is everywhere outside him and that his own higher Self is only a small part of this great Self.' (See the lecture of 4.9.1906.)

There is no longer any need for the qualitative gestures of nature to be excluded from perception. Every quality of perception has a significance and can become the basis for a broadened understanding and knowledge. The examples given in these lectures – such as the meadow saffron as symbol of a human being's melancholic disposition, in other words as an image of a particular human quality – point us in a certain direction, one which can help us to develop a modern science that includes the spiritual. We are, naturally, only pointed in the right direction; to travel this path requires a greater effort than is needed within current circumscribed views of nature, for its methods must of course be mastered. Upon this path, the perceived world is upheld both for a scientific striving and for an inner strengthening of soul. Thinking and observing are the two pillars which support the beginning of a path of practice that can lead us to a broadening of knowledge and understanding. This path passes on through further stages which are indicated in these lectures, but cannot be further elaborated here. It is my intention only to describe the significance of thinking and observation for the occult path of schooling. Any other 'way in' to an expansion of consciousness, which anticipates later stages of realization, has a significant consequence. Its results cannot be controlled and therefore do not contribute to human freedom. What one's own 'I' cannot achieve must then be replaced by another's 'I', by the 'I' of a guru, an occult teacher.

The guru and human freedom

All occult schooling that goes beyond the stages I have described here conceals great perils for the soul. These are drastically and impressively described in the great epics of the soul's journey, such as the wanderings of Odysseus. In these lectures are impressed upon us the falling apart of various capacities, and the splitting of the personality. Are we then not in need of someone to lead and safeguard our soul? Certainly. But the question is, what kind of relationship should exist between teacher and pupil, between master and apprentice? It is, above all, important to gain clarity in respect to various eastern esoteric practices which have been adopted and to some degree overlaid with western influences.

It may be of help here to pose the question: to what extent is such a practice determined by oneself or ruled by another? Rudolf Steiner describes the latter kind as existing when 'an initiate, living upon earth, is the leader, the guru of another', in which case the pupil relies wholly and in specific detail upon the guru. 'This is best achieved when one discards one's own self for the period of schooling and gives it over to the guru, who gives advice on every individual action. One's own self merges completely and therefore also selflessly with the other.' (See the second lecture of 2.9.1906.) The relationship of teacher to pupil is 'as strict as can be imagined. The guru is absolute authority for the pupil', who wholly subjects himself to the will of the teacher. Whoever chooses such a path of self-development not only gives up a stage of consciousness achieved over long epochs but also simultaneously works against his own constitution: for he does not strive to walk further on the path of his own biography, whose environment is the here and now, and is this specific cultural stage of development and no other. Instead he turns back and eludes the questions concerning consciousness in our modern age; this brings about a rift in his identity, whose source is the ongoing, unfolding progression of his biography.

It is understandable, of course, that given the continual demands made upon us by contemporary consciousness it can be satisfying to the soul to give itself over selflessly to another, not least because deep experiences are bound up with such a path which do not seem to hinder one's own identity since one can experience something like an expanding of one's being into someone else. And yet this kind of flowing out does not bring me closer to myself, but merely allows me to share in the soul-life of another. For we cannot discover the spiritual within our perceptions of the sense-world by being dependent on someone else's guidance.

The anthroposophical path of self-development through spiritual science cannot proceed in this way. As well as broadening our present capacities for thinking and observing, it also allows for a creation in the pupil's life of 'spaces of freedom' in regard even to very prevalent dependencies. In quite basic 'pre-exercises', which are fully subject to the practitioner's autonomy and self-possession, certain capacities are developed in a controlled and lucid way; these give the soul the necessary strength to withstand the dangers it may meet on its journey, which could threaten its integrity. These pre-exercises, of which there are six altogether, are also described as 'subsidiary exercises', because the capacities they develop (such as control of one's thoughts, initiative in one's actions, etc.) are to be developed both before and simultaneously with the stages on the path of knowledge. In his book *Knowledge of the Higher Worlds* and in the lectures of this volume, Rudolf Steiner speaks repeatedly of the need for guidance from a teacher when embarking on the path of self-development. He says, for example:

We must have a guru who shows us how we should develop our organs of perception, who tells us how he himself has proceeded in order to develop these. [See the lecture of 7.12.1905.]

Or:

Sometimes it is indeed absolutely necessary that the teacher should be physically present for the pupil, but this is more seldom the case than the pupil may believe. The pupil cannot, to begin with, judge the effect which the teacher has upon him. The teacher has ways and means which only gradually become clear to the pupil. Some single word or other, which the pupil believes to be casually spoken and without significance, turns out to be, after all, of great importance. Such a word works on unconsciously in the pupil's soul like a guiding, helping hand. If the teacher exercises a correct occult influence then the connection between him and the pupil is a genuine one.

From this one might assume that an uncritical dependency is being recommended, even that very subtle forms of control were at work, based on unconscious urges. If that were so, however, it would bring the anthroposophical spiritual-scientific path of schooling very close to the kind of total dependency of pupil upon teacher that was mentioned previously.

Such an idea, though, is quite contrary to what is truly intended, which is complete self-determination on the inner journey. Naturally enough, the person who broadens, develops and elevates his soul-capacities takes different paths towards the dangerous precipices and mountains of the soul than those travelled by conventional science. Yet in all other respects, the situation is the same: for this science has as its own context a particular level of experience and a more or less sure procedure and method of research. Occult science differs from it only inasmuch as its content is far older and its methods were always hidden, secret, occult. If I turn to a teacher, it is in order to make use of his accumulated wealth of experience, knowledge and method. This can occur, just as in the tradition of university science, in three ways: 1, through personal tutoring – a direct and personal teacher-pupil relationship; 2, through a systematic guidance in the form of lectures; 3, through the written word.

Naturally, in the latter case, there is an absence of direct human connection, of personal encounter; but this loss is counterbalanced by an increase in independence and freedom for the pupil. In the lectures of this volume a middle path is taken. They are transcripts of lectures which were not revised by the lecturer himself. Some of them are addressed to people who were themselves concerned with questions of inner development (members' lectures); others were given to people who were simply interested in the theme and wished to hear more. As transcripts, they lose the direct, living quality of a lecture and become 'literature'. In these lectures, Rudolf Steiner refers repeatedly to the teacher-pupil relationship as having to do with communication and information, just as it would in a basic introduction to scientific method; only in this case one's attention is turned towards regions inaccessible to the senses.

The content of this science is not, of course, an inert object, but a living and highly individual soul. It is therefore quite understandable that an appropriate method must be one that offers individual encouragement and advice; an approach based on personal contact becomes apparent at various points of these lectures. At the same time, Rudolf Steiner considered it extremely important to avoid all danger of personal dependency upon the teacher. He writes, for example, in the preface to the fifth edition of *Knowledge of the Higher Worlds*: 'At that time I had to say of much that was not described in the book, that it could be learnt by means of "word-of-mouth". By now, a great deal of such material has, in fact, been published. But such indications may well have given my readers a false impression; the personal relationship to this or that teacher of someone on the path of spiritual development, may have been taken to be far more essential than it should have been … a direct relationship to the objective spiritual world is much more important than a relationship to the personality of a teacher. The role of such a teacher will increasingly be simply that of a helper, as is already the case – in accordance with modern views – in any other branch of knowledge.'

The teacher, then, should no longer exercise authority or require belief any more than is the case 'in any other area of learning or life'. This is the new way in which a teacher supports and accompanies his pupil, and in which the pupil approaches his teacher in free, self-determining trust.

It is possible, since spiritual science has revealed and published its methods for the broadening and development of knowledge, that the emphasis on personal instruction will give way to an approach based on the written word, in the same way as scientific information is commonly communicated. This allows the pupil to retain a space of freedom as in any other branch of knowledge – but for spiritual science this is a quite new departure, unknown before in history. The pupil thereby becomes to a large degree independent of personal influences and connections. The written word becomes equal in importance to the personal teacher.

This development is one for which Rudolf Steiner strove through his preoccupation with the theory of knowledge, and which he ultimately achieved as a result of it. Nevertheless the new relationship between teacher and pupil, who can now also be called 'author' and 'reader', cannot be regarded as an anonymous one. On the contrary, the author bears an inner, spiritual responsibility for his communications; and therefore what the pupil takes in through him creates a real and living connection, which is described in these lectures as a relationship of trust. Anyone who distrusts such communications cannot take anything of them in, since he holds fast to the position of observer or critic and does not actively involve himself with what is being communicated. A conscious involvement, on the other hand, paves the way for a developing trust, for a connection that has a personal quality.

The figure of 'The Teacher' in Rudolf Steiner's Mystery

Play *The Guardian of the Threshold* (scene 6) expresses this kind of connection in an artistic form:

> Each one who in this earthly life
> received from me the Spirit's light
> must I accompany; whether he
> has given himself knowingly or not
> to be my pupil on the Spirit's path,
> I must guide him further on the journey
> which he, through me, in Spirit has begun.

This implies freedom for the pupil but not, however, for the teacher – for him it is a relationship that should be both conscious and dutiful.

Concerning the choice of lectures

In the following books by Rudolf Steiner there are detailed descriptions of method for broadening knowledge and understanding:

1. *Knowledge of the Higher Worlds: How is it Achieved?* (1904)
2. *Theosophy* (1904)
3. *The Stages of Higher Knowledge* (1905/1908)
4. *Occult Science: An Outline* (1910)
5. *The Guiding Spirit for Human Beings and Humanity* (1911)
6. *A Path to Self-Knowledge in Eight Meditations* (1911)
7. *The Threshold of the Spiritual World – Aphoristic Descriptions* (1913)
8. *Cosmology, Religion and Philosophy* (1922)

Given this wealth of descriptions composed intentionally for the reader, what justification is there for a selection of lecture transcripts? To begin with, this one: 'Whoever genuinely

wishes to make progress in an understanding of spiritual
science will experience the need to observe the spiritual
domain of life from ever-changing perspectives. It is only
natural that *every* such description will be to a certain extent
one-sided. This is far truer of descriptions of the spiritual
domain than it is of the sense-world.' (See the introduction to
The Threshold of the Spiritual World.)

It is also relevant to mention here something about the
significance of the breathing exercises: 'When the exercises
for intuition are practised they work not only upon the etheric
body, but also upon the sense-free capacities of the physical
body. However, one should not imagine that this results in an
effect on the physical body which is accessible to normal
sensory observation. The effects are such that they can only
be discerned by sense-free perception. They have nothing to
do with any outer knowledge. They arise when consciousness
has succeeded in maturing to the point of experiencing
intuition, having expunged all previously known outer and
inner experiences. The experiences accessible to the power of
intuition are intimate, delicate and subtle; whereas the human being's physical body is, at the present stage of
development, coarse by comparison and therefore strongly
hinders the success of the intuition-exercises. But if one
perseveres in them with the necessary energy and inner
calm, one can at last overcome the hindrances of the
physical body. The pupil of the spiritual path will notice
this because certain manifestations of the physical body,
which previously occurred without his conscious involvement, gradually come under his control. He also notices it
because he experiences, for a while, a need to order his
breathing (for example) to bring it into harmony with the
motions which his soul performs by means of these exercises.
The ideal, though, in self-development, would be for no
specifically physical exercises to be practised, not even such
breathing exercises, but rather for all that should occur
in the physical body to be accomplished only as a result

of the intuition-exercises themselves' (from *Occult Science: An Outline*).

Issues and aspects such as those discussed above are clarified in these selected lectures. Which brings us to a further justification: this selection particularly illuminates the differences between this path and other spiritual disciplines, allowing a clear perception of the tasks facing human beings in the present age. Similarly, it demonstrates how the teacher-pupil relationship can be one based on freedom and how Rudolf Steiner's own views developed towards advocating the greatest possible degree of personal freedom in such a relationship. This theme surfaces consistently in the lectures of this volume. As a result of the current receptivity towards ancient and worthy spiritual paths from a wide variety of cultures, the journey towards higher worlds appears all too easily to be one that is timeless and therefore unrelated to history. This means, however, that the human being is viewed to some extent as an entity with little need or capacity for change, for whom is still relevant what was valid thousands of years ago.

Yet it is not only the human being's consciousness but also his physical constitution which is subject to continuous change, and thus the spiritual discipline through which he extends his consciousness cannot remain the same. The choice of lectures was dictated in some degree by their concern with the particular characteristics of modern consciousness and its consequences for an expansion of knowledge and understanding, and for the path of self-development. Whoever is familiar with Rudolf Steiner's lectures will be aware that he seldom gave a lecture without making reference to the practice of self-development. How then is one to choose amongst thousands of lectures? In spite of the reasons given above, it was still hard to be sure whether the lectures most relevant to the theme had, in fact, been chosen. The unavoidable subjectivity of the editor was therefore mitigated by discussion with others and I would like to thank those friends who helped me with many suggestions.

At the same time it became clear that some themes were absent: there is no mention in this volume of mediumism, hallucination, clairvoyance, somnambulism or hypnosis. Neither are there explicit descriptions of the following: the Guardian of the Threshold; the splitting of the personality; the stages of higher knowledge – Imagination, Inspiration and Intuition; the different regions of the sense-free world – the world of souls and Spiritland. It was not the aim of this selection to deal with such matters.

The first lecture gives a kind of 'topographical sketch', a 'map' of the region to which the various paths of inner schooling aspire. Three historical paths of practice are differentiated: the yoga path; the Gnostic-Christian path; and the Rosicrucian-Christian path. The second lecture pursues the same theme and examines the accompanying states of consciousness; it also describes six preliminary or subsidiary exercises. The third lecture describes the eight stages of the oriental path and clarifies Gnostic-Christian practices. In the fourth lecture the Rosicrucian-Christian path is outlined. This is followed, in the fifth lecture, by a more detailed picture of the transformations which have taken place in the fabric of the world and the constitution of human beings up to the present day.

The sixth lecture presents inner development based on self-knowledge, gives an account of inner experiences and describes basic exercises. The seventh lecture offers seven exercises which strengthen thinking and make it a sure foundation for the broadening of human knowledge. The first part of the eighth lecture makes clear what effect an inwardly strengthened and living thinking has both for the human being and for the spiritual world and its inhabitants. The second part of the lecture deals with the way in which thinking can be permeated with feeling and will in meditation and describes in detail how this occurs.

The ninth lecture, 'The Three Decisions on the Path of Imaginative Cognition', occupies rather unusual territory; it proceeds beyond an elaboration of the strengthening of thought, to examine other practices which are fraught with great dangers. From this it becomes clear that less taxing paths of practice can lead to swift results, but that the spiritual contents revealed by means of them are nothing other than the burgeoning elemental powers which reside in the human body. This description can help us form our own judgements. The last three lectures tackle the problem of the inner path from the perspective of modern consciousness and describe the path which proceeds by means of thinking and observation.

I. The Path of Knowledge and Its Stages: The Rosicrucian Spiritual Path[1]

Berlin, 20 October 1906

TODAY A picture of the path of knowledge will be given, and the fruits of this path will also be shown. You already know some of the major points of view which thereby come into consideration. However, for those of you who have already heard lectures pertaining to the path of knowledge, something new will be offered if we discuss the path of knowledge as can occur only in intimate circles of students of spiritual science.[2] The main matter at hand is to discuss this path of knowledge in so far as it is traced through the Rosicrucian, western spiritual stream, which has guided European culture spiritually by invisible threads since the fourteenth century.[3]

The Rosicrucian movement worked in complete concealment up until the last third of the nineteenth century. What was true Rosicrucianism could not be found in books and was also forbidden to be spoken of publicly. Only in the last 30 years have a few of the Rosicrucian teachings been made known to the outer world through the theosophical movement, after having been taught earlier only in the most strictly closed circles. The most elementary teachings of the Rosicrucians are included in what is called theosophy today – but only the most elementary.[4] It is only possible bit by bit to allow mankind to look more deeply into this wisdom which has been fostered in these Rosicrucian schools in Europe since the end of the fourteenth century.

To begin with, we would like to make clear that there is not just one kind of path of knowledge, but three paths to consider. Yet this should not be understood as if there were three truths. There is only one truth, just as the view revealed from the peak of a mountain is the same for all who stand there. There are, however, various ways by which the peak of the mountain can be reached. During the ascent, one has at every point a different view. Only if one is at the top – and one can ascend to the peak from various sides – can one have a free and full view from one's own perspective. So it is also with the three paths of knowledge. One is the oriental path of yoga, the second is the Christian-Gnostic path, and the third is the Christian-Rosicrucian path. These three paths lead to the single truth.

There are three different paths because human nature is different around our earth. One has to distinguish three types of human nature.[5] Just as it would not be right for someone trying to reach a mountain top to select a remote path rather than the one next to him, so it would also be wrong if a person wanted to take another spiritual path than the one appropriate to him. Many muddled ideas about this prevail today in the theosophical movement, which must still develop upwards from its initial stage. It is often supposed that there is only a single path to knowledge, by which is meant the yoga path. The oriental yoga path is not the only path to knowledge, however, and is in fact not a propitious path for those who live within European civilization. He who considers this matter only from outside certainly can have scarcely any insight into what we are concerned with here, because one could easily come to the conclusion that human nature actually appears to differ little in various lands. If one with occult powers observes the great differences in human types, it becomes clear that what is good for the orientals, and perhaps also for some other men in our culture, is by no means the proper path for everyone. There are people, but only a few within European circumstances, who could follow the oriental path of yoga. But for most Europeans, this is impracticable. It brings with it illusions and also the destruction of soul-forces. The eastern and western natures, although they do not appear so different to today's scientists, are totally different. An eastern brain, an eastern imagination, and an eastern heart work completely differently from the organs of westerners. What can be expected of someone who has grown up within eastern circumstances should never be expected of a westerner. Only one who believes that climate, religion, and social environment have no influence on the human spirit might also think that the external circumstances under which a spiritual training is undergone are also a matter of indifference. But one who knows the deeply spiritual influences exerted upon human nature by all these outer circumstances understands that the yoga path is impossible for those who remain within European culture, and can only be trod by those few Europeans who radically and fundamentally detach themselves from European circumstances.

Those persons who today are still inwardly upright and honest Christians, those who are permeated with certain principal themes of Christianity, may choose the Christian-Gnostic path, which differs little from the Cabbalistic path. For Europeans in general, however, the Rosicrucian path is the only right path. This European Rosicrucian path will be spoken of today, and indeed the different practices this path prescribes for people and also the fruits it holds for those who follow it will be described. No one should believe that this path is only for scientifically trained men or for scholars. The simplest person can tread it. If one takes this path, however, one will quickly be in the position to encounter every objection which can be made against occultism by European science. This was one of the main tasks of the Rosicrucian Masters: to arm those who take this path so that they could travel this path and defend occult knowledge in the world.[6] The simple man who holds only a few popular ideas about modern science, or even none at all, but who has an honest craving for truth can tread the Rosicrucian path alongside trained men and scholars.

Great distinctions exist among the three paths of knowledge. The first important distinction is in the relationship of the pupil to the occult teacher, who gradually becomes the guru or who mediates the relationship to the guru. A characteristic of the oriental Yoga schools is that this relationship is the strictest imaginable. The guru is an unconditional authority for the pupil. If that were not the case, this training could not have the right outcome. An oriental yoga training without a strong submission to the authority of the guru is totally impossible. The Christian-Gnostic or Cabbalistic path allows a somewhat looser relationship to the guru on the physical plane. The guru leads his pupil to Christ Jesus; he is the mediator. With the Rosicrucian path, the guru becomes always more a friend whose authority rests on inner agreement. Here it is not possible to have any relationship but one of strong personal trust. Should but the slightest mistrust arise between teacher and pupil, then the essential bond which must remain between them would be ruptured, and any forces which play between teacher and pupil would no longer work. It is easy for the pupil to form false ideas about the role of his teacher. It might seem to the pupil that he needs to speak to his teacher now and then, or that his teacher must often be physically near him. Certainly it is sometimes an urgent necessity for the teacher to approach the pupil physically, but this is not so often the case as the pupil may believe. The effect that the teacher exercises on his pupil cannot be judged in the right way at the beginning of their relationship. The teacher has means which only gradually reveal themselves to the pupil. Many words which the pupil believes to have been spoken by chance are actually of great importance. They may work unconsciously in the pupil's soul, as a force of right, leading and guiding him. If the teacher exercises these occult influences correctly, then the real bond is also there between him and his pupil. In addition, there are the forces of loving participation working at a distance, forces that are always at the teacher's disposal and which later are ever more revealed to the pupil if he finds the entrance to the higher worlds. But absolute trust is an unconditional necessity; otherwise it is better to dissolve the bond between the teacher and the pupil.

Now the various precepts which play a certain role in the Rosicrucian training should be mentioned briefly. These things need not meet him in the exact sequence in which they are enumerated here. According to the individuality, the occupation and the age of the pupil, the teacher will have to extract this or that from the different spheres, and rearrange them. Only an overview of the information shall be given here.

What is highly essential for the Rosicrucian training is not sufficiently attended to in all occult trainings. This is the cultivation of clear and logical thinking, or at least the striving for it! All confused and prejudiced thinking must first be eliminated. A person must accustom himself to viewing the relationships in the world broadly and unselfishly. The best exercise for one wishing to undergo this Rosicrucian path unpretentiously is the study of the elementary teachings of spiritual science.[7] It is unjustified to object: what good does it do me to learn about the higher worlds, the different races and cultures, or to study reincarnation and karma when I can't see and verify it all for myself? This is not a valid objection because occupying one's thoughts with these truths purifies the thinking and disciplines it so that people become ripe for the other measures that lead to the occult path. For the most part, people think in ordinary life without bringing order into their thoughts. The guiding principles and epochs of human development and planetary evolution, the great viewpoints which have been opened by the initiates, bring thought into ordered forms. All of this is a part of Rosicrucian training. It is called the Study. The teacher will therefore suggest that the pupil think deeply into the elementary teachings about reincarnation and karma, the three worlds, the Akashic Record, and the evolution of the earth and the human races. The range of elementary spiritual science as it is diffused in modern times is the best preparation for the normal person.

For those, however, who wish to cultivate even sharper faculties of thinking and to undertake a still more rigorous moulding of the soul life, the study of books written expressly for bringing thinking into disciplined paths is recommended. Two books written for this purpose – in which there is no mention of the word 'theosophy' – are my two books *Truth and Science* and *The Philosophy of Freedom*.[8] One writes such a book in order to fulfil a purpose. Those who have a foundation in an intensive training in logical thinking and who wish to arrive at a wider study would do well to submit their spirits once to the 'gymnastics for soul and spirit' which these books require. That gives them the foundation upon which Rosicrucian study is erected.

When one observes the physical plane, one perceives certain sense impressions: colours and light, warmth and cold, smells and tastes, and impressions from the senses of hearing and touch. One connects all of these with one's activity of thought and intellect. Intellect and thought belong still to the physical plane. You can perceive all that on the physical plane. Perceptions on the astral plane are completely different in appearance. Perceptions are again entirely different on the devachanic plane, not to mention in even higher spirit regions.[9] The person who has not yet acquired a glimpse into the higher worlds can still try to picture them to himself. I am also seeking to give a view of these worlds through pictures in my current manner of representation. He who ascends to the higher regions sees for himself how they work on him. On every plane a person has new experiences. But there is one which remains the same through all worlds up to Devachan itself, one which never changes: that is logical, trained thinking. Once on the Buddhi plane, this thinking no longer has the same value as on the physical plane. There, another form of thinking must enter. But for the three worlds below the Buddhi plane, for the physical, astral, and devachanic planes, the same form of thinking is valid. One who therefore schools himself in orderly thinking through this study in the physical plane will find in this thinking a good guide in the higher worlds. He will not falter as easily as one who seeks to enter the spirit realms with confused thinking. Therefore, the Rosicrucian training advises a person to discipline his thinking in order to move freely in the higher worlds. He who reaches up into these worlds learns new methods of perception, which were not there on the physical plane, but he can master these with his thinking.

The second thing which the pupil must learn on the Rosicrucian path of knowledge is Imagination. The pupil prepares for this in that he gradually learns to immerse himself in pictorial concepts which represent the higher worlds in the sense of Goethe's words, 'All that is transitory is but a likeness.' As man ordinarily goes through the physical world, he takes things up as they appear to his senses, but not that which lies behind. He is pulled down in the physical world as if by a dead weight. Man only becomes independent of this physical world when he learns to consider the objects around him as symbols. He must, for this reason, seek to acquire a moral relationship to them. The teacher can give him much guidance in learning to regard outward appearances as symbols of the spirit, but the pupil can also do a great deal for himself. He can, for example, look closely at a meadow saffron and a violet. If I see the meadow saffron as a symbol for a melancholy disposition, then I have regarded it not only as it outwardly comes to meet me but also as a symbol of a certain quality. In the violet, one can behold a symbol for a calm, innocent disposition. So you can go from object to object, from plant to plant, from animal to animal and regard them as symbols for the spiritual. In this way, you make your imaginative capacities fluid and release them from the sharp contours of sense perception. One comes then to behold the symbol for a characteristic quality in every species of animal. One perceives one animal as a symbol for strength, another as a symbol for slyness. We must try to pursue such things not fleetingly but earnestly and step by step.

Fundamentally, all human language is spoken in symbols. Language is nothing but a speaking in symbols. Every word is a symbol. Even science, which claims to view every object objectively, must make use of language, in that its words work symbolically. If you speak of the wings of the lungs, you know that there are actually no wings, yet you nevertheless cherish this designation. He who wishes to remain on the physical plane would do well not to lose himself too strongly in these symbols, but the advanced occult pupil will not lose himself in them. If one investigates, one will perceive the primordial depths in which human language is founded. Such deep natures as Paracelsus and Jacob Boehme owed much of their development to the opportunities they had – which they did not shun – for studying the imaginative significance of language through conversations with vagrants and farmers. There the words 'nature', 'soul', and 'spirit' worked completely differently. There they worked more strongly. When out in the country the farmer's wife plucks a goose's feathers, she actually calls the interior of the feather 'the soul'. The pupil must find for himself such symbols in language. In this way he loosens himself from the physical world and learns to raise himself to the realm of Imagination. If the world is thus viewed as a likeness of man, it has a strong effect. If the pupil practises this for a long time, he will notice corresponding effects. In observing a flower, for example, something gradually loosens from the flower. The colour, which once clung to the surface of the blossom, ascends like a small flame and hovers freely in space. Imaginative cognition forms itself out of these things. Then it is as if the surfaces of all objects loosen. The whole space fills with colours, the flames hovering in space. In this way, the whole world of light seems to detach itself from physical reality. When such a colour picture detaches itself and hovers freely in space, it soon begins to adhere to something. It presses towards something. It does not just stand still arbitrarily; it encloses a being, which now itself appears in the colour as spiritual being. The colour which the pupil has detached from the objects of the physical world clothes the spiritual beings of astral space.

Here is the point where the occult teacher's counsel must intervene, as the pupil could very easily lose his bearings. This could happen for two reasons. The first is that each pupil must go through a definite experience. The images which are peeled off from the physical objects – they are not only colours, but also aural and olfactory sensations – may present themselves as strange, hideous or perhaps beautiful shapes, as animal heads, plant forms or even hideous human faces. This first experience represents a mirror-image of the pupil's own soul. The particular passions and desires, the evils that still lie within the soul, appear before the advancing pupil as in a mirror in astral space. Here he requires counsel of the occult teacher, who can tell him that it is not an objective reality that he has seen but a mirror-image of his own inner being.

You will understand just how dependent the pupil is on his teacher's advice when you hear more about the manner in which these pictures appear. It is often emphasized that everything is reversed in astral space, that everything appears as a mirror-image. The pupil can, for this reason, easily be misled through illusions, especially with respect to a mirroring of his own being. The mirror-image of a passion does not only appear as an approaching animal – that would still be quite manageable – but it is something quite different with which one must reckon. Let us suppose that a person has a hidden evil passion. The reflection of such a desire or lust often appears in an alluring form, whereas a good characteristic may not appear at all alluring. Here again we are discussing something which has been wonderfully portrayed in an ancient saga. You find a picture of this in the legend of Hercules. As Hercules goes on his way, good and evil characteristics stand before him. Vices are clothed in the enticing form of beauty, but virtues are in modest garb.

Still other hindrances can stand in the pupil's way. Even when he is already in a position to see things objectively, there is still the other possibility of his inner will directing and influencing these phenomena as an outer force. He must bring himself to the point where he can see through this and understand the strong influence that the wish has on the astral plane. All things which have a directing force here in the physical world cease to exist when one arrives in the imaginative world. If on the physical plane you imagine yourself to have done something you actually have not done, you will soon be persuaded by the facts of the physical world that this is not so. This is not the case in astral space. There, pictures of your own wishes deceive you, and you must have knowing guidance which will piece together how these imaginative pictures work in order to perceive their true significance.

The third task in the Rosicrucian training is to learn the occult script. What is this occult script? There are certain pictures, symbols, which are formed by simple lines or the joining of colours. Such symbols constitute a definite occult sign-language. Let us take the following as an example. There is a certain process in the higher worlds which also operates in the physical world: the whirling of a vortex. You can observe this whirling of a vortex when you look at a star cluster, as in the constellation of Orion, for example. There you see a spiral, only it is on the physical plane. But you can view this also on all planes. It can present itself in the form of one vortex entwining itself into another. This is a figure to be found on the astral plane in all possible forms. When you understand this figure, you can grasp through it how one race transforms itself into another.[10] At the time of formation of the first sub-race of our present main race, the sun stood directly in the sign of Cancer. At that time, one race entwined itself in the other; for this reason, one has this occult sign for Cancer. All the signs of the zodiac are occult signs. One must only come to know and understand their meaning.

The pentagram is also such a sign. The pupil learns to connect certain sensations and feelings with it. These are the counterpart of astral processes. This sign-language, which is learned as occult script, is nothing other than a reproduction of the laws of the higher worlds. The pentagram is a sign which expresses various meanings. As the letter B is used in many different words, so can a symbol in the occult script have diverse meanings. The pentagram, hexagram, angle and other figures can be combined into an occult script which acts as a signpost in the higher worlds.[11] The pentagram is the sign for the fivefold organization of man, for secrecy, and also for that which underlies the species-soul of the rose. When you connect the petals of the rose's image, you get a pentagram. Just as the letter B signifies something different in the words 'build' and 'bond', so do the signs in the occult script also signify various things. One must learn to order them in the right way. They are the signposts on the astral plane. One who has learned to read the occult script bears the same relationship to one who only sees these symbols as a literate person does to an illiterate one in the physical world. Our symbols for writing on the physical plane are for the most part arbitrary. Originally, however, they were likenesses of the astral sign-language. Take an ancient astral symbol, Mercury's staff with the snake. That has become the letter E in our system of writing. Or take the letter W which depicts the wave-movements of water. It is the soul-sign of man and at the same time a sign for the Word. The letter M is nothing other than an imitation of the upper lip. In the course of evolution, it has all become more and more arbitrary. On the occult plane, by contrast, necessity prevails. There one can live these things.

The fourth step is the so-called 'rhythm of life'. People know such a life-rhythm only very slightly in everyday life. They live carelessly and egotistically. At most, for the children in school, the lesson plan still bears a certain life-rhythm in that the sequence of daily lessons is repeated from week to week. But who does that in normal life? None the less, one can ascend to a higher development only by bringing rhythm and repetition into one's life. Rhythm holds sway in all nature. In the revolutions of the planets around the sun, in the yearly appearance and withering of the plants, in the animal kingdom, and in the sexual life of the animals, everything is ruled rhythmically. Only man is permitted to live without rhythm in order that he can become free. However, he must of his own accord bring rhythm again into the chaos. A good rhythm is established by undertaking occult exercises every day at a definite time. The pupil must carry out his meditations and concentration exercises daily, at the same hour, just as the sun sends its forces down to earth at the same time each spring. This is a way of bringing rhythm into life. Another is one in which the occult teacher brings the proper rhythm into the pupil's breathing. Inhaling, holding the breath, and exhaling must be brought into the rhythm for a short period daily, as determined by the experience of the teacher. Thus through man a new rhythm is put in place of the old one. Making life rhythmic in such a way is a prerequisite for ascent into the higher worlds. But no one can do this without the guidance of a teacher. It should be brought to awareness here only as a principle.

The fifth step is that in which one learns the correspondence between microcosm and macrocosm. This consists of the teacher instructing the pupil on how to concentrate his thoughts on certain parts of the body. Those of you who heard the lecture about the relationship of the senses to the higher worlds will recall that the whole cosmos took part in the formation of the human physical body.[12] The eye was created by light, by the spirits who work in light. Every point of the physical body stands in connection with a particular force in the cosmos. Let us examine the point at the root of the nose. There was a time when the etheric head protruded way beyond the physical body. Even in Atlantean times, the forehead was a point where the etheric head stood far out beyond the physical head, as is still the case today with the horses and other animals.[10] With horses the etheric head today still protrudes beyond the physical. In modern man this point in the etheric head has been brought under the protection of the physical head and this gives him the capacity to develop those parts of the physical brain which enable him to call himself 'I'. This organ, which enables man to call himself 'I', is connected with a definite process which took place during the Atlantean development of the earth. The occult teacher now instructs his pupil thus: direct your thoughts and concentrate them on this point! Then he gives him a mantra. In this way, a certain force in this part of the head is aroused which corresponds to a certain process in the macrocosm. In such a way a correspondence between microcosm and macrocosm is evoked. Through a similar concentration on the eye, the pupil acquires knowledge of the sun. One finds the entire spiritual organization of the macrocosm spiritually within one's own organs.

When the pupil has practised this long enough, he may go on to immerse himself in the things he has thus discovered. He may, for instance, seek out in the Akashic Record that point during the Atlantean epoch in which the root of the nose reached the condition upon which he had concentrated. Or he finds the sun in concentrating on the eye. This sixth step, this immersion in the macrocosm, is called contemplation. This gives the pupil cosmic knowledge, and through it he expands his self-knowledge beyond the personality. This is something different from the beloved chatter about self-knowledge. One finds the self not when one looks within, but rather when looking without. This is the same self which produced the eye brought forth by the sun. When you wish to seek that part of the self which corresponds to the eye, then you must seek it in the sun. You must learn to perceive as your self that which lies outside you. Looking only within oneself leads to a hardening in oneself, to a higher egotism. When people say, 'I need only let myself speak,' they have no idea of the danger that lies therein. Self-knowledge may only be practised when the pupil of the white path has bound himself to self-renunciation. When he has learned to say to each thing,

'That am I,' then he is ripe for self-knowledge, as Goethe expresses in the words of Faust:

Thou leadest past mine eyes the long array
Of living things, mak'st known to me my brethren
Within the silent copse, the air, the water.

All around us are parts of our self. This is represented, for example, in the myth of Dionysus. It is for this reason that the Rosicrucian training places such a great value upon an objective and quiet contemplation of the external world: if you wish to know yourself, behold yourself in the mirror of the outer world and its beings! What is in your soul shall speak to you far more clearly from the eyes of companions than if you harden yourself and sink into your own soul. That is an important and essential truth which no one who wishes to walk on the white path may ignore. There are many people today who have transformed their ordinary egotism into a more refined egotism. They call it theosophical development, when they have allowed their ordinary, everyday selves to rise as high as possible. They wish to bring out the personal element. The true occult knowledge, by contrast, shows man how his inner nature is elucidated when he learns to perceive his higher self in the world.

When a person has developed himself through the contemplation of these convictions, when his self flows out over all things, when he feels the blossom that grows before him as he feels his finger moving, when he knows that the whole earth and the whole world is his body, then he learns to know his higher self. Then he speaks to the flower as to a member of his own body: you belong to me, you are a part of myself. Gradually he experiences what is called the seventh step of the Rosicrucian path: godliness. This represents the element of feeling which is necessary to lead man up into the higher worlds, where he may not merely think about the higher worlds but learn to feel in them. Then the fruits of his striving to learn, under the constant guidance of his teacher, will be shown to him, and he need not fear that his occult path might lead him into an abyss. All things which have been described as dangers of occult development do not come into question if one has been guided in the right way. When this has happened, the occult seeker becomes a true helper of humanity.

During Imagination, the possibility arises for the individual to go through a certain portion of the night in a conscious condition. His physical body sleeps as usual, but a part of his sleep-condition becomes animated by significant dreams. These are the first heralds of his entrance into the higher worlds. Gradually, he leads his experiences over into his ordinary consciousness. He then sees astral beings in his entire environment, even here in the room between the chairs, or out in the woods and meadows.

Man reaches three stages during imaginative knowledge. On the first stage, he perceives the beings which stand behind physical sense-impressions. Behind the colour red or blue stands a being, behind each rose, behind each animal stands a species- or group-soul. He becomes day-clairvoyant. If he now waits for a while and practises Imagination quietly, and steeps himself in the occult script, he also becomes day-clairaudient. On the third level, he becomes acquainted with all the things one finds in the astral world which draw man down and lead him into evil, but which actually are intended to lead him upwards. He learns to know Kamaloca.[13]

Through that which forms the fourth, fifth, and sixth parts of Rosicrucian training, that is, the life-rhythm, the relation of microcosm to macrocosm, and contemplation of the macrocosm, the pupil reaches three further stages. In the first, he attains knowledge of the conditions of life between death and a new birth. This confronts him in Devachan. The next is the ability to see how forms change from one state to another, transmutation, the metamorphosis of form. Man did not always have the lungs he has today, for example; he acquired them first in Lemurian times.[10] During the preceding Hyperborean epoch they had another form; before that, another form, because he found himself in an astral condition; and before that, yet another form, because he was in Devachan. One could also say: at this stage, man becomes acquainted with the relationships between the different globes, which is to say that he experiences how one globe or condition of form passes over into another. As a last step, before he passes over into still higher worlds, he beholds the metamorphosis of the conditions of life. He perceives how the different beings pass through different kingdoms, or rounds, and how one kingdom passes over into another. Then he must ascend to still higher stages.

What has been pursued here will give you enough material to ponder over for the present. Those things must be really pondered over; that is the first step to ascend to the heights. Therefore, it is a good thing to have the path sketched once in an orderly way. It may be possible to take a journey on the physical plane without a map of the country. On the astral plane, however, to be given such a map is necessary. Regard these communications as a kind of map, and they will be useful to you not only in this life but also when you step through the portal into the higher worlds. Whoever takes up these things through spiritual science will be served well by this map after death. The occultist knows how wretched it often is for those who arrive on the other side and have no idea where they really are and what they are experiencing. One who has lived with the teachings of spiritual science knows his way about and can characterize these things to himself. If man would not shrink from treading the path of knowledge, this would bring him great benefit in the other world.

II. Three Paths of Practice[14]

Stuttgart, 2 September 1906

YOU WILL have gathered from yesterday's study how important it is to develop a feeling of fellowship, which means overcoming all regard for your own ego if you wish to penetrate more deeply into the spiritual life. For example, anyone who aspires to occult development must among other things get rid of the following form of egoism. He must not say: 'What good is it for me to hear about occult things from others when I cannot see them for myself?' That implies a lack of trust. He must trust a person who has reached a certain stage of development. People work together, and if someone has achieved more than others, he will not have achieved it for himself alone but for all the others, and they are called upon to listen to him. By this means his own powers are enhanced, and his hearers, through the very fact of having first given him their trust, will gradually become able to gain knowledge for themselves. You should not want to take a second step before the first.

There are three paths of occult development: the eastern, the Christian-Gnostic and the Christian-Rosicrucian, or simply the Rosicrucian. They are distinguished above all by the extent to which the pupil surrenders himself to his teacher. What, then, happens to someone who enters on occult development? What are the necessary preconditions for it?

Let us first consider the life of an ordinary human being nowadays. From early till late he is occupied with his work and his daily experiences; he makes use of his intellect and his outer senses. He lives and works in what we call the waking state. But that is only one state; between waking and sleeping there is another. In this state he is aware of pictures, dream pictures, passing through his soul. These pictures are not directly related to the external world and ordinary reality. We may call this the dream-state, and it is interesting to study how it takes its course. Many people suppose that dreams are nonsense, but this is not so. Even with people today dreams have a meaning, but not that of experiences in waking life. When we are awake, our mental pictures always correspond to definite facts and experiences; in our dreams they do not. For instance, you may dream that you hear the clatter of horses' hooves, and when you wake up you realize that you were hearing the ticking of the clock by your bedside. Dreams are symbolic pictures. You may have a dream which tells a whole story. A student, for instance, may dream about a duel and all its preliminary details, from the request for pistols to the report of the shot which wakes him – and then he realizes that he has knocked down the chair that stood by his bed. Or again, a peasant woman may dream that she is on her way to church. She enters, she hears the priest utter lofty sayings, with his arms moving. Suddenly his arms turn into wings and then the priest starts to crow. She wakes up and hears the cock crowing outside!

You can see from these examples that in dreams we live in a very different sort of time from that of our waking consciousness. The actual cause of the dream I have quoted was the last event in point of time. The reason is that such a dream flashes through the soul in a moment and has its own inner time. You must picture it in this way: when you wake up and remember all the details you extend this inner time yourself, so that the events seem to have occurred in that extended period. This will also help you to get some idea of how time appears in the astral world.[9] A small experience thus creates a long dramatic course of events. The dream flashes through the soul in a moment and in a flash arouses a whole series of pictures. In this way you yourself transpose time into the dream.

Inner conditions may also be represented symbolically in dream. For instance, you may have a headache and dream that you are in a cellar with a lot of cobwebs. Or the beating of your heart or a feeling of being hot may be represented in a dream by a fiery stove. Some people who possess a particular inner sensitivity may have a different experience. They may dream, for instance, that they are in an unhappy situation. Here the dream is prophetic – a symbol of some latent illness which will come out in a few days' time. Many people even dream of the remedy for such an illness. In short, our manner of perception in dreams is quite different from that of ordinary life.

The third state is that of dreamless sleep, sleep without consciousness, when nothing comes before the soul. Now if you begin to be aware of higher worlds as a result of inner development, the first indication you will notice is that your dreams become more regular and meaningful. Above all, you will gain knowledge through your dreams, provided only that you pay careful attention to them. Later, you may notice that your dreams become more frequent, until you come to feel that you have been dreaming all night through. Again, you may notice that your dreams are concerned with things which do not exist at all in the outside world and which you cannot possibly experience physically. You will find that in your dreams you no longer see things which originate in the outer world or symbolic conditions such as those I described above, but, as I have just said, you will experience pictures of things which have no existence in the sense-world, and you will then notice that your dreams are saying something important. For instance, you may dream that a friend of yours is in danger from fire and you may see him getting nearer and nearer to the danger. The next day you may learn that this friend was taken ill during the night. You did not actually see him falling ill; you saw a symbolic picture of it. Thus your dreams may be influenced from higher worlds, so that you experience something which does not exist in the physical world; that is how impressions from higher worlds pass over into dreams. This is a very important bridge to higher occult development.

Someone might say that all this was only dreamt – how can any significance be read into it? But that is a wrong approach. Take the following example. It is said that Edison once dreamt how to make an electric light bulb; he remembered the dream and made the light bulb in accordance with it. Suppose someone had then come along and said: 'The lamp is no good – it was only a dream.' You can see that what matters is not the mere fact of dreaming but whether the dream has significance for life. Quite often dreams of this sort go unheeded because we fail to notice them. That is wrong. It is just these delicate points that we should attend to; then we shall make progress.

Later comes a stage when the nature of reality is disclosed to the pupil in dream, and he can then test the dream by the reality. When he has advanced so far that he has the whole picture-world present before him in daylight and not only during sleep, he is then able to analyse with his intellect whether what he sees is true. This means that it is wrong to use dream-pictures as a foundation for wisdom; the pupil must wait for them to enter into his daytime experience. If he exercises conscious control over them, a stage is soon reached when the pupil not only sees what is physically present but can truly perceive the astral element in a human being, his soul and his aura. He then learns to understand what the shapes and colours in the astral body signify – what passions, for example, they express. So he learns gradually to spell out, as it were, the soul-world. But he must always realize that everything there is symbolical.

Here it might be objected that if you see symbols only, some particular event might be symbolized by all sorts of images, and you could never be sure that a given image has a consistent meaning. But when you reach a certain stage one image always does stand for one thing, just as in the ordinary world one object is always represented by the same mental concept. For instance, you will find that a given passion is always represented for everyone by the same image. The important thing is to learn how to read the images correctly.

Now you can understand why the sacred books of all religions tend to speak almost entirely through symbolic images. Wisdom, for example, may be described as light; the reason is that to anyone who is occultly developed the wisdom of man and other beings always appears as astral light. Passions appear as fire. The ancient religious documents do not tell only of things on the physical plane, but also of events on higher planes. They owe their origin to seers and are concerned with higher worlds; hence they have to speak to us in pictures. Everything narrated from the Akashic Record has for the same reason been presented in pictures of this kind.[7]

The next condition experienced by the pupil is called 'continuity of consciousness'. When an ordinary person is completely withdrawn from the sense-world in sleep he is unconscious. This is no longer so with a pupil who has reached the stage just mentioned. By day and by night, with no interruption, he lives in a state of fully clear consciousness, even when his physical body is at rest.

After some time the pupil's entry into a new but quite specific state of consciousness is marked by the fact that sounds and words are added to the images. The images speak to him in an intelligible language. They tell him what they are, without any possibility of deception. These are the sounds and speech of Devachan, the Music of the Spheres. Everything speaks forth its own name and its relation to other things. This comes in addition to astral sight, and it marks the seer's entry into Devachan. Once a person has reached this devachanic state, the lotus flowers, the chakras or wheels begin to revolve at specific places in the astral body, turning like the hands of a clock from left to right.[9] These are the sense-organs of the astral body, but their mode of perception is an active one. The eye, for example, is at rest; it allows the light to enter and only then perceives it. The lotus flowers, on the other hand, perceive only when they are in motion and take hold of an object. The vibrations caused by the revolving

lotus flowers bring them into contact with the astral substance, and that is how perception on the astral plane occurs.

What are the forces which activate the lotus flowers, and
where do they come from? We know that during sleep the
exhausted forces of the physical and etheric bodies are re-
stored by the astral body; by its inherent regularity it can make
up for irregularities in the physical and etheric bodies. It is
these forces, normally used for overcoming fatigue, which
animate the lotus flowers. When a person enters on occult
development, he is thus really withdrawing certain forces
from his physical and etheric bodies. If these forces were to be
withdrawn permanently from the physical body, the person
would fall ill; he would find himself utterly exhausted. If
therefore he does not want to injure himself, morally as well
as physically, he must find something to replace these forces.

He must remind himself of the general rule: rhythm
restores power. Here you have an important occult principle.
Most people today lead lives devoid of any regular rhythm,
especially as regards their thoughts and their behaviour.
Anyone who allowed the distractions of the outer world to
gain a hold on him would be unable to avoid the dangers to
which his physical body would be exposed in the course of his
occult development by the withdrawal of these forces of
renewal. Hence he has to strive to introduce a rhythmic
element into his life. Of course he cannot arrange his days so
that each day passes exactly like another. But he can at least
pursue certain activities regularly, and indeed anyone who
wants to develop on the occult path will have to do this. Thus
he should, for example, do certain exercises of meditation and
concentration at a chosen time every morning. He can also
bring rhythm into his life if in the evening he reviews the
events of the day in reverse order. If he can bring in further
regularities, so much the better: in that way his life will take
its course in harmony with the laws of the world. Everything
in the system of nature is rhythmical – the course of the sun,
the passage of the seasons, of day and night, and so on. Plants,

too, grow rhythmically. It is true that the higher we go in the kingdoms of nature the less rhythm we find, but even in animals a certain rhythm can be observed. For instance, animals mate at regular times. Only man now leads an unrhythmical, chaotic life: nature has deserted him.

Man's task, therefore, is deliberately to infuse some rhythm into this chaotic life, and he has available certain means through which he can bring this harmony and rhythm into his physical and etheric bodies. Both these bodies will then gradually develop such rhythms that they will correct themselves when the astral body withdraws. If they are forced out of their proper rhythm during the day, they will of their own accord regain the right kind of movement when they are at rest.

The means available consist in the following exercises, which must be practised in addition to meditation:

1. *Thought control.* This means preventing, at least for a short time every day, all sorts of thoughts from drifting through the mind, and bringing a certain ordered tranquillity into the course of thinking. You must take a definite idea, set it in the centre of your thinking, and then logically arrange your further thoughts in such a way that they are all closely linked with the original idea. Even if you do this for only a minute, it can be of great importance for the rhythm of the physical and etheric bodies.

2. *Initiative in action.* You must compel yourself to some action, however trivial, which owes its origin to your own initiative, to some task you have laid on yourself. Most actions derive not from your own initiative but from your family circumstances, your education, your calling and so on. You must therefore give up a little time to performing actions which derive from yourself alone. They need not be important; quite insignificant actions fulfil the same purpose.

3. *Tranquillity.* Here the pupil learns to regulate his emotions so that he is not at one moment up in the skies and at the next down in the dumps. Anyone who refuses to do this for

fear of losing his originality in action or his artistic sensibility can never go through occult development. Tranquillity means that you are master of yourself in the most intense pleasure and in the deepest grief. Indeed, we become truly receptive to the joys and sorrows of the world only when we do not give ourselves over egotistically to them. The greatest artists owe their greatest achievements precisely to this tranquillity, because through it they have opened their eyes to subtle and inwardly significant impressions.

4. *Freedom from prejudice.* This, the fourth characteristic, sees good in everything and looks for the positive element in all things. Relevant to this is a Persian legend told of Christ Jesus. One day Christ Jesus saw a dead dog lying by the wayside; he stopped to look at the animal while those around him turned away in disgust. Then Jesus said: 'What beautiful teeth the dog has!' In that hideous corpse he saw not what was ugly or evil but the beauty of the white teeth. If you can acquire this mood, you will look everywhere for the good and the positive, and you will find it everywhere. This has a powerful effect on the physical and etheric bodies.

5. *Faith.* Next comes faith, which in its occult sense implies something rather different from its ordinary meaning. During occult development you must never allow your judgement of the future to be influenced by the past. Under certain circumstances you must exclude all that you have experienced hitherto, so that you can meet every new experience with new faith. The occultist must do this quite consciously. For instance, if someone comes up to you and tells you that the church steeple is crooked and at an angle of 45 degrees, most people would say that is impossible. The occultist must always leave a way open to believe. He must go so far as to have faith in everything that happens in the world; otherwise he bars the way to new experiences. You must always be open to new experiences; by this means your physical and etheric bodies will be brought into a condition which may be compared with the contented mood of a brooding hen.

6. *Inner Balance*. This is a natural outcome of the other five qualities. The pupil must keep the six qualities in mind, take his life in hand, and be prepared to progress slowly in the sense of the proverb about drops of water wearing away a stone.

Now if anyone acquires higher powers through some artificial means without attending to all this, he will be in a bad way. In ordinary life today the spiritual and the physical are intermingled, somewhat like a blue and yellow liquid in a glass of water. Occult development sets going a process rather like the work of a chemist who separates the two liquids. Soul and body are separated in a similar way, and the benefits of the mingling are lost. An ordinary person, because the soul stays in close relation to the body, is not subjected to the more grotesque passions. But as a result of the separation I have been talking about, the physical body, with all its attributes, may be left to itself, and this can lead to all manner of excesses. Thus a person who has embarked on occult development, but has not taken care to cultivate moral qualities, may manifest certain traits which as an ordinary human being he had long ago ceased to exhibit. He may suddenly become a liar, vengeful, quick to anger; all sorts of characteristics which had previously been toned down may appear in a violent form. This may happen even if someone who has neglected moral development becomes unduly absorbed in the teachings of Theosophy.

We have seen that a person must first pass through the stage of spiritual sight and only then comes to the stage of spiritual hearing. While he is still at the first stage he has of course to learn how the images are related to their objects. He would find himself plunged into the stormy sea of astral experiences if he were left to fend for himself. For this reason he needs a guide who can tell him from the start how these things are related and how to find his bearings in the astral world. Hence the need to find a guru on whom he can strictly rely. In this connection three different ways of development can be distinguished.

1. *The eastern way*, also called *yoga*. Here an initiated person living on the physical plane acts as the guru of another, who entrusts himself to his guru completely and in all details. This method will go best if during his occult development the pupil eliminates his own self entirely and hands it over to his guru, who must even advise him on every action he may take. This absolute surrender of one's own self suits the Indian character, but there is no place for it in European culture.

2. *The Christian way*. Here, in place of individual gurus, there is one great Guru, Christ Jesus Himself, for everyone. The feeling of belonging to Christ Jesus, of being one with Him, can take the place of surrender to an individual guru. But the pupil has first to be led to Christ by an earthly guru, so that in a certain sense he still depends on a guru on the physical plane.

3. *The Rosicrucian way*, which leaves the pupil with the greatest possible independence. The guru here is not a leader but an adviser; he gives directions for the necessary inner training. At the same time he takes good care that, parallel with the occult training, there is a definite development of thinking, without which no occult training can be carried through. This is because there is something about thinking which does not apply to anything else. When we are on the physical plane, we perceive with the physical senses only what is to be found on that plane. Astral perceptions are valid for the astral plane; devachanic hearing is valid only in Devachan. Thus each plane has its own specific form of perception. But one activity – logical thinking – goes through all worlds. Logic is the same on all three planes. Thus on the physical plane you can learn something which is valid also for the higher planes; and this is the method followed by Rosicrucian training when on the physical plane it gives primary attention to thinking, and for this purpose uses the means available on the physical plane. A penetrative thinking can be culti-vated by studying theosophical truths, or by practising mental

exercises. Anyone who wishes further training for the intellect can study books such as *Truth and Science* and *The Philosophy of Freedom*, which are written deliberately in such a way that a thinking trained by them can move with certainty on the highest planes. Even a person who studies these books and knows nothing of Theosophy might find his way about in the higher worlds. But, as I have said, the teachings of Theosophy act in the same way.

Here, then, the guru is only the friend and adviser of the pupil, for by training his reason the pupil will be training the best guru for himself. But he will of course still need a guru to advise him on how to make progress in freedom.

Among Europeans, the Christian way is best suited to those whose feelings are most strongly developed. Those who have more or less broken away from the Church and rely rather on science, but have been led by science into a doubting frame of mind, will do best with the Rosicrucian way.

III. Oriental and Christian Training[14]

Stuttgart, 3 September 1906

YESTERDAY WE concluded by outlining the three methods of occult development: the eastern, the Christian and the Rosicrucian. Today we will begin by going more closely into the details which distinguish these three paths. But first I should say that no occult school sees in its teaching and requirements anything like a moral law valid for all mankind. The requirements apply only to those who deliberately choose to devote themselves to a particular occult training. You can, for instance, be a very good Christian and fulfil everything that the Christian religion prescribes for the laity without undergoing a Christian occult training. It goes without saying that you can be a good man and come to a form of the higher life without any occult training.

As I said earlier, the eastern training calls for strict submission to the guru.[15] I will describe briefly the kind of instruction that an eastern teacher gives. You will realize that the actual instructions cannot be given publicly; I can indicate only the stages of the path. The instructions can be divided into eight parts:

1. Yama
2. Niyama
3. Asanam
4. Pranayama
5. Pratyahara
6. Dharana
7. Dhyanam
8. Samadhi

1. *Yama* includes all the abstentions required of anyone who wishes to undergo yoga training: Do not lie, do not kill, do not steal, do not lead a dissolute life, desire nothing.

The injunction *Do not kill* is very stringent and applies to all creatures. No living creature may be killed or even injured, and the more strictly this rule is observed the further will the pupil progress. Whether this rule can be observed in our civilization is another matter. Every killing, even of a flea, impedes occult development. Whether someone is obliged to do it – that again is a different question.

You will understand the command *Do not lie* if you recall what I said about the astral plane, where to lie is to kill and every lie is a murder. Lying therefore comes into the same category as killing.

The precept *Do not steal* also has to be applied most strictly. A European might claim that he does not steal. But the eastern yogi does not look at it so simply. In the regions where these exercises were first promulgated by the great teachers of humanity, conditions were much simpler: stealing was easy to define. But a yoga teacher would not agree that Europeans do not steal. For example, if I unjustifiably appropriate another man's labour, or if I procure for myself a profit which may be legally permissible but which involves the exploitation of another person – all this the yoga teacher would call stealing. With us, social relations have become so complex that many people violate this commandment without the slightest awareness of doing so. Suppose you have money and deposit it in a bank. You do nothing with it; you exploit no one. But suppose now the banker starts speculating and exploits other people with your money. In the occult sense you will be responsible for it, and the events will burden your karma. You can see that this precept requires deep consideration if you are entering on a path of occult development.

With regard to the injunction *Do not lead a dissolute life*, take a person with private means whose capital is invested without his knowledge in a distillery; he is just as culpable as the producer of strong drinks. The fact that he knew nothing about it makes no difference to his karma. There is only one way of keeping to the right path with these abstentions: strive to need nothing. Even if you have great possessions, in so far as you strive to have no needs you will injure no one.

The injunction *Desire nothing* is especially hard to carry out.

It means that the pupil must strive to have no needs, no desire for anything in the world, and to do only what the outer world demands of him. He must even suppress any feeling of pleasure at doing good to someone; he must be moved to help not by any such feeling but simply by the sight of suffering. And if he has to spend money, he must not think of his own wishes or desires but must say to himself: 'I need this to maintain my body or to meet the needs of my spirit, as everyone else does. I do not desire it, but am considering only how best to live my life in the world.'

In yoga training this concept of *Yama* is, as I have said, taken most strictly; it could not be transplanted to Europe as it stands.

2. *Niyama*. This means the observance of religious customs. In India, where these rules are chiefly applied, a problem is solved which causes many difficulties in European civilization. For us it is very easy to say that we have passed beyond dogmas; we hold to the inner truth only and have no use for outer forms. The further a European has got away from religious observances, the more exalted does he imagine himself to be. The Hindu takes the opposite view; he holds firmly to the rites of his religion and no one may touch them, but anyone is free to form his own opinion of them. There are sacred rites which have come down from very ancient times and signify something very profound. An uneducated person will have very elementary ideas about them; a more highly cultured human being will have different and better ideas, but no one will say that anyone else's ideas are wrong. The wise and the unlearned observe the same customs. There are no dogmas, only rites. Hence these deeply religious customs can be observed by all, and in them the wise and the simple are brought together. Thus the rites are socially unifying. No one is restricted in his opinions by conforming to a strict ritual.

The Christian religion has followed the opposite principle. Not customs but opinions have been imposed on people, and the consequence is that formlessness has become the rule in

our social life. So begins a complete disregard of all observances that could draw human beings together; every form that
expresses symbolically a higher truth is gradually rejected.
This is a great loss for human development, especially for
development in the eastern sense.

In Europe today there are plenty of people who think they
have learnt to do without dogmas, yet it is precisely the free-
thinkers and the materialists who are the worst fanatics for
dogmas. The dogma of materialism is much more oppressive
than any other. The infallibility of the Pope is no longer valid for
many people, but instead we have the infallibility of the professor. Even the most liberal-minded, whatever they may say to the
contrary, are victims of the dogmas of materialism. Think of the
dogmas which burden lawyers, doctors and so on. Every university professor teaches his own dogma. Or think how people suffer
from the dogma of the infallibility of public opinion, of the
newspapers! The eastern teacher of yoga does not demand that
the ceremonies which unite the learned and unlearned together
should be abandoned; these sacred ancient rites are symbols of
the highest wisdom. No culture is possible without such formal
observances; to believe otherwise is an illusion. Suppose for
instance a colony is founded with no forms or accepted customs.
Clearly a colony such as that, with no Church, no religious
services or observances, could exist quite well for a time, because
its people would continue to live in accordance with the rules
and conventions they had brought with them. But as soon as
these were lost the colony would collapse, for every culture must
embody a certain pattern which will give expression to its inner
character. Modern civilization must recover the forms it has lost;
it must learn again how to give external expression to its inner
life. In the long run social life is conditioned by its pattern, its
formal customs. The ancient sages knew this, and hence they
held firmly to religious practices.

3. *Asanam* means the adoption of a certain bodily posture
in meditation. This is much more important for the oriental
than for the European, because the European body is no

longer so sensitive to the flow of certain subtle currents. The body of the oriental is even nowadays more delicately organised; it responds readily to the currents which pass from East to West, from North to South, from the heights to the depths. Spiritual currents flow through the universe, and it is for this reason that churches are built with a particular orientation. It is for this reason also that the yoga teacher makes his pupil adopt a special posture; the pupil has to keep his hands and feet in a particular position, so that the currents may flow through his body in the right direction. If the Hindu did not bring his body into this harmony, he would risk losing all the benefits of his meditation.

4. *Pranayama* is breathing, yoga-breathing. It is an essential and detailed part of eastern yoga training. Christian training pays almost no attention to it, but in Rosicrucian training it has regained some importance.

What does breathing signify in occult development? You can find the answer in the injunctions not to kill and not to injure any living creature. The occult teacher says: 'By breathing you are slowly, continually, killing your surroundings.' What does this mean? We breathe the air in, use it to furnish our blood with oxygen and then breathe it out again. What does this involve? We inhale the air with its oxygen; we combine the oxygen with carbon and we exhale carbon dioxide, in which no man or animal can live. We breathe in oxygen and breathe out carbon dioxide, which is a poison; and this means that with every breath we draw we are dealing death to other beings in our environment. Bit by bit we are killing our whole environment: we inhale the breath of life and exhale air which we can make no further use of. The occult teacher is concerned to alter this. If there were only men and animals in the world, all the oxygen would soon be used up and all living creatures would die. It is thanks to the plants that this does not happen, for in plants the breathing process is the reverse of ours. They assimilate carbon dioxide, separate the carbon from the oxygen, and use the carbon to build up their bodies. They liberate oxygen, and human beings and animals breathe it in again. So do the plants renew the life-giving air; otherwise all life would long ago have been destroyed. We owe our life to the plants, and in this way plants, animals and human beings are complementary.

But this process will change in the future, and since anyone who is undergoing occult training must begin to do what others will achieve at some time in the future, he must learn not to kill with his breath. That is Pranayama, the science of the breath. Our modern materialistic age places health under the sign of fresh air; but our modern way of achieving health through fresh air is one that terminates in death. A yogi, on the other hand, will retire into a cave and as far as possible will breathe the air he has himself exhaled – unlike the European, who is always wanting to open windows. A yogi has learnt the art of contaminating the air as little as possible because he has learnt how to use it up. How does he do it? The secret has always been known to the European occult schools, where it was called the finding of the Stone of the Wise, the Philosopher's Stone.

At the turn of the eighteenth to the nineteenth century a good deal of information about occult development leaked out. The Stone of the Wise was often mentioned in published writings, but one can see that the author understood little of it, even though it all came from the right sources. In 1797 a local Thuringian newspaper printed an article about the Stone of the Wise which included, *inter alia*, the following: 'The Stone of the Wise is something one has only to recognize, for every man has seen it. It is something which everyone holds in his hand for part of almost every day, but without knowing that it is the Philosopher's Stone.' This is an enigmatic way of indicating that the Philosopher's Stone can be found everywhere. Yet this strange expression is literally true.

This is how it comes about. The plant, as it builds up its body, takes in the carbon dioxide and retains the carbon for its body-building purposes. Human beings and animals eat the plants, take in the carbon, and give it up as carbon dioxide when they breathe out. So we have a carbon cycle. In the future there will be a great change. Man will learn to extend the range of his innate powers and will gradually come to do for himself what at present he leaves to the plant. Just as man passed through the plant and animal kingdoms in the course of his evolution, so will he in a certain sense retrace his steps. He will himself become plant; he will take up the plant-nature into himself and accomplish the whole plant-process within himself. He will retain the carbon dioxide and will consciously build up his body with it, as the plant now builds up its own body unconsciously. He will prepare the necessary oxygen in his own organs, unite it with carbon to form carbon dioxide, and then deposit the carbon again in himself. Thus he will be able to build up his bodily structure. Here is an idea which opens up a great perspective for the future; and when it comes about man will cease to be a killer with his breath.

Now we know that carbon and diamond are the same substance; diamond is more thoroughly crystallized and a more transparent form of carbon. Hence we need not think that in the future people will go about looking very dark-skinned. Their bodies will consist of soft, transparent carbon. At that stage man will have found the Philosopher's Stone and he will transform his own body into it.

Anyone undergoing occult development has to anticipate this process as far as possible. He must deprive his breath of the capacity to kill, and must organize his breathing so that the air he exhales is usable and can be breathed again. How is this to be accomplished? You have to bring rhythm into your breathing. The teacher gives the necessary instructions. Breathing in, holding your breath and breathing out again – this must be done rhythmically, if only for a short period. With every rhythmical exhalation the air is improved, slowly but surely. Here the old saying applies – drops of water wear away the stone. The chemists cannot yet confirm this; their instruments are too coarse to detect the finer substances, but the occultist knows that breath imbued with rhythm is life-promoting and contains more than the normal amount of oxygen. The breath can be purified also, and at the same time, by meditation. This, too, contributes, if only by a very little, towards bringing the plant-nature back into man, so that he may become a being who does not kill.

5. *Pratyahara*, the curbing of sense-perception. Nowadays in ordinary life a person receives a continual stream of sense-impressions and allows them all to work on him. The occult teacher says to the pupil: 'You must concentrate on a single sense-impression for a specified number of minutes and pass on to another only by your own free choice.'

6. *Dharana*, when the pupil has done that for a while he must learn to make himself deaf and blind to all sense-impressions; he must turn away from them and try to hold in his thought only the concepts they leave behind. If he thus lives in concepts only, and controls his thoughts and links one concept to another by his own free choice, he has reached the condition known as *Dharana*.

7. *Dhyanam*. There are concepts – often disregarded by Europeans – which do not derive from sense-impressions. We have to form them for ourselves – mathematical concepts, for example. No perfect triangle exists in the outer world; it can only be conceived in thought, and the same is true of a circle. Then there is a whole range of concepts which anyone undertaking occult training must study intensively. They are symbolic concepts which are connected with some objects – for example, the hexagram, or the pentagram, symbols which occultism can explain. The pupil must keep his mind sharply concentrated on such symbolic objects, not to be found in the outer world. It is the same with another kind of concept: for example, that of the species Lion, which can be laid hold of only in thought. On these, too, the pupil must focus his attention. Finally, there are moral ideas, such for example as the following from *Light on the Path*: 'Before the eye can see, it must be incapable of tears.'[16] This, too, cannot be experienced outwardly, but only inwardly. This meditation on concepts which have no sense-perceptible counterpart is called *Dhyanam*.

8. Finally, *Samadhi*, the most difficult of all. After concentrating for a very long time on an idea which has no sense-perceptible counterpart, you allow your mind to rest in it and your soul to be filled with it. Then you let the idea go, so that nothing is left in your consciousness. But you must not fall asleep, as would then normally happen; you must remain conscious. In that state the secrets of the higher worlds begin to reveal themselves. This state can be described as follows. You are thinking, for you are conscious, but you have no thoughts, and into this thinking without thoughts the spiritual powers are able to pour their content. But as long as you yourself fill your thinking, they cannot come in. The longer you can hold in your consciousness this activity of thinking without thoughts, the more will the supersensible world reveal itself to you.

These are the eight realms with which a teacher of eastern yoga deals.

Now we will speak about the Christian way of occult training, as far as this is possible, and we shall see how it differs from the eastern way. This Christian way can be followed with the advice of a teacher who knows what has to be done and can rectify mistakes at every step. But in Christian training the great Guru is Christ Jesus Himself. Hence it is essential to have a firm belief in the presence and the life on earth of the Christ. Without this, a feeling of union with Him is impossible. Further, we must recognize that in the Gospel of St John we have a document which originates with the great Guru Himself and can itself be a source of instruction. This Gospel is something we can experience in our own inner being and not something we merely believe. Whoever has absorbed it in the right way will no longer need to prove the reality of Christ Jesus, for he will have found Him.

In Christian training you must meditate on this Gospel, not simply read and reread it. The Gospel begins: 'In the beginning was the Word, and the Word was with God and the Word was God...' The opening verses of this Gospel, rightly understood, are sentences for meditation and must be inwardly absorbed in

the condition of *Dhyanam*, as described above. If in the morning,
before other impressions have entered the soul, you live for five
minutes solely in these sentences, with everything else excluded
from your thoughts, and if you continue to do this over the years
with absolute patience and perseverance, you will find that these
words are not only something to be understood; you will realize
that they have an occult power, and you will indeed experience
through them a transformation of the soul. In a certain sense you
become clairvoyant through these words, so that everything in
St John's Gospel can be seen with astral vision.

Then, under the direction of the teacher, and after meditating again on the five opening verses, the pupil allows the
first chapter to pass through his mind for seven days. During
the following week, after again meditating on the five opening
verses, he goes on to the second chapter, and so in the same
way up to the twelfth. He will soon learn how powerful an
experience this is; how he is led into the events in Palestine
when Christ Jesus lived there, as they are inscribed in the
Akashic Record, and how he can actually experience it all.
And then, when he reaches the thirteenth chapter, he has to
experience the separate stages of Christian initiation.

The first stage is the Washing of the Feet. We must understand the significance of this great scene. Christ Jesus bends
down before those who are lower than himself. This humility
towards those who are lower than we are, and at whose expense
we have been able to rise, must be present everywhere in the
world. If a plant were able to think, it would thank the minerals
for giving it the ground on which it can lead a higher form of life,
and the animal would have to bow down before the plant and
say: 'To thee I owe the possibility of my own existence.' In the
same way man should recognize what he owes to all the rest of
nature. So also, in our society, a person holding a higher position
should bow before those who stand lower and say: 'But for the
diligence of those who labour on my behalf, I could not stand
where I do.' And so on through all stages of human existence up
to Christ Jesus Himself, who bows down in meekness before the

Apostles and says: 'You are my ground, and to you I fulfil the saying, "He who would be first must be last, and he who would be Lord must be the servant of all".' The Washing of the Feet betokens this willingness to serve, this bowing down in perfect humility. This is a feeling that everyone committed to occult development must have.

If the pupil has permeated himself with this humility, he will have experienced the first stage of Christian initiation. He will know by two signs, an outer and an inner, that he has gone thus far. The outer sign is that he feels as though his feet were being bathed with water. The inner sign is an astral vision which will quite certainly come: he sees himself washing the feet of a number of persons. This picture rises up in his dreams as an astral vision, and every pupil has the same vision. When he has experienced it, he will have truly absorbed this whole chapter.

The second stage is that of the Scourging. When the pupil has reached this point, he must, while he reads of the Scourging and allows it to act upon him, develop another feeling. He must learn to stand firm under the heavy strokes of life, saying to himself: 'I will stand up to whatever pains and sorrows come to me.' The outer sign of this is that the pupil feels a kind of prickling pain all over his body. The inner sign is that in a dream-vision he sees himself being scourged.

The third stage is that of the Crowning with Thorns, and for this he has to acquire yet another feeling: he learns to stand firm even when he is scorned and ridiculed because of all that he holds most sacred. The outer sign of this is that he experiences a severe headache; the inward symptom is that he has an astral vision of himself being crowned with thorns.

The fourth stage is that of the Crucifixion. A new and quite definite feeling must be developed. The pupil must cease to regard his body as the most important thing for him; his body must become as indifferent to him as a piece of wood. He then comes to look quite objectively on the body he carries with him through life; it has become for him the wood of the Cross.

He need not despise it, any more than he does any other tool. The outer sign for having reached this stage is that during the pupil's meditation red marks (stigmata) appear at those places on his body which are called the sacred wounds. They do indeed appear on the hands and feet, and on the right side of the body at the level of the heart. The inward sign is that the pupil has a vision of himself hanging on the Cross.

The fifth stage is that of the Mystical Death. Now the pupil experiences the nothingness of earthly things, and indeed dies for a while to all earthly things.

Only the most scanty descriptions can be given of these later stages of Christian initiation. The pupil experiences in an astral vision that darkness reigns everywhere and that the earthly world has fallen away. A black veil spreads over that which is to come, and while he is in this condition the pupil comes to know all that exists as evil and wickedness in the world. This is the Descent into Hell. Then he experiences the tearing away of the curtain and the world of Devachan appears before him. This is the rending of the veil of the Temple.

The sixth stage is that of the Burial. Just as at the fourth stage the pupil learnt to regard his own body objectively, so now he has to develop the feeling that everything else around him in the world is as much part of what truly belongs to him as his own body is. The body then extends far beyond its skin. The pupil is no longer a separate being; he is united with the whole planet. The earth has become his body; he is buried in the earth.

The seventh stage, that of the Resurrection, cannot be described in words. Hence occultism teaches that the seventh stage can be conceived only by a person whose soul has been entirely freed from the brain, and only to such a human being could it be described. Hence we cannot do more than mention it here. The Christian teacher indicates the way to this experience.

When a person has lived through this seventh stage, Christianity has become an inner experience of the soul. He is now wholly united with Christ Jesus; Christ Jesus is in him.

IV. Rosicrucian Training and Mysteries of the Earth[14]

Stuttgart, 4 September 1906

YESTERDAY WE described the various stages by which pupils of the eastern and the Christian occult schools came to higher knowledge. Today I will try to describe, in a similar way, the stages of Rosicrucian training.

You must not imagine that the Rosicrucian training contradicts the other two. It has existed since the fourteenth century, and it had to be introduced because mankind then needed a different form of training. Among the initiates it was foreseen that a time would come when because of the gradual increase of knowledge human beings would be confused in matters of religious faith. Therefore a form of instruction had to be created for those who felt within themselves the discord between faith and knowledge. In the Middle Ages the most learned men were also those of the greatest faith and piety; and for a long time afterwards those who had made headway in scientific knowledge could not conceive of any contradictions between knowledge and faith. We are usually told that faith was shaken by the ideas of Copernicus, but that is quite wrong. After all, Copernicus dedicated his book to the Pope! It is only in quite recent times that this conflict has gradually developed. The Masters of Wisdom saw that this was bound to happen and that a new path would have to be found for those whose faith had been destroyed.

For persons much occupied with science, the necessary path towards initiation is the Rosicrucian, for the Rosicrucian method shows that the highest knowledge of mundane things is thoroughly compatible with the highest knowledge of spiritual truths. It is precisely through the Rosicrucian path

that those who have been led away from Christian belief by
what they take to be science can learn to understand Christianity truly for the first time. By this method anyone can
come to a deeper grasp of the truth of Christianity. Truth is
one, but it can be reached along different paths – just as at the
foot of a mountain there are various paths, but they all meet
at the summit.

The essence of Rosicrucian training may be described in
two words: true self-knowledge. The Rosicrucian pupil has to
distinguish two things, not merely theoretically but practically, so that they become part of his everyday life. There are
two forms of self-knowledge – the lower form, called by the
Rosicrucian pupil 'self-mirroring', which should serve to
overcome the lower self, and the higher form of self-knowledge, which is born out of self-renunciation.

What is the lower form of self-knowledge? It consists in the
recognition of our everyday self, of what we are and of what
we bear within us: in other words, an examination of our own
soul-life. But we must make it quite clear to ourselves that by
this means we cannot reach the higher self. When we look into
ourselves we see only what we are, and that is just what we
have to grow out of in order to surmount the ordinary self. But
how is this to be done? Most people are convinced that their
characteristics are the best, and anyone who lacks these
characteristics is uncongenial to them. Once a person has
outgrown this idea, not only in theory but in feeling, he will
be on the way to true self-knowledge.

You can get out of the habit of self-admiration by a particular method which can be practised whenever you have five
minutes for it. You must start from the principle that all characteristics are one-sided; you must learn to recognize in what
respects yours are one-sided and then try to balance them.
This principle may not amount to much in theory, but in
practice it is highly effective. If you are industrious, you must
ask yourself whether your activity may not be wrongly applied. Quickness, too, is one-sided; it needs to be supplemented

by careful deliberation. Every quality has its polar opposite; you should cultivate its opposite and then try to harmonize the two extremes. For example, make haste slowly; be quick and yet deliberate; deliberate and yet not slow. Then the pupil will begin to grow beyond himself. All this is not part of meditation, but must be acquired alongside it.

It is by attention to small details that this harmony can be achieved. If your tendency is not to let anyone finish what he is saying, you must keep a watch on yourself and make up your mind that for six weeks you will keep silent, as far as possible, when someone else is talking. Then you must accustom yourself to speak neither too loudly nor too softly. Things such as this, which are generally not thought of, contribute essentially to inner self-development, and the more attention you pay to quite insignificant characteristics the better it will be. If you try not only to acquire certain moral, intellectual or emotional qualities but to get rid of some external habit this will be particularly effective. It is a question not so much of investigating your inner self as of endeavouring to perfect the qualities which you have not yet fully developed, and to complement those you already have by cultivating their polar counterparts. Self-knowledge is one of the hardest things to acquire, and it is precisely those who think they know themselves best who are most likely to be deceived: they think too much about themselves. You should get out of the habit of fixing your attention on yourself and constantly using the word 'I' – I think, I believe, I consider this right. Above all you must get rid of the notion that your opinion is worth more than that of other people. Suppose, for instance, that someone is very clever. If he displays his cleverness in the company of people who are not so clever, his behaviour will be very ill-timed; he will be doing it only to please his own egoism. He ought to adapt his response to the needs and capacities of others. Agitators are particularly apt to offend against this rule.

In addition to all this you must cultivate patience, in the

occult sense of the word. Most people who want to achieve something cannot wait; they imagine they are already fit to receive anything. This patience derives from strict self-training, and it, too, is related to the lower form of self-knowledge.

Higher self-knowledge begins only when we can say that our higher self is not in our ordinary 'I'. It is in the whole great world outside, in the sun and the moon, in a stone or an animal: everywhere can be found the same essential being that is in us. If a man says: 'I wish to cultivate my higher self and to withdraw from the world; I want to know nothing about anything material,' he entirely fails to understand that the higher self is everywhere outside, and that his own higher self is only a small part of the Great Self outside. Certain methods of so called 'spiritual' healers make this mistake, which can be very serious. They instil into patients the idea that matter has no real existence and so there can be no illnesses. This notion is based on a false self-knowledge, and, as I have said, it can be very dangerous. This healing method calls itself Christian, but in fact it is anti-Christian.

Christianity is an outlook which sees in everything a revelation of the Divine. Everything material becomes an illusion unless we look on it as an expression of the Divine. If we disown the external world, we are disowning the Divine; if we reject the material realm, in which God has revealed himself, we are rejecting the Divine. The important thing is not to gaze into ourselves but to seek to know the Great Self which shines down into us. The lower self says: 'Standing here I am cold.' The higher Self says: 'I am also the cold, for as part of the one Self I live in the cold and make myself cold.' Again the lower self says: 'I am here in the eye which beholds the sun.' The higher Self says: 'I am in the sun and in the sun's rays I look into your eyes.'

Really to go out of yourself is to renounce yourself. Hence the Rosicrucian training aims at drawing the lower self out of man. In the early days of Theosophy the gravest mistake was made when people were told to look away from the external world and to gaze into themselves. That is a great illusion, for then we find only the lower self, the fourth principle, which imagines itself to be divine but is not so at all. We must come out of ourselves if we are to know the Divine. 'Know thyself' means also 'Overcome thyself.'

The Rosicrucian training leads its pupils through the following stages, and these go hand in hand with the six exercises already mentioned: control of thought; initiative in action; tranquillity; lack of prejudice, or positiveness; faith; and inner balance. The training itself consists of the following:

1. *Study*. Without study, a modern European cannot get to know himself. He must try, first of all, to reproduce in himself the thoughts of the whole of humanity. He must learn to think in harmony with the world-order. He must say to himself: 'If others have thought this, it must be a possible human thought; I will test whether one can live with it.' He need not swear to it as a dogma, but by studying it he must get to know what it is. The pupil must learn about the evolution of sun and planets, of the earth and humanity. Thoughts of this kind, given to us for study, purify the spirit. By following the strict lines of these thoughts, we come to form strictly logical thoughts ourselves. This kind of study, again, purifies our thoughts, and so we learn to think with strict logic. If, for instance, we are reading a difficult book, the most important thing is not to comprehend its whole content but to enter into the author's line of thought and learn to think with him. Hence the pupil should find no book too difficult; if he does, it means only that he is too easy-going to think.

The best books are those we have to take up again and again, books we cannot understand immediately but have to study sentence by sentence. It does not matter so much what we study as how we study. If we study the great truths, for instance the planetary laws, we develop an important line of thought, and this is what really matters. If we say that we want more moral teaching and nothing about planetary systems, we show great egoism. True wisdom engenders a moral life.

2. *Imagination* or *imaginative knowledge* is the second thing we have to attain. What is it and how do we achieve it? As we go through the world we must observe it in the light of Goethe's saying: 'Everything transitory is but a symbol.' Goethe was a Rosicrucian and he can lead us into the life of the soul. Everything must become for us a symbol in manifold respects. Suppose, for instance, we are walking past a meadow saffron: in form and colour it is a symbol of mourning. Another flower, the convolvulus, is a symbol of helplessness; another flower, with its splash of red, is a sign of gaiety, and so on. A bird with bright colours may be a symbol of coquetry. The symbols may actually be expressed in the names: weeping willow, forget-me-not, and so on. The more we reflect in this way, so that external things become symbolic pictures of moral qualities, the more easily shall we attain to imaginative knowledge. We can see similar likenesses in human beings. For instance, we can study people's temperament from their gait – look at the slow, heavy step of the melancholic, the light, springy step of the sanguine type.

After some time spent on these exercises we can pass to exercises of real Imagination. Take, for example, a living plant, look at it carefully, sink yourself into it, then draw forth the inner feeling of your soul and lay it as it were in the plant, as is described in the book *Knowledge of the Higher Worlds*. All this stimulates the Imagination, and by this means the pupil acquires astral vision. After a time he will notice a little flame proceeding from the plant: that is the astral counterpart of its growth. Again, the pupil takes a seed and visualizes the whole plant, as it will later on be in reality. These are exercises of the Imagination; by their means one comes to see things surrounded by their astral element.

3. The third stage is called *learning the occult script*. There is in fact such a script, through which one can penetrate more deeply into things. An example will show you more exactly what I mean. With the close of the Old Indian civilization a new civilization began. The symbol for such an evolutionary

stage is the vortex. These vortices exist everywhere in the world. They occur in the nebulae – the Orion nebula, for instance. There, too, an old world is dying and a new one being born. When the Indian civilization was coming into being, the Sun was in the sign of Cancer; during the Persian civilization in Gemini; during the Egyptian civilization in Taurus; during the Graeco-Roman civilization in Aries. Since the astronomical sign for Cancer is ♋ = ♋, this was the sign for the rise of the Indian civilization.

Another example is the letter M. Every letter of the alphabet can be traced back to an occult origin. Thus M is the symbol of wisdom; it derives from the shape of the upper lip ⬳. It is also the sign for the waves of the seas ∿; hence wisdom may be symbolized by water. These signs indicate sounds which correspond with real things, and in the Rosicrucian training such studies are cultivated.

4. A *rhythmical element* is brought into breathing. It plays a less important part than it does in eastern training, but it belongs to the Rosicrucian training and a Rosicrucian knows that through meditation the air he breathes out is purified.

5. The *correspondence between microcosm and macrocosm* is emphasized. This means the connection between the great world and the small, or between man and the world outside him.

Man has emerged by gradual stages and his various members have been formed in the course of evolution. Now it is impossible for certain organs to arise in a being which has, for example, no astral body, and therefore they could not come into existence on the Sun, even in a preliminary form. The liver is an instance of this: it cannot exist without the etheric body, but it is actually created by the astral body. Similarly, no being can have warm blood unless it first appeared at a time when the ego was at least in course of preparation. True, the higher animals are warm-blooded, but they split off from man when the development of his ego was already under way. Hence we can say that the liver is closely related to the astral body, and warm blood to the ego.

In fact every one of man's organs, even the smallest, has its specific relationship to one member of his being. If the pupil concentrates his attention on himself objectively, as though on something outside himself – if for instance he concentrates on the point at the root of the nose and connects with it a particular saying given by his occult teacher, he will be guided to that which corresponds to this point and he will come to know it. If he concentrates on this point under definite guidance, he will come to know the nature of the ego. Another, much later exercise is directed towards the inner part of the eye; through this one learns to know the inner nature of light and of the sun. The nature of the astral can be learnt by concentrating on the liver, with the aid of certain specific words.

This is true self-development, when the pupil is taken out of himself by means of each organ on which he concentrates his attention. This method has become specially important in recent times because humanity has become deeply involved in matter. In this way one penetrates through the material to its creative cause.

6. Dwelling in, or sinking oneself into, the macrocosm. This is the same form of spiritual contemplation that we described as *Dhyanam*. The pupil sinks himself into the organ he is contemplating – for example, the inner part of the eye. After concentrating on it for a while, he drops the mental picture of the external organ and thinks only of that to which the eye leads him – the light. In this way he comes to the creator of the organ and so out into the macrocosm. He then feels his body increasingly growing larger and larger until it is as large as the earth, indeed even bigger than the earth, until all things are in it. And then he lives in all things.

7. The seventh stage corresponds to the eastern *Samadhi*. It is called divine blessedness because now the pupil ceases to think of this last concept, but he retains the power to think. The content of his thought falls away, but the activity of thought remains. And thus he comes to rest in the divine-spiritual world.

These stages of Rosicrucian training are more inward, and call for a subtle cultivation of the higher life of the soul. The widespread superficiality of our material epoch is a powerful obstacle to the necessary deepening of the whole inner life; it must be overcome. This form of training is particularly well suited to Europeans. Anyone who is in earnest can carry it out. But Goethe's saying 'It is indeed easy, but even the easy is hard' applies here.

We have gone into the various methods of training, and I will end by showing you something of the relationship between man and the whole earth, so that you will see how man is related to everything that happens on earth.

I have described the evolution of man and shown you how he can acquire a true inner being of his own. In the course of evolution the whole of humanity will attain to everything that the individual can achieve through occult training. But what will be happening to the earth while mankind is developing in this way? There is a great difference between the earth seen by the occultist and the earth known to the ordinary geologist or scientist. He looks on it as merely a sort of great lifeless ball, with an interior not very unlike its exterior, except that at most the interior substances are fluid. But it is not easy to understand how such a lifeless ball could have produced all the different kinds of beings on it.

We know that on this earth of ours various phenomena occur which deeply affect the fate of many people; but present-day science looks on this as a purely external relationship. Thus the fate of hundreds and thousands may be affected by an earthquake or a volcano. Does the human will have any influence on this, or is it all a matter of chance?

Are there dead laws which act with blind fury, or is there some connection between these events and the will of man? What is really happening when a man is killed by an earthquake? What does the occultist say about the interior of the earth?

The occult science of all epochs says the following about

the interior of the earth. We must think of the earth as consisting of a series of layers, not completely separated from one another like the skins of an onion, but merging into one another gradually.

1. The topmost layer, the mineral mass, is related to the interior as an eggshell is to the egg. This topmost layer is called the mineral earth.

2. Under it is a second layer, called the fluid earth; it consists of a substance to which there is nothing comparable on earth. It is not really like any of the fluids we know, for these all have a mineral quality. This layer has specific characteristics: its substance begins to display certain spiritual qualities, which consist in the fact that as soon as it is brought into contact with something living it strives to expel and destroy this life. The occultist is able to investigate this layer by pure concentration.

3. The 'air-earth'. This is a substance which annuls feelings: for instance, if it is brought into contact with any pain, the pain is converted into pleasure, and vice versa. The original form of a feeling is, so to speak extinguished, rather as the second layer extinguishes life.

4. The 'water-earth', or the 'form-earth'. It produces in the material realm the effects that occur spiritually in Devachan. There, we have the negative pictures of physical things. In the 'form-earth' a cube of salt, for example, would be destroyed, but its negative would arise. The form is as it were changed into its opposite; all its qualities pass out into its surroundings. The actual space occupied by the object is left empty.

5. The 'fruit-earth'. This substance is full of exuberant energy. Every little part of it grows out at once like sponge; it gets larger and larger and is held in place only by the upper layers. It is the underlying life which serves the forms of the layers above it.

6. The 'fire-earth'. Its substance is essentially feeling and will. It is sensitive to pain and would cry out if it were trodden on. It consists, as it were, entirely of passions.

7. The 'earth-mirror' or 'earth-reflector'. This layer gets its name from the fact that its substance, if one concentrates on it, changes all the characteristics of the earth into their opposites. If the seer disregards everything lying above it and gazes down directly into this layer, and if then, for example, he places something green before him, the green appears as red; every colour appears as its complementary opposite. A polaric reflection arises, a reversal of the original. Sorrow would be changed by this substance into joy.

8. The 'divisive' layer. If with developed power one concentrates on it, something very remarkable appears. For example, a plant held in the midst of this layer appears to be multiplied, and so with everything else. But the essential thing is that this layer disrupts the moral qualities also. Through the power it radiates to the earth's surface, it is responsible for the fact that strife and disharmony exist there. In order to overcome this disruptive force, men must work together in harmony.

That is precisely why this layer was laid down in the earth – so that people should be enabled to develop harmony for themselves. The substance of everything evil is prepared and organized there. Quarrelsome people are so constituted that this layer has a particular influence on them. This has been known to everyone who has written out of a true knowledge of occultism. Dante in his *Divine Comedy* calls this layer the Cain-layer. It was here that the strife between the brothers Cain and Abel had its source. The substance of this layer is responsible for evil having come into the world.

9. The 'earth-core'. This is the substance through whose influence black magic arises in the world. The power of spiritual evil comes from this source.

You will see that man is related to all the layers, for they are continually radiating out their forces. Humanity lives under the influence of these layers and has to overcome their powers. When human beings have learnt to radiate life on earth and have trained their breathing so that it promotes life, they will overcome the 'fire-earth'. When spiritually they overcome pain through serenity, they overcome the 'air-earth'. When concord reigns, the 'divisive' layer is conquered. When white magic triumphs, no evil remains on earth. Human evolution thus implies a transformation of the earth's interior. In the beginning the nature of the earth's body was such as to hold subsequent developments in check. In the end, when human powers have transformed the earth, it will be a spiritualized earth. In this way man imparts his own being to the earth.

Now there are occasions when the very substance of the passions of the fire-earth begins to rebel. Aroused by people's passions, it penetrates through the fruit-earth, forces its way through the channels in the upper layers and even flows up into and violently shakes the solid earth: the result is an earthquake. If this passion from the fire-earth thrusts up some of the earth's substance, a volcano erupts. All this is closely connected with man. In Lemurian times, the upper layer was still very soft and the fire-layer was near the surface. Human passions and the 'passion-substance' of this layer are related; when people give rein to evil passions they strengthen its passions, and that is what happened at the end of Lemurian times. Through their passions the Lemurians made the fire-earth rebellious, and in this way they brought the whole Lemurian continent to destruction. No other cause for this destruction could be found except in what they had them-selves drawn forth from the earth. Today the layers are thicker and firmer, but there is still this connection between human passions and the passion-layer in the interior of the earth; and it is still an accumulation of evil passions and forces that gives rise to earthquakes and volcanic eruptions.

How man's destiny and will are related to happenings in the earth can be seen from two examples which have been occultly investigated. It has been found that persons who have been killed in an earthquake appear in their next incarnation as people of high spiritual quality and faith. They had progressed far enough to be convinced by that final stroke of the transitoriness of earthly things. The effect of this in Devachan was that they learnt a lesson for their next lives: that matter is perishable but spirit prevails. They did not all come to realize that, but many of them are now living as people who belong to some spiritual-theosophical movement.

In the other example, the births which occurred during a time of frequent earthquakes were investigated. It was found that all those born at about the time of an earthquake, though not exactly in its area, were, surprisingly enough, people of a very materialistic cast of mind. The earthquakes were not the cause of this; rather it was these strongly materialistic souls, ripe for birth, who worked their way down into the physical world by means of their astral will and let loose the forces of the fire-earth layer, which proceeded to shake the earth at the time of their birth.

Man transforms his dwelling-place and himself at the same time, and when he spiritualizes himself, he spiritualizes the earth also. One day, at a later planetary stage, he will have ennobled the earth by his own creative power. Every moment when we think and feel, we are working on the great structure of the earth. The Leaders of mankind have insight into such relationships and seek to impart to human beings the forces which will work in the true direction of evolution. One of the latest of these impulses is the theosophical movement. Its purpose is to develop harmony and balance in the very depths of the human soul. Anyone who puts the assertion of his own opinion higher than love and peace has not thoroughly understood the idea of Theosophy. The spirit of love must penetrate even into the opinions a person holds. In the course of occult development he must unavoidably learn this, or he will get no further. He must renounce entirely his own opinions and must wish to be solely an instrument of the objective truth which comes from the spiritual world and flows through the world as the one great Truth. The more a person renounces himself and sets his own opinions aside, becoming instead a channel for the great Truth, the more does he manifest the true spirit of Theosophy.

All this is extraordinarily difficult today. But theosophical teaching is itself a promoter of peace. When we come together so that we may live within this teaching, it gives rise to peace. But if we introduce something from outside, we bring dissension in, and that should really be an impossibility. So the theosophical conception of the world must pass over into feeling – into something I would call a spiritual atmosphere – in which Theosophy lives. You must have a will to understand; then Theosophy will hover like a unifying spirit over our gatherings, and from there will spread its influence out through the world.[17]

V. The Ancient Yoga Civilization and the Michael Civilization of the Future[18]

Dornach, 30 November 1919

YOU HAVE seen from my past lectures that it is necessary, for a complete understanding of the human being, to distinguish the various members of the human organism and to realize the incisive difference between that which we may call the human head organization and that which constitutes the rest of the human organization. As you know, we can also subdivide this remaining organization, thus obtaining a three-fold constitution, but for the comprehension of the significant impulses in mankind's evolution with which we are faced at the present time and in the immediate future, the differentiation between head man and the organization of the rest of man is primarily important.[19]

Now, if we speak spiritual-scientifically about the human being by differentiating between head man and the rest of man, then these two organizations are, at the outset, pictures for us, pictures created by nature herself for the soul element, for the spiritual element, whose expression and manifestation they are. Man is placed in the whole evolution of earth humanity in a way which becomes comprehensible only if one considers how different is the position of the head organization in this evolution from that of the rest of the human organization. Everything connected with the head organization, which chiefly manifests as man's life of thought, is something that reaches far back in the post-Atlantean evolution of mankind. When we focus our attention upon the time which followed immediately after the great Atlantean catastrophe, that is, the time of the sixth, seventh, eighth millennium before the Christian era, we shall find a soul

mood holding sway in the regions of the civilized world
of that period which can hardly be compared with our
soul mood. The consciousness and whole conception of
the world of the human being of that time can scarcely
be compared with that which characterizes our sense perception and conceptual view of the world. In my *Occult
Science: An Outline* I have called this culture which reaches
back into such ancient times the *primeval Indian culture.*[10]
We may say: the human head organism of that time was
different from our present head organism to a great degree
and the reckoning with space and time was not characteristic of this ancient people as it is of us. In surveying
the world, they experienced a survey of immeasurable
spatial distances, and they had a simultaneous experience of
the various moments of time. The strong emphasis on
space and time in world conception was not present in
that ancient period.

The first indications of this we find towards the fifth and
fourth millennium in the period we designate the *primeval
Persian period.* But even then the whole mood of soul-life is
such that it can hardly be compared with the soul and
world mood of the human being of our age. In that ancient
time, the main concern of the human being is to interpret
the things of the world as various shades of light, brilliancy,
and darkness, obscurity. The abstractions in which we live
today are completely foreign to that ancient earth population.
There still exists a universal, all-embracing perception, a
consciousness of the permeation of everything perceptible
with light and its adumbration, shading, with various degrees
of darkness. This was also the way the moral world order
was conceived of. A human being who was benevolent and
kind was experienced as a light, bright human being, one
who was distrustful and selfish was experienced as a dark
man. Man's moral individuality was, as it were, aurically
perceived around him. And if we had talked to a human
being of this ancient, primeval Persian time about that

which we call today the order of nature, he would not have understood a word of it. An order of nature in our sense did not exist in his world of light and shadow. For him, the world was a world of light and shadow; and in the world of tones, certain timbres of sounding he designated as light, bright, and certain other timbres of sounding he designated as dark, shadowy. And that which thus expressed itself through this element of light and darkness constituted for him the spiritual as well as the nature powers. For him, there existed no difference between spiritual and natural powers. Our present-day distinction between natural necessity and human freedom would have appeared to him as mere folly, for this duality of human arbitrary will and the necessity of nature did not exist for him. Everything was to be included for him in one spiritual-physical unity. If I were to give you a pictorial interpretation of the character of this primeval-Persian world conception, I would have to draw the following line (it will receive its full meaning only through that which will follow):

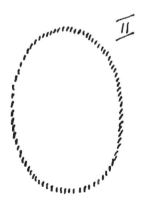

Then, after this soul mood of man had held sway for somewhat more than two thousand years, there appeared a

soul mood the echoes of which we can still perceive in the
Chaldean, in the *Egyptian* world conception, and in a special
form in the world conception whose reflection is preserved for
us in the Old Testament. There something appears which is
closer to our own world conception. There the first inkling of
a certain necessity of nature enters human thoughts. But this
necessity of nature is still far removed from that which we call
today the mechanical or even the vital order of nature; at that
time, natural events are conceived of as identical with Divine
Willing, with Providence. Providence and nature events are
still one. Man knew that if he moved his hand it was the Divine
within him, permeating him, that moved his hand, that
moved his arm. When a tree was shaken by the wind, the
perception of the shaking tree was no different for him from
the perception of the moving arm. He saw the same divine
power, as Providence, in his own movements and in the
movements of the tree. But a distinction was made between
the God without and the God within; he was, however,
conceived of as unitary, the God in nature, the God in man;
he was the same. And it was clear to human beings of that time
that there is something in man whereby Providence that is
outside in nature and Providence that is inside in man meet
one another.

At that time, man's process of breathing was sensed in this
way. People said: if a tree is shaking, this is the God outside,
and if I move my arm, it is the God inside; if I inhale the air,
work it over within me, and again exhale it, then it is the God
from outside who enters me and again leaves me. Thus the
same divine element was sensed as being outside and inside,
but simultaneously, in one point, outside and inside. People
said to themselves: by being a breathing being, I am a being
of nature outside and at the same time I am myself.

If I am to characterize the world conception of the third
culture period by a line, as I have done for the primeval
Persian world conception by the line of the preceding drawing, I shall have to characterize it through the following line:

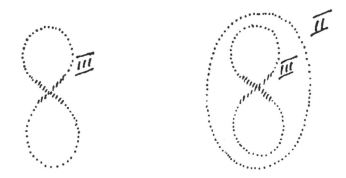

This line represents, on the one hand, the existence of nature outside, on the other hand, human existence – crossing over into each other at the one point, in the breathing process.

Matters become different in the fourth age, in the *Graeco-Latin age*. Here the human being is abruptly confronted by the contrast outside-inside, of nature existence and human existence. Man begins to feel the contrast between himself and nature. And if I am again to draw characteristically how man begins to feel in the Greek age, I will have to draw it this way: on the one hand he senses the external, and on the other the internal; between the two there is no longer the crossing point.

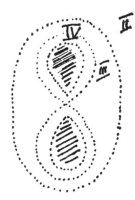

What man has in common with nature remains outside his consciousness. It falls away from consciousness. In Indian yoga an attempt is made to bring it into consciousness again. Therefore Indian yoga culture is an atavistic returning to previous evolutionary stages of mankind, because an attempt is made again to bring into consciousness the process of breathing, which in the third age was felt in a natural way as that in which one existed outside and inside simultaneously. The fourth age begins in the eighth pre-Christian century. At that time the late-Indian yoga exercises were developed which tried to call back, atavistically, that which mankind had possessed at earlier times, quite particularly in the Indian culture, but which had been lost.

Thus, this consciousness of the breathing process was lost. And if one asks why did Indian yoga culture try to call it back, what did it believe it would gain thereby, one has to answer: what was intended to be gained thereby was a real understanding of the outer world. For through the fact that the breathing process was understood in the third cultural age, something was understood within man that at the same time was something external.

This must again be attained; on another path, however. We live still under the after-effects of the culture in which a twofold element is present in the human soul mood, for the fourth period ends only around the year 1413, really only about the middle of the fifteenth century. We have, through our head organization, an incomplete nature conception, that which we call the external world; and we have through our inner organization, through the organization of the rest of man, an incomplete knowledge of ourselves [see following page, top].

That in which we could perceive a process of the world and at the same time a process of ourselves is eliminated; it does not exist for us.

It is now a question of consciously regaining that which has been lost. That means, we have to acquire the ability of taking

hold of something that is in our inner being, which belongs to the outer and the inner world simultaneously and reaches into both.

This must be the endeavour of the fifth post-Atlantean period, namely, the endeavour to find something in the human inner life in which an outer process takes place at the same time.

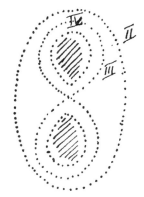
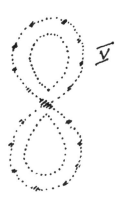

You will remember that I have pointed to this important fact; I have pointed to it in my last article in the *Sozialen Zukunft* [*The Social Future*] where I seemingly dealt with these things in their importance for social life, but where I clearly pointed to the very necessity of finding something which the human being lays hold of *within himself* and which he, at the same time, recognizes as a process of the *world*.[19] We as modern human beings cannot attain this by going back to yoga culture; that has passed. For the breathing process itself has changed. This, of course, you cannot prove clinically; but the breathing process has become a different one since the third post-Atlantean cultural period. Roughly speaking, we might say: in the third post-Atlantean cultural period the human being still breathed soul; today he breathes air. Not only our thoughts have become materialistic; *reality itself has lost its soul.*

I beg you, my dear friends, not to see something negligible in what I am now saying. For just consider what it means that reality itself, in which mankind lives, has been transformed so that the air we breathe is something *different* from what it was four millennia ago. Not only the consciousness of mankind has changed, oh no! – there was soul in the atmosphere of the earth. The air was the soul. This it is no longer today, or, rather, it is soul in a different way. The spiritual beings of *elemental nature* of whom I have spoken yesterday, they penetrate into you, they *can* be breathed if one practises yoga breathing today. But that which was attainable in *normal* breathing three millennia ago cannot be brought back artificially. That it may be brought back is the great illusion of the orientals. What I am stating here describes a reality. The ensouling of the air which belongs to the human being no longer exists. And therefore the beings – whom I should like to call the anti-Michaelic beings – are able to penetrate into the air and, through the air, into the human being, and in this way they enter into mankind, as I have described it elsewhere. We are only able to drive them away if we put in the place of yoga that which is the right thing for today. We must strive for this. We can only strive for the right thing for today if we become conscious of a much more subtle relation of man to the external world, so that in regard to our ether body something takes place which must enter our consciousness more and more, similar to the breathing process. In the breathing process, we inhale fresh oxygen and exhale unusable carbon. A similar process takes place in all our sense perceptions. Just think, my dear friends, that you see something – let us take a radical case – suppose you see a flame. There a process takes place that may be compared with inhalation, only it is much finer. If you then close your eyes – and you can make similar experiments with every one of your senses – you have the after-image of the flame which gradually changes – dies down, as Goethe said. Apart from the purely physical aspect, the human ether body is essentially engaged in this process of reception of the light impression and its eventual dying down. Something very significant is contained in this process: it contains the soul element which, three millennia ago, was breathed in and out with the air. And we must learn to realize the sense process, permeated by the soul element, in a similar way we have realized the breathing process three millennia ago.

You see, my dear friends, this is connected with the fact that man, three millennia ago, lived in a night culture. Yahveh revealed himself through his prophets out of the dreams of the night. But we must endeavour to receive in our intimate intercourse with the world not merely sense perceptions but also the spiritual element. It must become a certainty for us that with every ray of light, with every tone, with every sensation of heat and its dying down we enter into a soul-intercourse with the world, and this soul-intercourse must become significant for us. We can help ourselves to bring this about.

I have described to you the occurrence of the Mystery of Golgotha in the fourth post-Atlantean period which, if we wish to be accurate, begins with the year 747 BC and ends with the year AD 1413. The Mystery of Golgotha occurred in the first third of this period, and it was comprehended, at the outset, with the remnants of the ancient mode of thought and culture. This ancient way of comprehending the Mystery of Golgotha is exhausted and a new way of comprehension must take its place. The ancient way does no longer suffice, and many attempts that have been made to enable human thinking to grasp the Mystery of Golgotha have proved unsuitable to reach up to it.

You see, dear friends, all external-material things have their spiritual-soul aspect, and all things that appear in the spiritual-soul sphere have their external-material aspect. The fact that the air of the earth has become soul-void, making it impossible for man to breathe the originally ensouled air, had a significant spiritual effect in the evolution of mankind. For through being able to breathe in the soul to which he was originally related, as is stated at the beginning of the Old Testament, 'And God breathed into man the breath as living soul', man had the possibility of becoming conscious of the pre-existence of the soul, of the existence of the soul before it had descended into the physical body through birth or through conception. To the degree the breathing process ceased to be ensouled the human being lost the consciousness of the pre-existence of the soul. Even at the time of Aristotle in the fourth post-Atlantean period it was no longer possible to understand, with the human power of comprehension, the pre-existence of the soul. It was utterly impossible.

We are faced with the strange historical fact that the greatest event, the Christ Event, breaks in upon the evolution of the earth, yet mankind must first become mature in order to comprehend it. At the outset, it is still capable of catching the rays of the Mystery of Golgotha with the remnants of the power of comprehension originating in primeval culture. But this power of comprehension is gradually lost, and dogmatism moves further and further away from an understanding of the Mystery of Golgotha. The Church forbids the belief in the pre-existence of the soul – not because pre-existence is incompatible with the Mystery of Golgotha but because the human power of comprehension ceased to experience the consciousness of pre-existence as a force, the air having become soul-void. Pre-existence vanishes from head-consciousness. When our *sense processes become ensouled again*, we shall have established a crossing point, and in this crossing point we shall take hold of the human will that streams up, out of the third stratum of consciousness, as I have described it to you recently. Then we shall, at the same time, have the subjective-objective element for which Goethe was longing so very much. We shall have the possibility of grasping, in a sensitive way, the peculiar nature of the sense process of man in its relation to the outer world. Man's conceptions are very coarse and clumsy, indeed, which maintain that the outer world merely acts upon us and we, in turn, merely react upon it. In reality, there takes place a soul process from the outside towards the inside, which is taken hold of by the deeply subconscious, inner soul process, so that the two processes overlap. From outside, cosmic thoughts work into us; from inside, humanity's will works outwards. *Humanity's will and cosmic thought cross* in this crossing point, just as the objective and the subjective element once crossed in the breath. We must learn to feel how our will works through our eyes and how the activity of the senses delicately mingles with the passivity, bringing about the crossing of cosmic thoughts and humanity's will. We must develop this *new yoga will*. Then something will be imparted to us that is of like nature to that which was imparted to human beings in the breathing process three millennia ago. Our comprehension must become much more soul-like, much more spiritual.

Goethe's world conception strove in this direction. Goethe endeavoured to recognize the *pure phenomenon*, which he called the primal phenomenon, by arranging the phenomena which work upon man in the external world, without the interference of the luciferic thought which stems from the head of man himself; this thought was only to serve in the arranging of the phenomena. Goethe did not strive for the law of nature, but for the primal phenomenon; this is what is significant with him. If, however, we arrive at this pure phenomenon, this primal phenomenon, we have something in the outer world which makes it possible for us to sense the unfolding of our will in the perception of the outer world, and then we shall lift ourselves to something *objective-subjective*, as it still was contained, for instance, in the ancient Hebrew doctrine. We must learn not merely to speak of the contrast between the material and the spiritual, but we must recognize the interplay of the material and the spiritual in a unity precisely in sense perception. If we no longer look at nature merely materially and, further, if we do not 'think into it' a soul element, as Gustave Theodore Fechner did, then something will arise which will signify for us what the Yahveh culture signified for mankind three millennia ago.[20] If we learn, in nature, to receive the soul element together with sense perception, then we shall have the Christ relationship to outer nature. This Christ relationship to outer nature will be something like a kind of spiritual breathing process.

We shall be aided by realizing more and more, with our sound common sense, that pre-existence lies at the basis of our soul existence. We must supplement the purely egotistical conception of post-existence, which springs merely from our longing to exist after death, by the knowledge of the pre-existence of the soul. We must again rise to the conception of the real eternity of the soul. This is what may be called Michael culture. If we move through the world with the consciousness that with every look we direct outwards, with every tone we hear, something spiritual, something of the nature of the soul streams into us, and that at the same time we let our soul element stream out into the world, we have gained the consciousness which mankind needs for the future.

I return once more to the image: you see a flame; you shut your eyes and have the after-image which ebbs away. Is that merely a subjective process? Yes, says the modern physiologist. But this is not true. In the *cosmic ether* this signifies an objective process, just as in the air the presence of carbonic acid which you exhale signifies an objective process. You impress into the cosmic ether the image which you only sense as a receding after-image. This is not merely subjective, this is an objective process. You are dealing here with the objective element; you have the possibility of knowing that something which takes place within you is at the same time a delicate cosmic process, if you become but conscious of it. If I look at a flame, close my eyes, let it ebb away – it will ebb away even though I keep my eyes open, only then I will not notice it – then I experience a process that does not merely take place within me but that takes place in the world. But this is not only the case in regard to the flame. If I confront a human being and say: this person has said this or that, which may be true or untrue, this then constitutes a judgement, a moral or intellectual act of my inner nature. This ebbs away like the flame. It is an objective world process. If you think something good about your fellow man, it ebbs away and is an objective process in the cosmic ether; if you think something evil, it ebbs away as an objective process. You are unable to conceal your perceptions and judgements about the world. You seemingly carry them on in your own being, but they are at the same time an objective world process. Just as people of the third period were conscious of the fact that the breathing process is a process that takes place simultaneously within man and in the objective world, so mankind must become aware in the future that the soul element of which I spoke is at the same time an objective world process.

This transformation of consciousness demands greater strength of soul than is ordinarily developed by the human being of today. To permeate oneself with this consciousness means to permit the Michael culture to enter. Just as it was self-evident for the man of the second and third pre-Christian millennium to think of the *air* as ensouled – and it was ensouled – so must it become self-evident for us to think of *light* as ensouled; we must arouse this ability in us when we consider light the general representative of sense perception. We must thoroughly do away with the habit of seeing in light that which our materialistic age is accustomed to see in it. We must entirely cease to believe that merely those vibrations emanate from the sun of which, out

of the modern consciousness, physics and people in general
speak. We must become clear about the fact that the soul
element penetrates through cosmic space upon the pinions of
light; and we must realize, at the same time, that this was not the
case in the period preceding our age. That which approaches
mankind today through light approached mankind of that
former period through the air. You see here an objective
difference in the earth process. Expressing this in a comprehensive concept, we may say: *air-soul process, light-soul process*. This
is what may be observed in the evolution of the earth. The
Mystery of Golgotha signifies the transition from the one period
to the other.

Mystery of Golgotha

Air-soul process   Light-soul process

My dear friends, it does not suffice, for the present age nor
for the future age of mankind, to speak in abstractions about
the spiritual, to fall into some sort of nebulous pantheism; on
the contrary, we must begin to recognize that what today is
sensed as a merely material process is permeated by soul.

It is a question of learning to say the following: there was
a time prior to the Mystery of Golgotha when the earth had
an atmosphere which contained the soul element that belongs
to the soul of man. Today, the earth has an atmosphere which
is devoid of this soul element. The same soul element that was
previously in the air has now entered the light which embraces
us from morning to evening. This was made possible through
the fact that the Christ has united Himself with the earth.
Thus, also from the soul-spiritual aspect, air and light under-
went a change in the course of the earth evolution.

My dear friends, it is a childish presentation that describes
air and light in the same manner, purely materially, throughout the millennia in which *earth* evolution unfolded. Air and

light have changed inwardly. We live in an atmosphere and in a light sphere that are different from those in which our souls lived in previous earthly incarnations. To learn to recognize the externally material as a soul-spiritual element: this is what matters. If we describe purely material existence in the customary manner and then add as a kind of decoration that this material existence contains everywhere the spiritual, this will not produce genuine spiritual science. My dear friends, people are very strange in this respect; they are intent on withdrawing to the abstract. But what is necessary is the following: in the future we must cease to differentiate abstractly between the material and the spiritual, but we must look for the spiritual in the material itself and describe it as such; and we must recognize in the spiritual the transition into the material and its mode of action in the material. Only if we have attained this shall we be able to gain a true knowledge of man himself. 'Blood is a very special fluid',[21] but the fluid physiology speaks about today is not a 'special fluid', it is merely a fluid whose chemical composition one attempts to analyse in the same way any other substance is analysed; it is nothing special. But if we have gained the starting point of being able to understand the metamorphosis of air and light from the soul aspect, we shall gradually advance to the soul-spiritual comprehension of the human being himself, in every respect; then we shall not have abstract matter and abstract spirit, but spirit, soul and body working into one another. *This will be Michael-culture.*

This is what our time demands. This is what ought to be grasped with all the fibres of the soul life by those human beings who wish to understand the present time. Whenever something out of the ordinary had to be introduced into human world conception it met with resistance. I have often quoted the following neat example. In 1837 (not even a century ago), the learned Medical College of Bavaria was asked, when the construction of the first railroad from Fuerth to Nuremberg was proposed, whether it was

hygienically safe to build such a railroad. The Medical
College answered (I am not telling a fairy-tale, the documents
concerning it exist): such a railroad should not be built, for
people who would use such a means of transportation would
become nervously ill. And they added: should there be such
people who insist on such railroads, then it is absolutely
necessary to erect, on the right and left side of the tracks, high
plank walls to prevent the people whom the train passes from
getting concussion of the brain.[27] Here you see, my dear
friends, such a judgement is one thing; quite another is the
course which the evolution of mankind takes. Today we smile
about such a document as that of the Bavarian Medical
College of 1837; but we are not altogether justified in smiling,
for if something similar occurs today we behave in quite the
same manner. And, after all, the Bavarian Medical College
was not entirely wrong. If we compare the state of nerves of
modern mankind with that of mankind two centuries ago,
then we must say that people have become nervous. Perhaps
the Medical College has exaggerated the matter a bit, but
people did become nervous. Now, in regard to the evolution
of mankind it is imperative that certain impulses which try to
enter earth evolution really should enter and not be rejected.
That which from time to time wishes to enter human cultural
development is often very inconvenient for people, it does not
agree with their indolence, and what is duty in regard to
human cultural development must be recognized by learning
to read the objective facts, and must not be derived from
human indolence, not even from a refined kind of indolence.
I am concluding today's lecture with these words because
there is no doubt that a strongly increasing battle will take
place between anthroposophical cognition and the various
creeds. We can see the signs for this on all sides. The creeds
who wish to remain in the old beaten tracks, who do not wish
to arouse themselves to a new knowledge of the Mystery of
Golgotha, will reinforce their strong fighting position which
they already have taken up, and it would be very frivolous, my

dear friends, if we would remain unconscious of the fact that this battle has started.

I myself, you can be sure, am not at all eager for such a battle, particularly not for a battle with the Roman Catholic Church which, it seems, is forced upon us from the other side with such violence. He who, after all, thoroughly knows the deeper historical impulses of the creeds of our time will be very unwilling to fight time-honoured institutions. But if the battle is forced upon us, it is not to be avoided! And the clergy of our day is not in the least inclined to open its doors to that which has to enter: the spiritual-scientific world conception. Remember the grotesque quotation I read to you recently where it was said that people should inform themselves about anthroposophically-orientated spiritual science through the writings of my opponents, since Roman Catholics are forbidden by the Pope to read my own writings. This is not a light matter, my dear friends; it is a very serious matter! A battle which arises in such a manner, which is capable of disseminating such a judgement in the world, such a battle is not to be taken lightly. And what is more, it is not to be taken lightly since we do not enter it willingly. Let us take the example of the Roman Catholic Church, my dear friends – matters are not different in regard to the Protestant Church, but the Roman Catholic Church is more powerful – and we have to consider time-honoured institutions. If one understands the significance of the vestments of the priest when he reads the Holy Mass, the meaning of every single piece of his priestly garments, if one understands every single act of the Holy Mass, then one knows that they are sacred, time-honoured establishments. They are establishments more ancient than Christianity, for the Holy Mass is a ritual of the ancient Mystery culture, transformed in the Christian sense. And the modern clergy who use such weapons as described above, live in these rituals! Thus, if one has, on the one hand, the deepest veneration for the existing rituals and symbolism and sees, on the other hand, how insufficient is the defence of and how serious are the attacks against that which wishes to enter mankind's evolution, then one becomes aware of the earnestness that is necessary in taking a stand in these matters. It is truly something worth deep study and consideration. What is thus heralded from that side is only at its beginnings. And it is not right to sleep in regard to it; on the contrary, we have to sharpen our perception for it. During the two decades in which the anthroposophical movement has been fostered in Middle Europe, we could indulge in sectarian somnolence which was so hard to combat in our own ranks and which still today sits so deeply embedded in the souls of the human beings who have entered the anthroposophical movement. But the time has passed in which we might have been allowed to indulge in sectarian somnolence. That which I have often emphasized here is deeply true, namely, that it is necessary that we should grasp the world-historical significance of the anthroposophical movement and overlook trifles, but that we should also consider the small impulses as serious and great.

VI. The Way of Inner Development

Berlin, 7 December 1905

THE CONCEPTS concerning the supersensible world and its relationship with the world of the senses have been discussed here in a long series of lectures. It is only natural that, again and again, the question should arise: what is the origin of knowledge concerning the supersensible world? With this question or, in other words, with the question of the inner development of man, we wish to occupy ourselves today.

The phrase 'inner development of man' here refers to the ascent of the human being to capacities which must be acquired if he wishes to make supersensible insights his own. Now do not misunderstand the intent of this lecture. This lecture will by no means postulate rules or laws concerning general human morality, nor will it challenge the general religion of the age. I must stress this because when occultism is discussed the misunderstanding often arises that some sort of general demands or fundamental moral laws, valid without variation, are being established. This is not the case. This point requires particular clarification in our age of standardization, when differences between human beings are not at all acknowledged. Neither should today's lecture be mistaken for a lecture concerning the general fundamentals of the anthroposophical movement. Occultism is not the same as anthroposophy. The Anthroposophical Society is not alone in cultivating occultism, nor is this its only task. It could even be possible for a person to join the Anthroposophical Society and to avoid occultism altogether.[4]

Among the enquiries which are pursued within the Anthroposophical Society, in addition to the field of general ethics is also this field of occultism, which includes those laws of existence that are hidden from the usual sense observation in everyday human experience. By no means, however, are these laws unrelated to everyday experience. 'Occult' means 'hidden', or 'mysterious'. But it must be stressed over and over that occultism is a matter in which certain preconditions are truly necessary. Just as higher mathematics would be incomprehensible to the simple peasant who had never before encountered it, so is occultism incomprehensible to many people today. Occultism ceases to be 'occult', however, when one has mastered it. In this way, I have strictly defined the boundaries of today's lecture. Therefore, no one can object – this must be stressed in the light of the most manifold endeavours and of the experience of millennia – that the demands of occultism cannot be fulfilled, and that they contradict the general culture. No one is expected to fulfil these demands. But if someone requests that he be given convictions provided by occultism and yet refuses to occupy himself with it, he is like a schoolboy who wishes to create electricity in a glass rod yet refuses to rub it. Without friction, it will not become charged. This is similar to the objection raised against the practice of occultism.

No one is exhorted to become an occultist; one must come to occultism of one's own volition. Whoever says that we do not need occultism will not need to occupy himself with it. At this time, occultism does not appeal to mankind in general. In fact, it is extremely difficult in the present culture to submit to those rules of conduct which will open the spiritual world.

Two prerequisites are totally lacking in our culture. One is isolation, what spiritual science calls 'higher human solitude'. The other is overcoming the egotism which, though largely unconscious, has become a dominant characteristic of our time.

The absence of these two prerequisites renders the path of inner development simply unattainable. Isolation, or spiritual solitude, is very difficult to achieve because life conditions tend to distract and disperse, in brief, to demand sense-involvement in the external. There has been no previous culture in which people have lived with such an involvement in the external. I beg you not to take what I am saying as criticism, but simply as an objective characterization.

Of course, he who speaks as I do knows that this situation cannot be different, and that it forms the basis for the greatest advantages and greatest achievements of our time. But this is the reason that our time is so devoid of supersensible insight and that our culture is so devoid of supersensible influence. In other cultures – and they do exist – the human being is in a position to cultivate the inner life more and to withdraw from the influences of external life. Such cultures offer a soil where inner life in the higher sense can thrive. In the oriental culture there exists what is called yoga. Those who live according to the rules of this teaching are called yogis. A yogi is one who strives for higher spiritual knowledge, but only after he has sought for himself a master of the supersensible. No one is able to proceed without the guidance of a master, or guru. When the yogi has found such a guru, he must spend a considerable part of the day, regularly, not irregularly, living totally within his soul. All the forces that the yogi needs to develop are already within his soul. They exist there as truly as electricity exists in the glass rod before it is brought forth through friction. In order to call forth the forces of the soul, methods of spiritual science must be used which are the results of observations made over millennia. This is very difficult in our time, which demands a certain splintering of each individual struggling for existence. One cannot arrive at a total inward composure; one cannot even arrive at the concept of such composure. People are not sufficiently aware of the deep solitude the yogi must seek. One must repeat the same matter rhythmically with immense regularity, if only for a brief time each day, in total separation from all usual concerns. It is indispensable that all life usually surrounding the yogi ceases to exist and that his senses become unreceptive to all impressions of the world around him. He must be able to make himself deaf and dumb to his surroundings during the time which he prescribes for himself. He must be able to concentrate to such a degree – and he must acquire practice in this concentration – that a cannon could be fired next to him without disturbing his attention to his inner life. He must also become free of all memory impressions, particularly those of everyday life.

Just think how exceedingly difficult it is to bring about these conditions in our culture, how even the concept of such isolation is lacking. This spiritual solitude must be reached in such a way that the harmony, the total equilibrium with the surrounding world, is never lost. But this harmony can be lost exceedingly easily during such deep immersion in one's inner life. Whoever goes more and more deeply inward must at the same time be able to establish harmony with the external world all the more clearly.

No hint of estrangement, of distancing from external practical life, may arise in him lest he stray from the right course. To a degree, then, it might be impossible to distinguish his higher life from insanity. It truly is a kind of insanity when the inner life loses its proper relationship to the outer. Just imagine, for example, that you were knowledgeable concerning our conditions on earth and that you had all the experience and wisdom which may be gathered here. You fall asleep in the evening, and in the morning you do not wake up on earth but on Mars. The conditions on Mars are totally different from those on earth; the knowledge that you have gathered on earth is of no use to you whatsoever. There is no longer harmony between life within you and external life. You probably would find yourself in a Martian insane asylum within an hour. A similar situation might easily arise if the development of the internal life severs one's connection with the external world. One must take strict care that this does not happen. These are great difficulties in our culture.

Egotism in relation to inward soul properties is the first obstacle. Present humanity usually takes no account of this. This egotism is closely connected with the spiritual development of man. An important prerequisite for spiritual development is not to seek it out of egotism. Whoever is motivated by egotism cannot get very far. But egotism in our time reaches deep into the innermost soul. Again and again the objection is heard, 'What use are all the teachings of occultism, if I cannot experience them myself?' Whoever starts from this presumption and cannot change has little chance of arriving at higher development. One aspect of higher development is a most intimate awareness of human community, so that it is immaterial whether it is I or someone else having the experience. Hence I must meet one who has a higher development than I with unlimited love and trust. First, I must acquire this consciousness, the consciousness of infinite trust towards my fellow man when he says that he has experienced one thing or the other. Such trust is a precondition for working together. Wherever occult capacities are strongly brought into play, there exists unlimited trust; there exists the awareness that a human being is a personality in which a higher individuality lives. The first basis, therefore, is trust and faith, because we do not seek the higher self only in ourselves but also in our fellow human beings. Everyone living around one exists in undivided unity in the inner kernel of one's being.

On the basis of my lower self I am separated from other humans. But as far as my higher self is concerned – and that alone can ascend to the spiritual world – I am no longer separated from my fellow human beings; I am united with my fellow men; the one speaking to me out of higher truths is actually my own self. I must get away completely from the notion of difference between him and me. I must overcome totally the feeling that he has an advantage over me. Try to live your way into this feeling until it penetrates the most intimate fibre of your soul and causes every vestige of egotism to disappear. Do this so that the one further along the path than you truly stands before you like your own self; then you have attained one of the prerequisites for awakening higher spiritual life.

In situations where one receives guidance for the occult life, sometimes quite erroneously and confusedly, one may often hear that the higher self lives in the human being, that he need only allow his inner man to speak and the highest truth will thereby become manifest. Nothing is more correct and, at the same time, less productive than this assertion. Just try to let your inner self speak, and you will see that, as a rule, no matter how much you fancy that your higher self is making an appearance it is the lower self that speaks. The higher self is not found within us for the time being. We must seek it outside ourselves. We can learn a good deal from the person who is further along than we are, since there the higher self is visible. One's higher self can gain nothing from one's own egotistic 'I'. There where he now stands who is further along than I am, there will I stand sometime in the future. I am truly constituted to carry within myself the seed for what he already is. But the paths to Olympus must first be illuminated before one can follow them.

A feeling which may seem unbelievable is the fundamental condition for all occult development. It is mentioned in the various religions, and every practical occultist with experience will confirm it. The Christian religion describes it with the well-known sentence, which an occultist must understand completely, 'Except ye become as little children, ye shall not enter the kingdom of heaven.' This sentence can be understood only by he who has learned to revere in the highest sense. Suppose that in your earliest youth you had heard about a venerable person, an individual of whom you held the highest opinion, and now you are offered the opportunity to meet this person. A sense of awe prevails in you when the moment approaches that you will see this person for the first time. There, standing at the gateway of this personality, you might feel hesitant to touch the door handle and open it. When you look up in this way to such a venerable personality, then you have begun to grasp the feeling that Christianity intends by the statement that one should become like little children in order to enter the kingdom of heaven. Whether or not the subject of this veneration is truly worthy of it is not really important. What matters is the capacity to look up to something with a veneration that comes from the innermost heart.

This feeling of veneration is the elevating force raising us to higher spheres of supersensible life. Everyone seeking the higher life must write into his soul with golden letters this law of the occult world. Development must start from this basic soul-mood; without this feeling, nothing can be achieved. Next, a person seeking inner development must understand clearly that he is doing something of immense importance to the human being. What he seeks is no more nor less than a new birth, and that needs to be taken in a literal sense. The higher soul of man is to be born. Just as man in his first birth was born out of the deep inner foundations of existence and, as he emerged into the light of the sun, so does he who seeks inner development step forth from the physical light of the sun into a higher spiritual light. Something is being born in him which rests as deeply in most human beings as the unborn child rests in the mother.

Without being aware of the full significance of this fact, one cannot understand what occult development means. The higher soul, resting deep within human nature and interwoven with it, is brought forth. As man stands before us in everyday life, his higher and lower natures are intermingled, and that is fortunate for everyday life. Many persons among us would exhibit evil, negative qualities if it were not that there lives along with the lower nature a higher one which exerts a balancing influence. This intermingling can be compared with mixing a yellow with a blue liquid in a glass. The result is a green liquid in which blue and yellow can no longer be distinguished. So also is the lower nature in man mingled with the higher, and the two cannot be distinguished. Just as you might extract the blue liquid from the green by a chemical process, so that only the yellow remains and the unified green is separated into a complete duality, so the lower and higher natures separate in occult development. One draws the lower nature out of the body like a sword from the scabbard, which then remains alone. The lower nature comes forth appearing almost gruesome. When it was still mingled with the higher nature, nothing was noticeable. But once separated, all evil, negative properties come into view. People who previously appeared benevolent often become argumentative and jealous. This characteristic had existed earlier in the lower nature, but was guided by the higher. You can observe this in many who have been guided along an abnormal path. A person may readily become a liar when he is introduced into the spiritual world, because the capacity to distinguish between the true and the false is lost especially easily. Therefore, strictest training of the personal character is a necessary parallel to occult training. What history tells us about the saints and their temptations is not legend but literal truth.

He who wants to develop towards the higher world on any path is readily prone to such temptations unless he can subdue everything that meets him with a powerful strength of character and the highest morality. Not only do lust and passions grow – that is not even the case so much – but opportunities also increase. This seems miraculous. As through a miracle, the person ascending into the higher worlds finds previously hidden opportunities for evil lurking around him. In every aspect of life a demon lies in wait for him, ready to lead him astray. He now sees what he has not seen before. As through a spell, the division within his own being charms forth such opportunities from the hidden areas of life. Therefore, a very determined shaping of the character is an indispensable foundation for the so-called white magic, the school of occult development which leads man into the higher worlds in a good, true, and genuine way. Every practical occultist will tell you that no one should dare to step through the narrow portal, as the entrance to occult development is called, without practising these properties again and again. They build the necessary foundation for occult life.

First man must develop the ability to distinguish in every situation throughout his life what is unimportant from what is important, that is, what is perishable from the imperishable. This requirement is easy to indicate but difficult to carry out. As Goethe says, it is easy, but what is easy is hard. Look, for instance, at a plant or an object. You will learn to understand that everything has an important and an unimportant side, and that man usually takes interest in the unimportant, in the relationship of the matter to himself, or in some other subordinate aspect. He who wishes to become an occultist must gradually develop the habit of seeing and seeking in each thing its essence. For instance, when he sees a clock he must have an interest in its laws. He must be able to take it apart into its smallest detail and to develop a feeling for the laws of the clock. A mineralogist will arrive at considerable knowledge about a quartz crystal simply by looking at it. The occultist, however, must be able to take the stone in his hand and to feel in a living way something akin to the following monologue: 'In a certain sense you, the crystal, are beneath humanity, but in a certain sense you are far above humanity. You are beneath humanity because you cannot make for yourself a picture of man by means of concepts, and because you do not feel. You cannot explain or think, you do not live, but you have an advantage over mankind. You are pure within yourself, have no desire, no wishes, no lust. Every human, every living being has wishes, desires, lusts. You do not have them. You are complete and without wishes, satisfied with what has come to you, an example for man, with which he will have to unite his other qualities.'

If the occultist can feel this in all its depth, then he has grasped what the stone can tell him. In this way man can draw out of everything something full of meaning. When this has become a habit for him, when he separates the important from the unimportant, he has acquired another feeling essential to the occultist. Then he must connect his own life with that which is important. In this people err particularly easily in our time. They believe that their place in life is not proper for them. How often people are inclined to say, 'My lot has put me in the wrong place. I am,' let us say, 'a postal clerk. If I were put in a different place, I could give people high ideas, great teaching,' and so on. The mistake which these people make is that they do not enter into the significant aspect of their occupation. If you see in me something of importance because I can talk to the people here, then you do not see the importance of your own life and work. If the mail-carriers did not carry the mail, the whole postal traffic would stop, and much work already achieved by others would be in vain.

Hence everyone in his place is of exceeding importance for the whole, and none is higher than the other. Christ has attempted to demonstrate this most beautifully in the thirteenth chapter of the Gospel of John, with the words, 'The servant is not greater than his lord; neither he that is sent greater than he that sent him.' These words were spoken after the Master had washed the feet of the Apostles. He wanted to say, 'What would I be without my Apostles? They must be there so that I can be there in the world, and I must pay them tribute by lowering myself before them and washing their feet.' This is one of the most significant allusions to the feeling that the occultist must have for what is important. What is important in the inward sense must not be confused with the externally important. This must be strictly observed.

In addition, we must develop a series of qualities. To begin with, we must become masters over our thoughts, and particularly our train of thought. This is called *control of thoughts*. Just think how thoughts whirl about in the soul of man, how they flit about like will-o'-the wisps. Here one impression arises, there another, and each one changes one's thoughts. It is not true that we govern our thoughts; rather our thoughts govern us totally. We must advance to the ability of steeping ourselves in one specific thought at a certain time of the day and not allow any other thought to enter and disturb our soul.

In this way we ourselves hold the reins of thought-life for a time.

The second quality is to find a similar relationship to our actions, that is, to exercise *control over our actions*. Here it is necessary to undertake actions, at least occasionally, which are not initiated by anything external. That which is initiated by our station in life, our profession, or our situation does not lead us more deeply into higher life. Higher life depends on personal matters, such as resolving to do something springing totally from one's own initiative even if it is an absolutely insignificant matter. All other actions contribute nothing to the higher life.

The third quality to be striven for is *even-temperedness*. People fluctuate back and forth between joy and sorrow. One moment they are beside themselves with joy, the next they are unbearably sad. Thus, people allow themselves to be rocked on the waves of life, on joy or sorrow. But they must reach equanimity and steadiness. Neither the greatest sorrow nor the greatest joy must unsettle their composure. They must become steadfast and even-tempered.

Fourth is the *understanding for every being*. Nothing expresses more beautifully what it means to understand every being than the legend which is handed down to us, not by the Gospel but by a Persian story. Jesus was walking across a field with his disciples, and on the way they found a decaying dog. The animal looked horrible. Jesus stopped and cast an admiring look upon it, saying, 'What beautiful teeth the animal has!' Jesus found within the ugly the one beautiful aspect. Strive at all times to approach what is wonderful in every object of outer reality, and you will see that everything contains an aspect that can be affirmed. Do as Christ did when he admired the beautiful teeth of the dead dog. This course will lead you to the great ability to tolerate, and to an understanding of every thing and of every being.

The fifth quality is *complete openness* towards everything new that meets us. Most people judge new things which meet them by the old which they already know. If anyone comes to tell them something new, they immediately respond with an opposing opinion. But we must not confront a new communication immediately with our own opinion. We must rather be on the alert for possibilities of learning something new. And learn we can, even from a small child. Even if one were the wisest person, one must be willing to hold back one's own judgement and to listen to others. We must develop this ability to listen, for it will enable us to meet matters with the greatest possible openness. In occultism, this is called faith. It is the power not to weaken through opposition the impression made by the new.

The sixth quality is that which everyone receives once he has developed the first five. It is *inner harmony*. The person who has the other qualities also has inner harmony. In addition, it is necessary for a person seeking occult develop-ment to develop his feeling for freedom to the highest degree. That feeling for freedom enables him to seek within himself the centre of his own being, to stand on his own two feet, so that he will not have to ask everyone what he should do and so that he can stand upright and act freely. This also is a quality which one needs to acquire.

If man has developed these qualities within himself, then he stands above all the dangers arising from the division within his nature. Then the properties of his lower nature can no longer affect him; he can no longer stray from the path. Therefore, these qualities must be formed with the greatest precision. Then comes the occult life, whose expression depends on a steady rhythm being carried into life.

The phrase 'carrying rhythm into life' expresses the unfold-ing of this faculty. If you observe nature, you will find in it a certain rhythm. You will, of course, expect that the violet blooms every year at the same time in spring, that the crops in the field and the grapes on the vine will ripen at the same time each year. This rhythmical sequence of phenomena exists everywhere in nature. Everywhere there is rhythm, everywhere repetition in regular sequence. As you ascend from the plant to beings with higher development, you see the

rhythmic sequence decreasing. Yet even in the higher stages
of animal development one sees how all functions are ordered
rhythmically. At a certain time of the year, animals acquire
certain functions and capabilities. The higher a being evolves,
the more life is given over into the hands of the being itself,
and the more these rhythms cease. You must know that the
human body is only one member of man's being. There is also
the etheric body, then the astral body, and, finally, the higher
members which form the basis for the others.

The physical body is highly subject to the same rhythm that
governs outer nature. Just as plant and animal life, in its
external form, takes its course rhythmically, so does the life of
the physical body. The heart beats rhythmically, the lungs
breathe rhythmically, and so forth. All this proceeds so
rhythmically because it is set in order by higher powers, by the
wisdom of the world, by that which the scriptures call the
Holy Spirit. The higher bodies, particularly the astral body,
have been, I would like to say, abandoned by these higher
spiritual forces, and have lost their rhythm. Can you deny that
your activity relating to wishes, desires, and passions is
irregular, that it can in no way compare with the regularity
ruling the physical body? He who learns to know the rhythm
inherent in physical nature increasingly finds in it an example
for spirituality. If you consider the heart, this wonderful organ
with the regular beat and innate wisdom, and you compare it
with the desires and passions of the astral body which unleash
all sorts of actions against the heart, you will recognize how its
regular course is influenced detrimentally by passion. However, the functions of the astral body must become as rhythmical
as those of the physical body.

I want to mention something here which will seem grotesque to most people. This is the matter of fasting. Awareness
of the significance of fasting has been totally lost. Fasting is
enormously significant, however, for creating rhythm in our
astral body. What does it mean to fast? It means to restrain the
desire to eat and to block the astral body in relation to this

desire. He who fasts blocks the astral body and develops no desire to eat. This is like blocking a force in a machine. The astral body becomes inactive then, and the whole rhythm of the physical body with its innate wisdom works upward into the astral body to rhythmicize it. Like the imprint of a seal, the harmony of the physical body impresses itself upon the astral body. It would transfer much more permanently if the astral body were not continuously being made irregular by desires, passions and wishes, including spiritual desires and wishes.

It is more necessary for the human being of today to carry rhythm into all spheres of higher life than it was in earlier times. Just as rhythm is implanted in the physical body by God, so man must make his astral body rhythmical. Man must order his day for himself. He must arrange it for his astral body as the spirit of nature arranges it for the lower realms. In the morning, at a definite time, one must undertake one spiritual action; a different one must be undertaken at another time, again to be adhered to regularly, and yet another one in the evening. These spiritual exercises must not be chosen arbitrarily, but must be suitable for the development of the higher life. This is one method for taking life in hand and for keeping it in hand. So set a time for yourself in the morning when you can concentrate. You must adhere to this hour. You must establish a kind of calm so that the occult master in you may awaken. You must meditate about a great thought content that has nothing to do with the external world, and let this thought content come to life completely. A short time is enough, perhaps a quarter of an hour. Even five minutes are sufficient if more time is not available. But it is worthless to do these exercises irregularly. Do them regularly so that the activity of the astral body becomes as regular as a clock. Only then do they have value. The astral body will appear completely different if you do these exercises regularly. Sit down in the morning and do these exercises, and the forces I described will develop. But, as I said, it must be done regularly, for the astral body expects that the same process will take place at the same time each day, and it falls into disorder if this does not happen. At least the intent towards order must exist. If you rhythmicize your life in this manner, you will see success in not too long a time; that is, the spiritual life hidden from man for the time being will become manifest to a certain degree.

As a rule, human life alternates among four states. The first state is the perception of the external world. You look around with your senses and perceive the external world. The second is what we may call imagination or the life of mental images which is related to, or even part of, dream life. There man does not have his roots in his surroundings, but is separated from them. There he has no realities within himself, but at the most reminiscences. The third state is dreamless sleep, in which man has no consciousness of his ego at all. In the fourth state he lives in memory. This is different from perception. It is already something remote, spiritual. If man had no memory, he could uphold no spiritual development.

The inner life begins to develop by means of inner contemplation and meditation. Thus, the human being sooner or later perceives that he no longer dreams in a chaotic manner; he begins to dream in the most significant way, and remarkable things reveal themselves in his dreams, which he gradually begins to recognize as manifestations of spiritual beings. Naturally the trivial objection might easily be raised that this is nothing but a dream and therefore of no consequence. However, should someone discover the dirigible in his dream and then proceed to build it, the dream would simply have shown the truth. Thus an idea can be grasped in an other-than-usual manner. Its truthfulness must then be judged by the fact that it can be realized. We must become convinced of its inner truth from outside.

The next step in spiritual life is to comprehend truth by means of our own qualities and of guiding our dreams consciously. When we begin to guide our dreams in a regular manner, then we are at the stage where truth becomes transparent for us. The first stage is called 'material cognition'. For this, the object must lie before us. The next stage

is 'imaginative cognition'. It is developed through meditation, that is through shaping life rhythmically. Achieving this
is laborious. But once it is achieved, the time arrives when
there is no longer a difference between perception in the usual
life and perception in the supersensible. When we are among
the things of our usual life, that is, in the sense world, and we
change our spiritual state, then we experience continuously
the spiritual, the supersensible world, but only if we have
sufficiently trained ourselves. This happens as soon as we are
able to be deaf and dumb to the sense world, to remember
nothing of the everyday world, and still to retain a spiritual life
within us. Then our dream-life begins to take on a conscious
form. If we are able to pour some of this into our everyday life,
then the next capacity arises, rendering the soul-qualities of
the beings around us perceptible. Then we see not only the
external aspect of things but also the inner, hidden essential
kernel of things, of plants, of animals, and of man. I know that
most people will say that these are actually different things.
True, these are always different things from those a person
sees who does not have such senses. The third stage is that in
which a consciousness, which is as a rule completely empty,
begins to be enlivened by continuity of consciousness. The
continuity appears on its own. The person is then no longer
unconscious during sleep. During the time in which he used
to sleep, he now experiences the spiritual world.

Of what does sleep usually consist? The physical body lies
in bed, and the astral body lives in the supersensible world. In
this supersensible world, you are taking a walk. As a rule, a
person with the type of disposition which is typical today
cannot withdraw very far from his body. If one applies the
rules of spiritual science, organs can be developed in the astral
body as it wanders during sleep – just as the physical body has
organs – which allow one to become conscious during sleep.
The physical body would be blind and deaf if it had no eyes
or ears, and the astral body walking at night is blind and deaf
for the same reason, because it does not yet have eyes and ears.

But these organs are developed through meditation which provides the means for training these organs. This meditation must then be guided in a regular way. It is being led so that the human body is the mother and the spirit of man is the father. The physical human body, as we see it before us, is a mystery in every one of its parts and, in fact, each member is related in a definite but mysterious way to a part of the astral body. These are matters which the occultist knows. For instance, the point in the physical body lying between the eyebrows belongs to a certain organ in the astral organism. When the occultist indicates how one must direct thoughts, feelings, and sensations to this point between the eyebrows through connecting something formed in the physical body with the corresponding part of the astral body, the result will be a certain sensation in the astral body. But this must be practised regularly, and one must know how to do it. Then the astral body begins to form its members. From a lump, it grows to be an organism in which organs are formed. I have described the astral sense organs in the periodical *Lucifer Gnosis*. They are also called lotus flowers. By means of special word sequences, these lotus flowers are cultivated. Once this has occurred, the human being is able to perceive the spiritual world. This is the same world he enters when passing through the portal of death, a final contradiction to Hamlet's 'The undiscover'd country from whose bourn no traveller returns'.

So it is possible to go, or rather to slip, from the sense world into the supersensible world and to live there as well as here. That does not mean life in never-never land, but life in a realm that clarifies and explains life in our realm. Just as the usual person who has not studied electricity would not understand all the wonderful workings in a factory powered by electricity, so the average person does not understand the occurrences in the spiritual world. The visitor at the factory will lack understanding as long as he remains ignorant of the laws of electricity. So also will man lack understanding in the realm of the spirit as long as he does not know the laws of the spiritual. There is nothing in our world that is not dependent on the spiritual world at every moment. Everything surrounding us is the external expression of the spiritual world. There is no materiality. Everything material is condensed spirit. For the person looking into the spiritual world, the whole material, sense-perceptible world, the world in general, becomes spiritualized. As ice melts into water through the effect of the sun, so everything sense-perceptible melts into something spiritual within the soul which looks into the spiritual world. Thus, the foundation of the world gradually manifests before the spiritual eye and the spiritual ear.

The life that man learns to know in this manner is actually the spiritual life he carries within himself all along. But he knows nothing of it because he does not know himself before developing organs for the higher world. Imagine possessing the characteristics you have at this time, yet being without sense-organs. You would know nothing of the world around you, would have no understanding of the physical body, and yet you would belong to the physical world. So the soul of man belongs to the spiritual world, but does not know it because it does not hear or see. Just as our body is drawn out of the forces and materials of the physical world, so is our soul drawn out of the forces and materials of the spiritual world. We do not recognize ourselves within ourselves, but only within our surroundings. As we cannot perceive a heart or a brain – even by means of X-rays – without seeing it in other people through our sense organs (it is only the eyes that can see the heart), so we truly cannot see or hear our own soul without perceiving it with spiritual organs in the surrounding world. You can recognize yourself only by means of your surroundings. In truth there exists no inner knowledge, no self-examination; there is only one knowledge, one revelation of the life around us through the organs of the physical as well as the spiritual. We are a part of the worlds around us, of the physical, the soul and the spiritual worlds. We learn from the physical if we have physical organs, from the spiritual world and from all souls if we have spiritual and soul organs. There is no knowledge but knowledge of the world.

It is vain and empty idleness for man to 'brood' within himself, believing that it is possible to progress simply by looking into himself. Man will find the God in himself if he awakens the divine organs within himself and finds his higher divine self in his surroundings, just as he finds his lower self solely by means of using his eyes and ears. We perceive ourselves clearly as physical beings by means of intercourse with the sense-world, and we perceive ourselves clearly in relation to the spiritual world by developing spiritual senses. Development of the inner man means opening oneself to the divine life around us.

Now you will understand that it is essential that he who ascends to the higher world undergoes, to begin with, an immense strengthening of his character. Man can experience on his own the characteristics of the sense-world because his senses are already opened. This is possible because a benevolent divine spirit, who has seen and heard in the physical world, stood by man in the most ancient times, before man could see and hear, and opened man's eyes and ears. It is from just such beings that man must learn at this time to see spiritually, from beings already able to do what he still has to learn. We must have a guru who can tell us how we should develop our organs, who will tell us what he has done in order to develop these organs. He who wishes to guide must have acquired one fundamental quality. This is unconditional truthfulness. This same quality is also a main requirement for the student. No one may train to become an occultist unless this fundamental quality of unconditional truthfulness has been previously cultivated.

When facing sense-experience, one can test what is being said. When I tell you something about the spiritual world, however, you must have trust because you are not far enough to be able to confirm the information. He who wishes to be a guru must have become so truthful that it is impossible for him to take lightly such statements concerning the spiritual world or the spiritual life. The sense-world corrects errors immediately by its own nature, but in the spiritual world we must have these guidelines within ourselves. We must be strictly trained, so that we are not forced to use the outer world for controls but only our inner self. We are only able to gain this control by acquiring already in this world the strictest truthfulness. Therefore, when the Anthroposophical Society began to present some of the basic teachings of occultism to the world, it had to adopt the principle: there is no law higher than truth. Very few people understand this principle. Most are satisfied if they can say they have the conviction that something is true, and then if it is wrong they will simply say that they were mistaken. The occultist cannot rely on his subjective honesty. There he is on the wrong track. He must always be in harmony with the facts of the external world, and any experience that contradicts these facts must be seen as an error or a mistake. The question of who is at fault for the error ceases to be important to the occultist. He must be in absolute harmony with the facts in life. He must begin to feel responsible in the strictest sense for every one of his assertions. Thus he trains himself in the unconditional certainty that he must have for himself and for others if he wishes to be a spiritual guide.

So you see that I needed to indicate to you today a series of qualities and methods. We will have to speak about these again in order to add the higher concepts. It may seem to you that these things are too intimate to discuss with others, that each soul has to come to grips with them on its own terms and that they are possibly unsuitable for reaching the great destination which should be reached, namely, the entrance into the spiritual world. This entrance will definitely be achieved by those who tread the path I have characterized.

When? One of the most outstanding participants in the theosophical movement, Subba Row, who died some time ago, has spoken fittingly about this.[23] Replying to the question of how long it would take, he said, 'Seven years, perhaps also seven times seven years, perhaps even seven incarnations, perhaps only seven hours.' It all depends on what the human being brings with himself into life. We may meet a person who seems to be very stupid, but who has brought with himself a concealed higher life that needs only to be brought out. Most human beings these days are much further than it seems, and more people would know about this if the materialism of our conditions and of our time would not drive them back into the inner life of the soul. A large percentage of today's human beings was previously much further advanced. Whether that which is within them will come forth depends on many factors. But it is possible to give some help. Suppose you have before you a person who was highly developed in his earlier incarnation, but now has an undeveloped brain. An undeveloped brain may at times conceal great spiritual faculties. But if he can be taught the usual everyday abilities, it may happen that the inner spirituality also comes forth.

Another important factor is the environment in which a person lives. The human being is a mirror-image of his surroundings in a most significant way. Suppose that a person is a highly developed personality, but lives in surroundings that awaken and develop certain prejudices with such a strong effect that the higher talents cannot come forth. Unless such a person finds someone who can draw out these abilities, they will remain hidden.

I have been able to give only a few indications to you about this matter.[24] I especially wanted to awaken in you this one understanding, that the higher life is not schooled in a tumultuous way but rather quite intimately, in the deepest soul, and that the great day when the soul awakens and enters into the higher life actually arrives like the thief in the night. The development towards the higher life leads man into a new world, and when he has entered this new world, then he sees the other side of existence, so to speak; then what has previously been hidden for him reveals itself. Maybe not everyone can do this; maybe only a few can do it, one might say to oneself. But that must not keep one from at least starting on the way that is open to everyone, namely, to hear about the higher worlds. The human being is called to live in community, and he who secludes himself cannot arrive at a spiritual life. But it is a seclusion in a stronger sense if he says, 'I do not believe this, this does not relate to me; this may be valid for the after-life.' For the occultist this has no validity. It is an important principle for the occultist to consider other human beings as true manifestations of his own higher self, because he knows then that he must find the others in himself. There is a delicate distinction between these two sentences: 'To find the others in oneself', and 'To find oneself in the others'. In the higher sense it means, 'This is you'. And in the highest sense it means to recognize oneself in the world and to understand that saying of the poet which I cited some weeks ago in a different connection: 'One was successful. He lifted the veil of the goddess at Sais. But what did he see? Miracle of miracles! He saw himself.' To find oneself – not in egotistical inwardness, but selflessly in the world without – that is true recognition of the self.

VII. Practical Training in Thinking[25]

Karlsruhe, 18 January 1909

I<small>T MAY</small> seem strange that an anthroposophist should feel called upon to speak about practical training in thinking, for there is a widespread opinion that anthroposophy is highly impractical and has no connection with life. This view can only arise among those who see things superficially, for in reality what we are concerned with here can guide us in the most ordinary affairs of everyday life. It is something that can be transformed at any moment into sensation and feeling, enabling us to meet life with assurance and to acquire a firm position in it.

Many people who call themselves practical imagine that their actions are guided by the most practical principles. But if we enquire more closely, it is found that their so-called 'practical thinking' is often not thinking at all but only the continuing pursuit of traditional opinions and habits. An entirely objective observation of the 'practical' man's thinking and an examination of what is usually termed 'practical thinking' will reveal the fact that it generally contains little that can be called practical. What to them is known as practical thought or thinking consists in following the example of some authority whose ideas are accepted as a standard in the construction of some object. Anyone who thinks differently is considered impractical because this thinking does not coincide with traditional ideas.

Whenever anything really practical has been invented, it has been done by a person without practical knowledge of that particular subject. Take, for instance, the modern postage stamp. It would be most natural to assume that it was invented by some practical post office official. It was not. At the beginning of the last century it was a complicated affair to mail a letter. In order to dispatch a letter one had to go to the nearest receiving office where various books had to be referred to and many other formalities complied with. The uniform rate of postage known today is hardly 60 years old, and our present postage stamp that makes this possible was not invented by a practical postal employee at all but by someone completely outside the post office. This was the Englishman Rowland Hill.[26]

After the uniform system of postage stamps had been devised, the English minister who then had charge of the mails declared in Parliament that one could not assume any simplification of the system would increase the volume of mail as the impractical Hill anticipated. Even if it did, the London post office would be entirely inadequate to handle the increased volume. It never occurred to this highly 'practical' individual that the post office must be fitted to the amount of business, not the business to the size of the post office. Indeed, in the shortest possible time this idea, which an 'impractical' man had to defend against a 'practical' authority, became a fact. Today, stamps are used everywhere as a matter of course for sending letters.

It was similar with the railways. When in 1837 the first railway in Germany was to be built, the members of the Bavarian College of Medicine were consulted on the advisability of the project and they voiced the opinion that it would be unwise to build railways.[27] They added that if this project were to be carried out then at least a high board fence would have to be erected on both sides of the line to protect the public from possible brain and nervous shock.

When the railway from Potsdam to Berlin was planned, Postmaster General Nagler said, 'I am now dispatching two stage-coaches daily to Potsdam and these are never full. If people are determined to throw their money out the window, they can do it much more simply without building a railway!'[28]

But the real facts of life often sweep aside the 'practical', that is to say, those who believe in their own ability to be practical. We must clearly distinguish between genuine thinking and so-called 'practical thinking' that is merely reasoning in traditional ruts of thought.

As a starting-point to our consideration I will tell you of an experience I had during my student days. A young colleague once came to me glowing with the joy of one who has just hit upon a really clever idea, and announced that he must go at once to see Professor X (who at the time taught machine construction at the university) for he had just made a great discovery. 'I have discovered,' he said, 'how, with a small amount of steam power and by simply rearranging the machinery, an enormous amount of work can be done by one machine.' He was in such a rush to see the professor that that was all he could tell me. He failed to find him, however, so he returned and explained the whole matter to me. It all smacked of perpetual motion, but after all, why shouldn't even that be possible? After I had listened to his explanation I had to tell him that although his plan undoubtedly appeared to be cleverly thought out it was a case that might be compared in practice with that of a person who, on boarding a railway carriage, pushes with all his might and then believes when it moves that he has actually started it. 'That,' I said to him, 'is the thought principle underlying your discovery.' Finally, he saw it himself and did not return to the professor.

It is thus quite possible to shut ourselves up within a shell fashioned by our own thoughts. In rare cases this can be observed distinctly, but there are many similar examples in life that do not always reach such a striking extreme as the one just cited. He who is able to study human nature more intimately, however, knows that a large number of thought processes are of this kind. He often sees, we might say, people standing in the carriage pushing it from within and believing that they are making it move. Many of the events of life would take a different course if people did not so often try to solve their problems by thus deluding themselves.

True practice in thinking presupposes a right attitude and proper feeling for thinking. How can a right attitude towards thinking be attained? Anyone who believes that thought is merely an activity that takes place within his head or in his soul cannot have the right feeling for thought. Whoever harbours this idea will be constantly diverted by a false feeling from seeking right habits of thought and from making the necessary demands on his thinking. He who would acquire the right feeling for thought must say to himself, 'If I can formulate thoughts about things, and learn to understand them through thinking, then these things themselves must first have contained these thoughts. The things must have been built up according to these thoughts, and only because this is so can I in turn extract these thoughts from the things.'

It can be imagined that this world outside and around us may be regarded in the same way as a watch. The comparison between the human organism and a watch is often used, but those who make it frequently forget the most important point. They forget the watchmaker. The fact must be kept clearly in mind that the wheels have not united and fitted themselves together of their own accord and thus made the watch 'go', but that first there was the watchmaker who put the different parts of the watch together. The watchmaker must never be forgotten. Through thoughts the watch has come into existence. The thoughts have flowed, as it were, into the watch, into the thing.

The works and phenomena of nature must be viewed in a similar way. In the works of man it is easy to picture this to ourselves, but with the works of nature it is not so easily done. Yet these, too, are the result of spiritual activities and behind them are spiritual beings. Thus, when a person thinks about things he only re-thinks what is already in them. The belief that the world has been created by thought and is still ceaselessly being created in this manner is the belief that can alone fructify the actual inner practice of thought.

It is always the denial of the spiritual in the world that

produces the worst kind of malpractice in thought, even in the field of science. Consider, for example, the theory that our planetary system arose from a primordial nebula that began to rotate and then densified into a central body from which rings and globes detached themselves, thus mechanically bringing into existence the entire solar system. He who propounds this theory is committing a grave error of thought.

A simple experiment used to be made in the schools to demonstrate this theory. A drop of oil was made to float in a glass of water. The drop was then pierced with a pin and made to rotate. As a result, tiny globules of oil were thrown off from the central drop creating a miniature planetary system, thus proving to the pupil – so the teacher thought – that this planetary system could come into existence through a purely mechanical process.

Only impractical thought can draw such conclusions from this little experiment, for he who would apply this theory to the cosmos has forgotten one thing that it ordinarily might be well to forget occasionally, and that is himself. He forgets that it is he who has brought this whole thing into rotation. If he had not been there and conducted the whole experiment, the separation of the little globules from the large drop would never have occurred. Had this fact been observed and applied logically to the cosmic system, he then would have been using complete healthy thinking. Similar errors of thought play a great part especially in science. Such things are far more important than one generally believes.

Considering the real practice of thought, it must be realized that thoughts can only be drawn from a world in which they already exist. Just as water can only be taken from a glass that actually contains water, so thoughts can only be extracted from things within which these thoughts are concealed. The world is built by thought, and only for this reason can thought be extracted from it. Were it otherwise, practical thought could not arise. When a person feels the full truth of these words, it will be easy for him to dispense with abstract thought. If he can confidently believe that thoughts are concealed behind the things around him, and that the actual facts of life take their course in obedience to thought – if he feels this, he will easily be converted to a practical habit of thinking based on truth and reality.

Let us now look at that practice of thinking that is of special importance to those who stand upon an anthroposophical foundation. The one who is convinced that the world of facts is born of thought will grasp the importance of the development of right thinking.

Let us suppose that someone resolves to fructify his thinking to such a degree that it will always take the right course in life. If he would do this, he must be guided by the following rules and he must understand that these are actual, practical and fundamental principles. If he will try again and again to shape his thinking according to these rules, certain effects will result. His thinking will become practical even though at first it may not seem so. Other additional mental experiences of quite a different kind also will come to the one who applies these fundamental principles.

Let us suppose that somebody tries the following experiment. He begins today by observing, as accurately as possible, something in the outer world that is accessible to him – for instance, the weather. He watches the configuration of the clouds in the evening, the conditions at sunset, etc., and retains in his mind an exact picture of what he has thus observed. He tries to keep the picture before him in all its details for some time and endeavours to preserve as much of it as possible until the next day. At some time the next day he again makes a study of the weather conditions and again endeavours to gain an exact picture of them.

If in this manner he has pictured to himself exactly the sequential order of the weather conditions, he will become distinctly aware that his thinking gradually becomes richer and more intense. For what makes thought impractical is the tendency to ignore details when observing a sequence of events in the world and to retain but a vague, general impression of them. What is of value, what is essential and fructifies thinking, is just this ability to form exact pictures, especially of successive events, so that one can say, 'Yesterday it was like that; today it is like this.' Thus, one calls up as graphically as possible an inner image of the two juxtaposed scenes that lie apart in the outer world.

This is, so to speak, nothing else but a certain expression of confidence in the thoughts that underly reality. The person experimenting ought not to draw any conclusions immediately or to deduce from today's observation what kind of weather he shall have tomorrow. That would corrupt his thinking. Instead, he must confidently feel that the things of outer reality are definitely related to one another and that tomorrow's events are somehow connected with those of today. But he must not speculate on these things. He must first inwardly re-think the sequence of the outer events as exactly as possible in mental pictures, and then place these images side by side, allowing them to melt into one another. This is a definite rule of thought that must be followed by those who wish to develop factual thinking. It is particularly advisable that this principle be practised on those very things that are not yet understood and the inner connection of which has not yet been penetrated.

Therefore, the experimenter must have the confidence that such events of which he has as yet no understanding – the weather, for instance – and which in the outer world are connected with one another will bring about connections within him. This must be done in pictures only while abstaining from thinking. He must say to himself, 'I do not yet know what the relation is, but I shall let these things grow within me and if I refrain from speculation they will bring something about in me.' It may be easily believed that if he forms exact inner images of succeeding events and at the same time abstains from all thinking something may take place in the invisible members of his nature.

The vehicle of man's thought life is his astral body.[7] As long as the human being is engaged in speculative thinking, this astral body is the slave of the ego. This conscious activity, however, does not occupy the astral body exclusively because the latter is also related in a certain manner to the whole cosmos.

Now, to the extent we abstain from arbitrary thinking and simply form mental pictures of successive events, to that extent do the inner thoughts of the world act within us and imprint themselves, without our being aware of it, on our astral body. To the extent we insert ourselves into the course of the world through observation of the events in the world and receive these images into our thoughts with the greatest possible clarity, allowing them to work within us, to that extent do those members of our organism that are withdrawn from our consciousness become ever more intelligent. If, in the case of inwardly connected events, we have once acquired the faculty of letting the new picture melt into the preceding one in the same way that the transition occurred in nature, it shall be found after a time that our thinking has gained considerable flexibility.

This is the procedure to be followed in matters not yet understood. Things, however, that are understood – events of everyday life, for example – should be treated in a somewhat different manner.

Let us presume that someone, perhaps our neighbour, had done this or that. We think about it and ask ourselves why he did it. We decide he has perhaps done it in preparation for something he intends to do the next day. We do not go any further but clearly picture his act and try to form an image of what he may do, imagining that the next day he will perform such and such an act. Then we wait to see what he really does since he may or may not do what we expected of him. We take note of what does happen and correct our thoughts accordingly. Thus, events of the present are chosen that are followed in thought into the future. Then we wait to see what actually happens.

This can be done either with actions involving people or

something else. Whenever something is understood, we try to form a thought picture of what in our opinion will take place. If our opinion proves correct our thinking is justified and all is well. If, however, something different from our expectation occurs, we review our thoughts and try to discover our mistake. In this way we try to correct our erroneous thinking by calm observation and examination of our errors. An attempt is made to find the reason for things occurring as they did. If we are right, however, we must be especially careful not to boast of our prediction and say, 'Oh well, I knew yesterday that this would happen!'

This is again a rule based upon confidence that there is an inner necessity in things and events, that in the facts themselves there slumbers something that moves things. What is thus working within these things from one day to another are thought forces, and we gradually become conscious of them when meditating on things. By such exercises these thought forces are called up into our consciousness, and if what has been thus foreseen is fulfilled we are in tune with them. We have then established an inner relation with the real thought activity of the matter itself. So we train ourselves to think not arbitrarily but according to the inner necessity and the inner nature of the things themselves.

But our thinking can also be trained in other directions. An occurrence of today is also linked to what happened yesterday. We might consider a naughty child, for example, and ask ourselves what may have caused this behaviour. The events are traced back to the previous day and the unknown cause hypothesized by saying to ourselves, 'Since this occurred today, I must believe that it was prepared by this or that event that occurred yesterday or perhaps the day before.'

We then find out what had actually occurred and so discover whether or not our thought was correct. If the true cause has been found, very well. But if our conclusion was wrong, then we should try to correct the mistake, find out how our thought process developed, and how it ran its course in reality.

To practise these principles is the important point. Time must be taken to observe things as though we were inside the things themselves with our thinking. We should submerge ourselves in the things and enter into their inner thought activity. If this is done, we gradually become aware of the fact that we are growing together with things. We no longer feel that they are outside us and we are here inside our shell thinking about them. Instead we come to feel as if our own thinking occurred within the things themselves. When a person has succeeded to a high degree in doing this, many things will become clear to him.

Goethe was such a man. He was a thinker who always lived with his thought within the things themselves. The psychologist Heinroth's book in 1826, *Anthropology*, characterized Goethe's thought as 'objective'. Goethe himself appreciated this characterization. What was meant is that such thinking does not separate itself from things, but remains within them. It moves within the necessity of things. Goethe's thinking was at the same time perception, and his perception was thinking. He had developed this way of thinking to a remarkable degree. More than once it occurred that, when he had planned to do something, he would go to the window and remark to the person who happened to be with him, 'In three hours we shall have rain!' And so it would happen. From the little patch of sky he could see from the window he was able to foretell the weather conditions for the next few hours. His true thinking, remaining within the objects, thus enabled him to sense the coming event preparing itself in the preceding one.

Much more can actually be accomplished through practical thinking than is commonly supposed. When a person has made these principles of thinking his own, he will notice that his thinking really becomes practical, that his horizon widens, and that he can grasp the things of the world in quite a different way. Gradually his attitude towards things and people will change completely. An actual process will take place within him that will alter his whole conduct. It is of immense importance that he tries to grow into the things in this way with his thinking, for it is in the most eminent sense a practical undertaking to train one's thinking by such exercises.

There is another exercise that is to be practised especially by those to whom the right idea usually does not occur at the right time.

Such people should try above all things to stop their thinking from being forever influenced and controlled by the ordinary course of worldly events and whatever else may come with them. As a rule, when a person lies down for half an hour's rest, his thoughts are allowed to play freely in a thousand different directions, or on the other hand he may become absorbed with some trouble in his life. Before he realizes it such things will have crept into his consciousness and claimed his entire attention. If this habit persists, such a person will never experience the occasion when the right idea occurs to him at the right moment.

If he really wants this to happen, he must say to himself whenever he can spare a half hour for rest, 'Whenever I can spare the time, I will think about something I myself have chosen and I will bring it into my consciousness arbitrarily of my own free will. For example, I will think of something that occurred two years ago during a walk. I will deliberately recall what occurred then and I will think about it if only for five minutes. During these five minutes I will banish everything else from my mind and will myself choose the subject about which I wish to think.'

He need not even choose so difficult a subject as this one. The point is not at all to change one's mental process through difficult exercises but to get away from the ordinary routine of life in one's thinking. He must think of something quite apart from what enmeshes him during the ordinary course of the day. If nothing occurs to him to think about, he might open a book at random and occupy his thoughts with whatever first catches his eye. Or he may choose to think of something he saw at a particular time that morning on his way to work and to which he would otherwise have paid no attention. The main point is that it should be something totally different from the ordinary run of daily events, something that otherwise would not have occupied his thoughts.

If such exercises are practised systematically again and again, it will soon be noticed that ideas come at the right moments, and the right thoughts occur when needed. Through these exercises thinking will become activated and mobile – something of immense importance in practical life.

Let us consider another exercise that is especially helpful in improving one's memory.

One tries, at first in the crude way people usually recall past events, to remember something that occurred, let us say, yesterday. Such recollections are, as a rule, indistinct and colourless, and most people are satisfied if they can just remember a person's name. But if it is desired to develop one's memory, one can no longer be content with this. This must be clear. The following exercise must be systematically practised, saying to oneself, 'I shall recall exactly the person I saw yesterday, also the street corner where I met him, and what happened to be in his vicinity. I shall draw the whole picture as exactly as possible and shall even imagine the colour and cut of his coat and vest.' Most people will find themselves utterly incapable of doing this and will quickly see how much is lacking in their recollections to produce a really lifelike, graphic picture of what they met and experienced only yesterday.

Since this is true in the majority of cases, we must begin with that condition in which many people are unable to recollect their most recent experiences. It is only too true that most people's observations of things and events are usually inaccurate and vague. The results of a test given by a professor in one of the universities demonstrated that out of 30 students who took the test, only two had observed an occurrence correctly; the remaining 28 reported it inaccurately. But a good memory is the child of accurate observation. A reliable memory is attained, let me repeat, by accurate observation and it can also be said that in a certain roundabout way of the soul it is born as the child of exact observation.

But if somebody cannot at first accurately remember his experiences of yesterday, what should he do? First, he should try to remember as accurately as he can what actually occurred. Where recollections fail he should fill in the picture with something incorrect that was not really present. The essential point here is that the picture be complete. Suppose it was forgotten whether or not someone was wearing a brown or a black coat. Then he might be pictured in a brown coat and brown trousers with such and such buttons on his vest and a yellow necktie. One might further imagine a general situation in which there was a yellow wall, a tall person passing on the left, a short one on the right, etc.

All that can be remembered he puts into this picture and what cannot be remembered is added imaginatively in order to have a completed mental picture. Of course, it is at first incorrect but through the effort to create a complete picture he is induced to observe more accurately. Such exercises must be continued, and although they might be tried and failed 50 times, perhaps the fifty-first time he shall be able to remember accurately what the person he has met looked like, what he wore, and even little details like the buttons on his vest. Then nothing will be overlooked and every detail will imprint itself on his memory. Thus he will have first sharpened his powers of observation by these exercises and in addition, as the fruit of this accurate observation, he will have improved his memory.

He should take special care to retain not only names and main features of what he wishes to remember but also to retain vivid images covering all the details. If he cannot remember some detail, he must try for the time being to fill in the picture and thus make it a whole. He will then notice that his memory, as though in a roundabout way, slowly becomes reliable. Thus it can be seen how definite direction can be given for making thinking increasingly more practical.

There is still something else that is of particular importance. In thinking about some matters we feel it necessary to come to a conclusion. We consider how this or that should be done and then make up our minds in a certain way. This inclination, although natural, does not lead to practical thinking. All overly hasty thinking does not advance us but sets us back. Patience in these things is absolutely essential.

Suppose, for instance, we desire to carry out some particular plan. There are usually several ways that this might be done. Now we should have the patience first to imagine how things would work out if we were to execute our plan in one way and then we should consider what the results would be of doing it in another. Surely there will always be reasons for preferring one method over another, but we should refrain from forming an immediate decision. Instead, an attempt should be made to imagine the two possibilities and then we must say to ourselves, 'That will do for the present; I shall now stop thinking about this matter.' No doubt there are people who will become fidgety at this point, and although it is difficult to overcome such a condition it is extremely useful to do so. It then becomes possible to imagine how the matter might be handled in two ways, and to decide to stop thinking about it for a while.

Whenever it is possible, action should be deferred until the next day, and the two possibilities considered again at that time. You will find that in the interim conditions have changed and that the next day you will be able to form a different, or at least a more thorough decision than could have been reached the day before. An inner necessity is hidden in things and if we do not act with arbitrary impatience but allow this inner necessity to work in us – and it will – we shall find the next day that it has enriched our thinking, thus making possible a wiser decision. This is exceedingly valuable.

We might, for example, be asked to give our advice on a problem and to make a decision. But let us not thrust forward our decision immediately. We should have the patience to

place the various possibilities before ourselves without forming any definite conclusions, and we then should quietly let
these possibilities work themselves out within us. Even the
popular proverb says that one should sleep over a matter
before making a decision.

To sleep over it is not enough, however. It is necessary to
consider two or, better still, several possibilities that will
continue to work within us when our ego is not consciously
occupied with them. Later on, when we return again to the
matter in question, it will be found that certain thought forces
have been stirred up within us in this manner, and that as a
result our thinking has become more factual and practical.

It is certain that what a person seeks can always be found in
the world, whether he stands at the carpenter's bench, or follows
the plough, or belongs to one of the professions. If he will practise
these exercises, he will become a practical thinker in the most
ordinary matters of everyday life. If he thus trains himself, he will
approach and look at the things of the world in a quite different
manner from previously. Although at first these exercises may
seem related only to his own innermost life, they are entirely
applicable and of the greatest importance precisely for the outer
world. They have powerful consequences.

An example will demonstrate how necessary it is to think
about things in a really practical manner. Let us imagine that
for some reason or other a person climbs a tree. He falls from
the tree, strikes the ground, and is picked up dead. Now, the
thought most likely to occur to us is that the fall killed him. We
would be inclined to say that the fall was the cause and death
the effect. In this instance cause and effect seem logically
connected. But this assumption may completely confuse the
true sequence of facts, for the person may have fallen as a
consequence of heart failure. To the observer the external
event is exactly the same in both cases. Only when the true
causes are known can a correct judgement be formed. In this
case it might have been that the person was already dead
before he fell and the fall had nothing to do with his death. It

is thus possible to invert completely cause and effect. In this instance the error is evident, but often they are not so easily discernible. The frequency with which such errors in thinking occur is amazing. Indeed, it must be said that in the field of science conclusions in which this confusion of cause and effect is permitted are being drawn every day. Most people do not grasp this fact, however, because they are not acquainted with the possibilities of thinking.

Still another example will show you clearly how such errors in thinking arise and how a person who has been practising exercises like these can no longer make such mistakes. Suppose someone concludes that man as he is today is a descendent of the ape. This means that what he has come to know in the ape – the forces active in this animal – have attained higher perfection and man is the result. Now, to show the meaning of this theory in terms of thought, let us imagine that this person is the only human being on earth, and that besides himself there are only those apes present that, according to his theory, can evolve into human beings. He now studies these apes with the utmost accuracy down to the most minute detail and then forms a concept of what lives in them. Excluding himself and without ever having seen another person let him now try to develop the concept of a human being solely from his concept of the ape. He will find this to be quite impossible. His concept 'ape' will never transform itself into the concept 'man'.

If he had cultivated correct habits of thinking, this person would have said to himself, 'My concept of the ape does not change into the concept of man. What I perceive in the ape, therefore, can never become a human being, otherwise my concept would have to change likewise. There must be something else present that I am unable to perceive.' So he would have to imagine an invisible, supersensible entity behind the physical ape that he would be unable to perceive but that alone would make the ape's transformation into man a possible conception.

We shall not enter into a discussion of the impossibility of this case, but simply point out the erroneous thinking underlying this theory. If this person had thought correctly he would have seen that he could not possibly conceive of such a theory without assuming the existence of something supersensible. Upon further investigation you will discover that an overwhelmingly large number of people have committed this error of thinking. Errors like these, however, will no longer occur to the one who has trained his thinking as suggested here.

For anyone capable of thinking correctly a large part of modern literature (especially that of the sciences) becomes a source of unpleasant experience. The distorted and misguided thinking expressed in it can cause even physical pain in a person who has to work his way through it. It should be understood, however, that this is not said with any intent to slight the wealth of observation and discovery that has been accumulated by modern natural science and its objective methods of research.

Now let us consider 'short-sighted' thinking. Most people are unconscious of the fact that their thinking is not factual, but that it is for the most part only the result of thought habits. The decisions and conclusions therefore of a person whose thought penetrates the world and life will differ greatly from those of one whose ability to think is limited or nil. Consider the case of a materialistic thinker. To convince such a man through reasoning, however logical, sound and good, is not an easy task. It is usually a useless effort to try to convince a person with little knowledge of life through reason. Such a person does not see the reasons that make this or that statement valid and possible if he has formed the habit of seeing nothing but matter in everything and simply adheres to this habit of thinking.

Today it can generally be said that people are not prompted by reasons when making statements but rather by the thinking habits behind these reasons. They have acquired habits of thought that influence all their feelings and sensations, and when reasons are put forth, they are simply the mask of the habitual thinking that screens these feelings and sensations. Not only is the wish often the father of the thought, but it can also be said that all our feelings and mental habits are the parents of our thoughts. He who knows life knows how difficult it is to convince another person by means of logical reasoning. What really decides and convinces lies much deeper in the human soul.

There are good reasons for the existence of the anthroposophical movement and for the activities in its various branches. Everyone who has participated in the work of the movement for any length of time comes to notice that he has acquired a new way of thinking and feeling. For the work in the various branches is not merely confined to finding logical reasons for things. A new and more comprehensive quality of feeling and sensation is also developed.

How some people scoffed a few years ago when they heard their first lectures in spiritual science. Yet today how many things have become self-evident to these same people who previously looked upon these things as impossible absurdities. In working in the anthroposophical movement one not only learns to modify one's thinking, one also learns to unfold a wider perspective of soul life.

We must understand that our thoughts derive their colouring from far greater depths than are generally imagined. It is our feelings that frequently impel us to hold certain opinions. The logical reasons that are put forward are often a mere screen or mask for our deeper feelings and habits of thinking.

To bring ourselves to a point at which logical reasons themselves possess a real significance for us, we must have learned to love logic itself. Only when we have learned to love factuality and objectivity will logical reason be decisive for us. We should gradually learn to think objectively, not allowing ourselves to be swayed by our preference for this or that thought. Only then will our vision broaden in the sense that we do not merely follow the mental ruts of others but in such a way that the reality of the things themselves will teach us to think correctly.

True practicality is born of objective thinking, that is, thinking that flows into us from the things themselves. It is only by practising such exercises as have just been described that we learn to take our thoughts from things. To do these exercises properly we should choose to work with sound and wholesome subjects that are least affected by our culture. These are the objects of nature.

To train our thinking using the things of nature as objects to think about will make really practical thinkers of us. Once we have trained ourselves in the practical use of this fundamental principle, our thinking, we shall be able to handle the most everyday occupations in a practical way. By training the human soul in this way a practical viewpoint is developed in our thinking.

The fruit of the anthroposophical movement must be to place really practical thinkers in life. What we have come to believe is not of as much importance as the fact that we should become capable of surveying with understanding the things around us. That spiritual science should penetrate our souls, thereby stimulating us to inner soul activity and expanding our vision, is of far more importance than merely theorizing about what extends beyond the things of the senses into the spiritual. In this, Anthroposophy is truly practical.

VIII. Occult Science and Occult Development[29]

London, 1 May 1913

THE THEME we are to consider today leads at once into a sphere which belongs to all humanity, apart from distinctions.

We are to speak, in the first place, of that realm of man's aspiration which in its true, original form can be described in no human language but only in the language of thought – I refer to the realm of occult science.

Through his human faculties man strives for occult knowledge and may also acquire it, but occult knowledge has a greater significance for the world than it has merely within the human soul. In the world around us we can distinguish different substances and materials through which its various phenomena and manifestations are given expression. In the Primal Principle, the essential nature of which can hardly be expressed in words of human language, all creatures, all things of the earth and all worlds are rooted. But the individual differentiations of this Primal Principle come to expression in the physical world in the substances of earth, of water, of air, of fire, of ether, and so forth.

One of the finest, most highly attenuated substances within the reach of human faculties is called *Akasha*.[9] The manifestations of beings and of phenomena in the Akasha are the most delicate and ethereal of any that are accessible to man. What a person acquires in the way of occult knowledge lives not only in his soul but is inscribed into the Akasha-substance of the world. When we make a thought of occult science come alive in our souls, it is at once inscribed into the Akasha-substance and this is of significance for the general evolution of the world. For no being in the whole world other than man is able to make in the Akasha-substance the inscriptions that can be called by the name of occult science.

It is important to bear in mind one characteristic feature of the Akasha-substance, namely, that in the spiritual world between death and a new birth man lives in this substance, just as here on the earth he lives in the atmosphere.

If a seer, using the means at his disposal, were to come into contact with human souls living between death and rebirth he would be able to observe the following:

In the present cycle of evolution – formerly it was different – a person who here on the earth is never able to kindle to life within him thoughts and ideas belonging to spiritual science, cannot be seen, even when he is actually present, by a soul living between death and a new birth. But when a human being living on the earth causes a thought or an idea from the domain of spiritual science to quicken within him so that it can be inscribed into the Akasha-substance, he becomes visible to the souls who are living between death and rebirth. Profoundly shattering impressions may come to a seer who has prepared himself patiently for clairvoyant vision when he enters into relation with souls who have passed through the gate of death. I will give you an actual example.

A seer found a man who had passed through the gate of death, leaving behind him his wife and children whom he dearly loved. This man and his family were kindly, good-hearted people but had no inclination whatever for spiritual knowledge; they had not outgrown the religious traditions through which certain souls today still feel connected with the spiritual world.

Some little time after he had passed through the gate of death, this man said to himself: 'I have left behind on the earth my wife and children; they were the very sunshine of my life, but my spiritual sight cannot reach them. I have nothing but the remembrance of the time I spent together with them on the earth.'

An entirely different picture can be seen if a soul still on the

earth forms strongly spiritual thoughts and ideas. In this case,
when another soul, living between death and a new birth,
looks down upon one he has left behind, he can follow his
soul-life at the present time because it is inscribing itself into
the Akasha-substance.

This is an indication of how anthroposophical teaching will
bridge the gulf between the so-called living and the so-called
dead; and already now we can see how human beings who
have some understanding of the spiritual may be a blessing to
the so-called dead by reading to them in thought the truths of
spiritual science. If, either reading aloud or to ourselves, we
follow in thought the ideas and concepts of spiritual science,
at the same time feeling that one or more who have passed
through death are there in front of us while we read, then this
reading becomes very real to them, because such thoughts are
inscribed into the Akasha-substance. Such reading may be of
the greatest service, not only to those on the other side of
death who while they were on earth concerned themselves
with spiritual science but also to those who during their
earthly life would have nothing to do with it.

The question may be asked: as the dead are living in the
spiritual world, do they need such reading of spiritual science
by those on the earth? There are many who believe that it is
only necessary to have passed through the gate of death in
order to experience everything that can be attained only by
dint of great effort on the earth, through spiritual science.
Such people also believe that after death a human being will
be able to acquire all occult knowledge, because he will then
be in the spiritual world. This, however, is not the case.

Just as here on the earth there live beings other than man,
who perceive everything that man is able to perceive by means
of his senses, whereas – as in the case of the animals – they are
unable to form ideas or concepts of it, so it is with souls living
in the supersensible worlds. Although these souls see the
beings and facts of the higher spiritual worlds, they can form
no concepts or ideas of them if people here on the earth do not

inscribe such concepts and ideas into the Akasha Chronicle.

This mission of human life upon earth is by no means without purpose; on the contrary it has very deep meaning and purpose. If human souls had never lived on the earth, the spiritual worlds would still be in existence but there would be no occult knowledge of these spiritual worlds. In the course of world-evolution the earth has reached a point at which spiritual knowledge can be developed by spiritual beings organized and constituted as people are on the earth. What has been inscribed into the Akasha-substance through spiritual science would never have been there if this science had not existed on the earth.

If a person tries to put the life of his soul on the earth to the test, he will discover in the first place that during our present age he has applied his faculties for the acquisition of knowledge to aims other than the attainment of spiritual knowledge. These faculties have been used for the acquisition of data, of knowledge produced by means of the senses and through the intellect that is bound to the brain. Thus human knowledge is of two kinds: the one pertains only to experience acquired by means of the senses, which needs the organ of the intellect in order to transform it into knowledge; the other kind is spiritual science. The knowledge that belongs only to the sense-world forms the one stream; the other consists of what human beings inscribe through spiritual science into the Akasha Chronicle. For spiritual science develops ideas and concepts which are then inscribed forever in the Akasha Chronicle.

All science, all knowledge pertaining to experiences acquired through the senses, to technical things, to the commercial and industrial life of mankind, when inscribed in the Akasha-substance has this effect: the Akasha-substance discards it, thrusts it away, and the medley of ideas and concepts is obliterated. If these facts are perceived with the eyes of a seer, a conflict may be observed in the Akasha-substance between the impressions made by the occult knowledge acquired by man – impressions which are eternal – and those made by thoughts based upon the senses, which are only transitory. This conflict arises from the fact that when man first began to inhabit the earth as man (that is to say, in the ancient epoch of Lemuria), he was already then destined by sublime spiritual beings to acquire spiritual science.[10]

But through what we call the luciferic influence, through the encroachment of luciferic beings, man diverted his power of thought and other powers of soul which he would otherwise have used for the acquisition of occult knowledge only, to the study of things belonging exclusively to the physical world.

There are many who say that whereas ordinary science is accessible to everybody, spiritual or occult science can be made intelligible only to those who are able to see into the spiritual worlds.

This is a fundamental error, for in the depths of his own soul every person is capable, even before he becomes a seer, of recognizing the truths of spiritual science. Admittedly, occult truths can be *discovered* only by the seer, but when they have been discovered, and expressed in the normal language of human reason, they can be intelligible to every human soul who has the will to remove the obstacles to such understanding that exist within himself.

As a result of the luciferic impulses it became possible at a later period in the evolution of the earth for another being, whom we call Ahriman, to acquire influence over the souls of human beings.[30] And only when the possibility of understanding spiritual science is held back through ahrimanic influence in the soul does that understanding remain unattainable. If the being we call Ahriman did not work in every human soul, if our souls were free from his influence, then an idea or thought belonging to spiritual science would need only to be spoken and the soul, through its subconscious relationship to this truth, would feel: this idea, this statement of spiritual science, is true. In every human soul there is a life which the everyday consciousness understands and can account for and a subconscious soul-life which lies submerged as if in the depths of an ocean and only from time to time is brought to light. In the depths of the soul there lies, for example, the fear that is present in every human being – the fear of the spiritual. This fear is the outcome of Ahriman's influence and would not exist if Ahriman had not gained power over the souls of human beings. The reason why a man is usually unconscious of such fear is that it works in the deepest foundations of his soul and plays no part in what he can account for with his everyday consciousness.

Sometimes this fear knocks at the door of a person's ordinary consciousness without any knowledge on his part of what is inwardly disquieting him; and then he looks for something that will act as an opiate, that will deaden this feeling of fear. He finds this opiate in materialistic thoughts, theories and ideas. Materialistic theories are not devised on a logical basis, although it may be believed that this is the case; they are devised as the result of a dread of the spiritual, which is the consequence of Ahriman's influence upon the soul. Hence the preparatory condition for an actual understanding of spiritual truths is much less a knowledge of physical science than an education of the soul in the virtue of moral courage, spiritual courage. Therefore we may say that occult science must be explored by the seer, but it can be understood by every human soul if this soul will only liberate within itself all the moral courage at its command and so frustrate the obstacles proceeding from Ahriman.

Should anyone wish to understand occult truths through the original moral forces of his soul he may make the following attempt: he may allow spiritual science to work upon his soul without saying to himself, 'I agree with this,' or, 'I do not agree with it.' He may assimilate the ideas and concepts given by the seer and allow them to work upon his soul; and if he has absorbed the occult knowledge with inner enthusiasm and not as the result of mere curiosity, he will have an experience that may be compared with a feeling of soaring without physical ground under his feet, with a feeling as if he were hovering in the air.

This attempt will have a completely different effect according to whether it is carried out by a person with religious, reverential inclinations towards spiritual life or by someone accustomed to materialistic thinking. One who has no actual occult knowledge but whose inclinations and feelings with regard to the spiritual world have nevertheless a religious quality may feel somewhat insecure as the result of this attempt but very much less so than a materialist who has no feeling of attraction to the spiritual world. The latter will experience a strong feeling of fear, of insecurity. The materialist may convince himself through this experience that the effect of occult ideas and concepts upon him is that they give rise to dread and terror. And then he may say to himself: 'This proves to me not only that I am full of fear of this realm but that fear is one of my intrinsic tendencies.'

If, for example, Ernst Haeckel or Herbert Spencer had made this attempt they would have convinced themselves not only that occult knowledge is not contradictory or impossible of belief but that in the inmost depths of their souls they were full of fear; and they would soon have forgotten all doubt and disbelief in what they had been wont to consider fantastic spiritual teachings, and would have admitted to themselves that to overcome this fear was of very great significance. Having made this confession they would soon have abandoned their opposition to the spiritual teachings. They would have said to themselves: 'I must endeavour to strengthen moral courage within myself.' Then, perhaps, they would have taken their own self-training in hand and if they had succeeded in overcoming this fear would have said: 'Now that we have become stronger souls we no longer have any doubts as to the truth of spiritual science.' This experience, arising from the strengthening of moral courage within the soul, is a victory over Ahriman, whose influence can be perceived in the science of Ernst Haeckel and the philosophy of Herbert

Spencer. It is Ahriman who has inspired souls to take a materialistic direction. If only a small portion of mankind, as a result of genuine knowledge, will work in the way above indicated to strengthen their moral courage, these materialistic theories will gradually disappear from the world.

Occult knowledge is necessary for the whole process of evolution, as it is inscribed in the Akasha-substance. The importance of this can be evident from a brief outline of the evolution of humanity on the earth.

Man's evolution on earth advances in stages from one civilization-epoch to another; during these successive epochs the souls of men dwell, as individualities, in bodies belonging to the several civilizations. All the souls here this evening were incarnated in bodies that belonged to earlier periods of culture. Each individual soul advances in accordance with the karma it has built up for itself.

As well as this evolution of individual souls which depends upon their karma, we must recognize the evolution of mankind as a whole which advances from epoch to epoch. A Grecian body, an Egyptian, Chaldean, ancient Persian or ancient Indian body was, in the finer parts of its structure, quite different from one of the present age.

Distinction must be made between the inner progress of the 'I' and the astral body from incarnation to incarnation, and the outer progress and change in the physical and etheric bodies from one race to another, from one nation to another, from one epoch to another. This progress of the physical and the etheric bodies from one epoch to another would not be perceptible to those who study anatomy and physiology, but it happens, nevertheless, and can be recognized through occult science. The human physical body will be quite different when, in the normal course of evolution, our souls appear again on the earth in future incarnations.

In the present epoch of human life a delicate organ is being developed in man. It is not perceptible to anatomists and physiologists, yet it exists as an anatomical structure. This rudimentary organ is situated in the brain, near the organ of speech.

The development of this organ in the convolutions of the brain is not the result of the karma of individual souls but of human evolution as a whole on the earth; and in the future all people will possess it, no matter what the development of the souls incarnating in the bodies may be, and irrespective of the karma connected with these souls.

In a future incarnation this organ will be possessed by human beings who at the present time may be opposed to Anthroposophy as well as by those who are now in sympathy with it. This organ will in future time be the physical means, the physical instrument, for the application of certain powers of the soul; just as, for example, Broca's organ in the third convolution of the brain is the organ of the human faculty of speech.

When this new organ has developed it may either be used rightly by mankind, or it may not. Those people will be able to use it rightly who are now preparing the possibility of having in their next incarnation a true remembrance of the present one. For this physical organ will be the physical means for remembering an earlier incarnation – which in the case of by far the greater majority of people is possible now only through higher development, through initiation. But a faculty which in the present epoch it would be possible to acquire only through initiation will later on become the common property of mankind. Our modern knowledge was formerly the special knowledge possessed by the Atlantean initiates only; everyone can now possess it. In the same way, remembrance of former lives on earth is possible at present only for initiates but in times to come it will be possible for every human soul.

The initiate is able to attain certain knowledge without the use of a physical organ, but this knowledge can become the common property of mankind only when a physical organ through which it can be acquired is developed in mankind as a whole in the course of evolution.

The reincarnated souls must, however, be able to use this organ in the right way and only those who in the present incarnation have inscribed occult thoughts and ideas in the Akasha-substance will be capable of this.

One often hears it asked: what is the use of believing in former lives when mankind in general can remember nothing about them? But from what is known of life, how much more surprising it would be if people in general were even now able to remember their former lives. If we ask ourselves what is necessary to enable us to remember anything, we shall have to reply: we can remember only that about which we have previously *thought*.

Everyday life can teach us that this is so. Suppose someone on getting up in the morning cannot find his cuff-links, no matter where he looks. Why is he not able to find them? Because while he was putting them away he was not thinking of what he was doing. Let him, however, try every evening while putting his links away to think quite consciously: I am putting my cuff-links away in this place. Then he will never be uncertain but will go straight to the place where he has put them; the thought brings the process back into his memory.

When we are living in a future incarnation we shall only be able to remember those that are past if we can grasp the true nature of the soul which continues from one incarnation to another. A person who does not study occult science in the present life can acquire no knowledge of the constitution and nature of the soul, and if he has no such knowledge how should he, when he is again incarnated, remember that to which he never gave a thought in the earlier incarnation?

Through the study of spiritual science, which includes, among other things, the study of the intrinsic nature of the soul, we prepare in ourselves that which will enable us in a future incarnation to remember what happened in the present one. There are, however, many people nowadays who are not willing to devote themselves to the study of this knowledge. These human beings will be reborn, perhaps in their next incarnation, with the above-mentioned organ for the remembrance of former lives *physically* developed; but they have not prepared themselves in such a way as to be able to remember the past.

What, then, is the significance of spiritual science or Anthroposophy in the life of the present day, in addition to all that has been said? Through Anthroposophy we become able to use in the right way the organ that will be developed in human beings of the future, the organ for the remembering of former lives on earth. In our present incarnation we must inscribe in the Akasha-substance the knowledge we acquire in order that in our next incarnation we may be able to use this organ – which is developing in man whether he wishes it or not. In the future there will be people who are able to use this organ for remembering past lives and others who are not able. Certain illnesses will appear in the latter, owing to the presence in their physical bodies of an organ which they are unable to use. To have an organ and be unable to use it gives rise to nervous diseases in a very definite form, and those that will be caused in cases of this kind will be far worse than any yet known to man.

When we study the connection of facts in this way we begin to get an idea of the mission and purpose of Anthroposophy and of the importance of understanding life and mankind through this knowledge. But lest the impression made upon you by what has been said should lead to any misunderstanding, I will mention yet another fact which may mitigate anything that was painful in that impression. Although a genuine occultist realizes that Anthroposophy must enter into the spiritual life of our present time in order that the human being of the future may be able to use the organ for remembering past lives and remain physically in good health, nevertheless it cannot be said categorically that a person who in this epoch is not ready to accept Anthroposophy will suffer in his following incarnations in the sense referred to above. For a long time to come it will still be possible for a human being, even if he has neglected to use this organ in the present life, to put this right in the next, for there will be several more opportunities for him to regain health and acquire anthroposophical knowledge. The time will come, however, when this possibility will cease.

For this reason, even if we have not yet reached the crucial moment, we are nevertheless living in the epoch when Anthroposophy must be membered into the spiritual life of mankind. Anthroposophy is an essential development in the general progress of mankind and does not stem from the personal opinions of individuals.

And so especially in our own time the possibility will be given for the subjective development of the human soul, leading to personal vision of the spiritual worlds, to genuine occult development. It may be said that every individual who will apply the original forces within his soul, undisturbed by ahrimanic influences, can understand everything that is revealed from the spiritual worlds; hence in a certain sense it is possible for every human being to unfold consciousness of the spiritual worlds by undergoing occult development. At the present time, three particular powers of the soul may well be developed in order to establish an occult link with the supersensible worlds.

The first of these powers is that of thinking. We live in relation with the world around us by forming thoughts about our surroundings. In ordinary, everyday life a person thinks thoughts which are caused through impressions made on the senses, or through the intellect that is bound up with the brain. In my book *Knowledge of the Higher Worlds: How is it Achieved?* it is said that through meditation, concentration and contemplation, through strengthening his life of soul, a person can make this power of thinking independent of external life. I want to call your attention here to how the power of thinking within the soul, which otherwise is developed only through thought about the external world, can be made essentially free and independent of everything belonging to the body. That is to say, through such development it becomes possible for the soul to think, to form thoughts within itself, without using the brain as an instrument. This is easy to understand if we consider the chief characteristic of ordinary, everyday thinking which is dependent upon the impressions conveyed through the senses.

The chief characteristic of ordinary thinking is that each single act of thinking injures the nervous system, and above all, the brain; it destroys something in the brain. Every thought means that a minute process of destruction takes place in the cells of the brain. For this reason sleep is necessary for us, in order that this process of destruction may be made good; during sleep we restore what during the day was destroyed in our nervous system by thinking. What we are consciously aware of in an ordinary thought is in reality the process of destruction that is taking place in our nervous system.

We now endeavour to practise meditation by devoting ourselves to contemplation, for instance, of the saying: *Wisdom lives in the Light.* This idea cannot originate from sense-impressions because according to the external senses it is not so.

In this example, by means of meditation we hold the thought back so far that it does not connect itself with the brain. If in this way we unfold an inner activity of thinking that is not connected with the brain, through the effects of such meditation upon the soul we shall feel that we are on the right path. As in meditative thinking no process of destruction is evoked in our nervous system, this kind of thinking never causes sleepiness, however long it may be continued, as ordinary thinking may easily do.

It is true that the opposite often occurs when someone is meditating, for people often complain that when they devote themselves to meditation they at once fall asleep. But that is because the meditation is not yet as it should be. It is quite natural that in meditation we should, to begin with, use the kind of thinking to which we have always been accustomed; it is only gradually that we can accustom ourselves to give up thinking about external things. When this point is reached meditative thinking will no longer make us sleepy, and we shall then know that we are on the right path.

When the inner power of thinking can thus be developed without using the thinking faculty of the body, then and only then shall we acquire knowledge of the inner life and recognize our real self, our higher 'I'.

The path to true knowledge of the human self is to be found in the kind of meditation just described, which leads to the liberation of inner thought-power. Only through such knowledge do we realize that this human self is not confined within the limits of the physical body; on the contrary, we come to recognize that this self is connected with the phenomena of the world around us. Whereas in ordinary life we see the sun here, the moon there, the mountains, hills, plants and animals, we now feel ourselves united with everything we see or hear; we are a part of it all, and for us there is now only one external world – our own body. In ordinary life we are here and the external world is around us, but after the development of the independent power of thinking, we are outside our body, one with all that we otherwise see; our body in which we live is now outside us; we look back upon it as the only world upon which we can now gaze.

In this way, by liberating the power of thinking, we can actually emerge from the physical body and contemplate it as something external. Even more can be done. For example, we can give a positive answer to the question: why do we wake up every morning? During sleep our physical body lies in the bed and we are actually outside it, just as is the case during meditative thinking. On waking we return to our physical body, being drawn back to it by countless forces, as by a magnet. A person usually knows nothing of this. But if through meditation he has made himself free, he is *consciously* drawn back by the same force which, on waking from sleep, draws his soul back into his physical body without consciousness on his part.

We also learn through meditation how the human being

comes down from the higher worlds in which he lived between death and a new birth, and how he unites with the forces and substances provided by parents, grandparents and so forth. In short, we learn to know the forces that draw human beings back from their life between death and a new birth to new incarnations.

As a fruit of such meditation one may look back over a great part of the life spent in the spiritual world between death and a new birth, before conception took place. But through this kind of meditation one can, as a rule, look back only to a certain point that lies before the present incarnation; it would not be possible to look further back into earlier incarnations themselves. To do this at the present time, as the organ referred to above has not yet developed in the human brain, another kind of meditation is necessary. This other kind can become effective only if feeling is brought into the meditation. All meditation as now described may also be permeated with feeling.

We will now consider the subject-matter which, in the process of meditation itself, must be permeated by feeling. If, for instance, we take: 'Wisdom radiates in the Light', and we feel inspired through the radiation of wisdom, if we feel uplifted, if we feel inwardly aglow, if we can live in and meditate upon the content of these words with inner zeal, then we have in our souls something more than meditation in thoughts. The power of feeling we then activate in the soul is the power we otherwise use in *speech*. Speech comes into being when thoughts are permeated with inner feeling. This is the origin of speech, and Broca's organ in the brain comes into existence in this way: the thoughts of the inner life that are permeated with feeling become active in the brain, and build the organ that is the physical instrument of speech.

When our meditation is really permeated by such feelings we hold back in our souls the force that in everyday life we employ in speaking. Speech may be said to be the embodiment of the inner soul-force which gives expression to these thoughts. If now, instead of allowing the soul-force to be applied in speaking, we develop meditation from these thoughts that are permeated with feeling, if we continue this meditation to further and further stages, we gradually gain the power – now actually without the physical organ but through initiation – to look back into earlier lives on earth and also to investigate the period between earthly lives, the period which always lies between death and a new birth.

Through cultivating the withholding of speech within the soul or, as the occultist says, withholding the 'word' within the soul, we can eventually look back to the primeval beginning of our earth, back to what the Bible calls the creative act of the Elohim.[31] We can look back to the time when repeated earth-lives actually began for human beings. For the occult development we attain through withholding the word, or withholding speech, enables us to look into the successive epochs, in so far as these are connected with our earth, with the spiritual life of our planet. We become able to behold the beings of the higher Hierarchies, in so far as they are connected with the spiritual life of the earth.

But these two clairvoyant faculties, which are developed in meditation through thoughts and through thoughts permeated with feeling, cannot lead us to experiences lying before the epoch of the present earth, experiences connected with earlier planetary incarnations of our earth.[10] This requires the development of the third meditative power, of which we will now speak briefly.

We can further permeate the content of our meditation with impulses of *will* in such a way that if we meditate, for instance, on 'The Wisdom of the World radiates in the Light', we may now really feel the impulse of our will united with that activity; we can feel our own being united with the radiating power of the light, and let this light shine and vibrate through the world. We must feel the impulse of our will to be united with this meditation.

When our meditation is filled with impulses of the will, we are holding back a force which otherwise would pass into the

pulsation of the blood. It is easy to realize that the inner life
of the 'I' can pass over into the pulsation of the blood when
we remember that we grow pale when we are afraid and blush
when we are ashamed; these are the signs that the soul-force
is passing over into the pulsing of the blood. If the same force
which influences the blood is activated in such a way that it
does not descend into the physical but remains in the soul
only, this is the beginning of the third form of meditation
which we can influence through impulses of will.

He who achieves these three forms of occult development
feels, when he liberates the power of thought, as though he
had an organ at the root of the nose – these organs are
described as 'lotus flowers'[7] – by means of which he can
become aware of his 'I' or Self that extends far into space.[9]

A person who by meditation has cultivated thoughts permeated with feeling becomes gradually conscious, through
this developed force which would otherwise have become
speech, of the so-called 16-petalled lotus flower in the region
of the larynx. By means of this lotus flower he can comprehend what is connected with temporal things, from the
beginning of the earth's existence until its end. By means of
this organ he also learns to recognize the occult significance
of the Mystery of Golgotha, which I will speak of in my
next lecture.[32]

Through the soul-force which in normal everyday life
would extend to the blood and its pulsation but is held back,
an organ develops in the region of the heart. By means of this
organ the nature of the earlier incarnations of the earth –
known in occultism as the Saturn-, Sun- and Moon-evolutions
– may be understood. Reference is made to this organ in my
book *Occult Science: An Outline*.

As you will now realize, occult development is achieved by
means of faculties and possibilities that are actually present in
the life of the human soul.

The first occult power that has been mentioned stems from
a higher development of the power of thinking, the power that

is otherwise applied only for thoughts connected with the external world.

The second power is only a higher development of the force which in everyday life is applied by every human being through the body, in speech, in the development of the organ for the word.

The third power is a higher cultivation of the force that exists in the human soul to cause the blood to pulsate faster or slower, to direct a greater or smaller amount of blood to one or another organ of the body; to direct it more to the centre when we grow pale, more to the surface when we blush, to direct it more or less strongly to the brain, and so on.

When a person cultivates these forces that are present within him, but in ordinary life are used for his outer, bodily existence only, occult development begins. The findings of occult investigation can be understood today by every human being who is willing to clear away obstacles to comprehension. What can be learnt as the result of occult development is occult science, and in the present cycle of man's existence occult science must flow into the human soul in order that it may learn to know its own being – which is independent of the body. The forms of all the substances in the external world, such as earth, water, air, etc., pass away; the forms of the *Akasha*-substance endure. Through its inner life, our soul must feel itself connected with the Akasha-substance, and in future time it will have the wish to remember what it is experiencing in the present epoch. The possibility of acquiring ideas and concepts that can lead to this remembrance results from the study of occult science, which means that the knowledge gained through occult development must be spread abroad and accepted.

I have therefore tried in this lecture to bring home to you that in addition to the impulses underlying the development of humanity, the spreading of anthroposophical occult knowledge and the pointing of the way to occult development are vitally necessary. It is not by means of words based upon

ordinary human considerations that I have tried to elucidate
the mission of spiritual science, but through the study of facts
which are the findings of occult research. Whoever will allow
these facts to work upon his soul will realize that anyone who
understands their full significance cannot possibly deny the
need to spread the knowledge of spiritual science at the
present time. There is certainly no need to become fanatical
in order to recognize the necessity of anthroposophical development; what is needed is to understand the facts that lie at
the foundation of man's occult life. Truth to tell, it can only
be ignorance of these facts that still keeps mankind away from
anthroposophical life.

Among the spiritual movements of our time, Anthroposophy as it is here understood will be the least fanatical, and the
one that proceeds most decisively from objective considerations. It is necessary to affirm repeatedly that all kindred
theories and teachings must finally unite in anthroposophical
circles in deeply-rooted, living *feeling*.

There is an objective spiritual life, the reflection of which
in the world of maya is the life by which we are surrounded.
Occult development is a step from semblance towards reality.
And because genuine understanding of these facts can lead to
nothing else than the impulse to take the necessary steps, the
future destiny of Anthroposophy or spiritual science will be
secure, because more and more souls will have the wish to
recognize the objective truth regarding the World Spirit.

The anthroposophical fire that can be kindled in us is only
an outcome of the Cosmic Fire which streams forth spiritually
from the beginning to the end of existence.

It is this that I wanted to say to you in this lecture
concerning the mission of the anthroposophical movement in
the spiritual life of the present day.

IX. The Three Decisions on the Path of Imaginative Cognition[33]

Berlin, 2 March 1915

A WEEK ago we considered souls nearly related to us who, if they are to be located now, must be sought in spiritual worlds.[34] Certain things were said about these souls which can throw light upon the whereabouts of beings in the spiritual world. Today I propose to direct our study more to that path to the spiritual world which the human soul can take while it is still in the body, in order to find those spiritual realms referred to last time as the dwelling place of the souls of the so-called dead. It must be emphasized over and over that the way into the spiritual worlds that is suitable for souls of the present day requires manifold preparation. Some of this preparation is difficult, but it is necessary. Today I wish to point to certain matters connected with the path of knowledge from the point of view of what may be called 'imaginative cognition'.

It is very familiar to you, my dear friends, that the human soul can have experiences in the spiritual world only when it is not using the instrument of the body. Everything we can gain through the instrument of the body can yield only experiences of what is present in the physical world. If we wish to have experience of the spiritual worlds, we must find the possibility of working with the soul outside the physical body. Now although it is difficult, it is possible for the human being today to experience the spiritual world while outside the body. Moreover it is always possible, once observations of the spiritual worlds have been made, for another who is not himself capable of this to judge them with really sound human reason – not with the kind of reason that is called sound, but with reason that is genuinely sound. But today we are going to speak of the actual way in which the human soul on the one hand emerges from the physical body, and on the other hand how it enters the spiritual world. A week ago we spoke of this from another point of view, and as today I want to consider it from the standpoint of imaginative cognition, many pictures will be discussed which will remain to be pursued in your meditations. If you do this, you will see that this path of knowledge is of great significance.

The spiritual world can be entered, as it were, through three portals. The first may be called the Portal of Death, the second the Portal of the Elements, and the third the Portal of the Sun. Those who wish to tread the entire path of knowledge must pass through all three portals.

The Portal of Death has from time immemorial been described by all Mystery teachings. This Portal of Death can only be attained if we strive to reach it through what has long been known to us as meditation, that is to say, complete surrender and devotion to certain thoughts or perceptions which are suited to our individuality and which we place so entirely in the centre of our consciousness that we identify ourselves wholly with them. Human effort, of course, weakens very easily along this particular path, because there truly are and must be inner hindrances and obstacles to be overcome. It is a matter of repeating, again and again, the silent inner efforts to devote oneself so completely to the given thoughts and perceptions that one forgets the whole world and lives wholly in these thoughts and perceptions. After constant repetition, however, one gradually begins to perceive that the thoughts that have been made the centre of the consciousness are taking on a kind of independent life. One receives the feeling that, 'Hitherto I have only "thought" this thought; I have placed it at the centre of my consciousness; but now it is beginning to unfold a particular life and inner agility of its own.' It is as if one were in the position of being able to produce a real being within oneself. The thought begins to become an inner structure. It is an important moment when one notices that this thought or perception has a life of its own, so that one feels oneself to be the sheath of this thought, of this perception. One can then say to oneself: 'My efforts have enabled me to provide a stage on which something is developing which now, through me, is coming to a particular life of its own.'

This awakening, this enlivening of the thought, is a moment of great significance in the life of the meditator. He is then deeply stirred by the objective reality of the spiritual world; he realizes that the spiritual world, so to speak, is concerning itself with him, that it has approached him. Naturally, it is not a simple matter to reach this experience, for before doing so one must go through various sensations that one would not, from one's own inclination, gladly go through. There is a certain feeling of isolation, for example, a feeling of loneliness to be undergone – a feeling of being forsaken. One cannot grasp the spiritual world without previously feeling forsaken by the physical world, without feeling that this physical world does many things which crush one, which wear one down. But we must come through this feeling of isolation to be able to bear the inner animation to which the thought awakens, to which it is born. Much resistance now confronts the human being; from within himself there is much resistance to what leads to true perception of this inner awakening of the thought to life.

One feeling in particular comes – an inner feeling that we simply do not wish to have. We do not admit this, however, but say instead: 'Oh, I can never attain that; it sends me to sleep; my thinking and inner elasticity forsake me, they will not continue.' In short, one chooses involuntarily all sorts of evasions of what one must experience: that the thought which thus becomes enlivened becomes substantial. It becomes substantial and forms itself into a kind of being. And then one has not merely the feeling but the vision that the thought is, at first, like a little rounded seed which germinates into a being with definite form, which from outside our head continues inside so that the thought seems to tell us: 'You have identified yourself with it, you are within the thought, and now, you extend with the thought into your own head; but you are essentially still outside.' The thought takes on the form of a winged human head, flowing out into infinity and then extending into one's own body through the head. The thought, therefore, grows into a winged Angel's head. One must actually achieve this. It is difficult to have this experience and we therefore like to believe that in this moment when the thought grows in this way we lose all possibility of thinking. We believe we shall lose ourselves at this moment. The body we have known hitherto and into which the thought extends is felt to be like an abandoned automaton. Besides, there are present in the spiritual world all kinds of hindrances which prevent this from becoming visible to us. This winged Angel's head really becomes inwardly visible, but there are all conceivable hindrances preventing its becoming visible. The point thus reached is the real threshold of the spiritual world. When one reaches the point I have just described, one is actually on the threshold of the spiritual world. But there, at first quite invisible to one, stands the power whom we have always called Ahriman. One does not see him. And it is Ahriman who hinders us from seeing that which I have described as the germinating thought-being. Ahriman does not wish one to see it. He wants to hinder this. And because it is primarily on the path of meditation that one reaches this point it always becomes easy for Ahriman to erase what one must come to, if one clings to the prejudices of the physical world. And truly, one must say: the human being does not believe how very much he clings to the prejudices of the physical world; neither can he imagine that there is another world whose laws are different from those of the physical world. I cannot mention today all the prejudices which people bring with them to the threshold of the spiritual world, but I will allude to one of the principal and more intimate prejudices.

You see, people speak of the physical world from a monistic world view, from unity; they repeatedly say that they can only grasp the world by contemplating the whole world as a unity.

We have sometimes had to go through curious experiences in this respect. When the spiritual-scientific movement began in Berlin a good many years ago, with only a few members, there were several who felt they were not wholly in sympathy with it. One lady, for instance, came to us after a few months and said that spiritual science was not for her because it required too much thinking, and she found that thinking wiped out everything precious for her, making her fall into a kind of sleep; besides which, she said, there is only one thing of real value, and that is unity! The unity of the world which the monist seeks in so many areas – and not the materialistic monist alone – had become a fixed idea with her. Unity, unity, and again unity! That was her quest.

In German culture we have the philosopher Leibnitz, an emphatically monadological thinker who did not seek for unity but for the many 'Monads' who to him were essences of soul. It was clear to him that in the spiritual world there can be no question of unity but only of multiplicity. There are monists and pluralists. The monists speak only of unity and oppose the pluralists who speak of multiplicity. You see, however, the fact is that both unity and multiplicity are concepts which are of value only in the physical world, so people believe that they must be of value in the spiritual world as well. But that is not so. People must realize that although unity can be glimpsed, it must immediately be superseded for it reveals itself as multiplicity. It is unity and multiplicity at the same time. Nor can ordinary calculation, physical mathematics, be carried into the spiritual world. One of the very strongest and at the same time most subtle of ahrimanic temptations is the desire to carry into the spiritual world, just as they are, concepts acquired in the physical world. We must approach the threshold without 'bag or baggage', without being weighed down with what we have learned in the physical world; we must be ready to leave all this at the threshold. All concepts – precisely those we have taken the most trouble to acquire – must be left behind and we must be prepared for the fact that in the spiritual world new concepts will be given; we will become aware of something entirely new. This clinging to what the physical world gives is extremely strong in the human being. He would like to take with him into the spiritual world what he has conquered in the physical. He must have the possibility, however, of standing before a completely clean slate, of standing before complete emptiness and of allowing himself to be guided only by the thoughts which then begin to come to life. This entrance into the spiritual world has been called fundamentally the Gate of Death, because it really is a greater death than even physical death. In physical death we are persuaded to lay aside the physical body; but on entering the spiritual world we must resolve to lay aside our concepts, our notions and our ideas, and allow our being to be built up anew.

Now we confront the winged thought-being of which I have spoken. We already confront it if we really give all our effort to living in a thought. All we need to know then is that when the moment comes which makes claims upon us that are different from those we have imagined, we must really stand firm, we must not, as it were, retreat. This retreat is in most cases unconscious. We weaken, but the weakening is only the sign that we do not wish to lay bag and baggage aside. The whole soul, with everything it has acquired on the physical plane, must perish if it is to enter the spiritual world. That is why it is quite correct to call this portal the Portal of Death. And then we look through this winged thought-being as through a new spiritual eye that one acquires, or through a spiritual ear – for we also hear, we also feel – and by these means we become aware of what is present in the spiritual world.

It is even possible, my dear friends, to speak of particular experiences which one can have upon entering the spiritual world. For one to be able to have these experiences, nothing else is necessary than perseverance in the meditation I have previously described. It is particularly important to be very clear that certain experiences that one brings to the threshold of the spiritual world must be laid aside before entering. Experiences have hence really shown that the spiritual world that confronts one is usually different from that which one would like to have. This then is the first portal: the Portal of Death.

The second portal now is the Portal of the Elements. This Portal of the Elements will be the second one to be passed through by those who give themselves up to zealous meditation. But it is also possible for a man to encourage his own organization in such a way that he can actually reach the second portal without having passed through the first. This is not good for a real knowledge, but it may happen that one reaches this point without first going through the first portal. A real appropriate knowledge will only yield itself if one has passed through the first portal and then approached the second portal consciously. This second portal shows itself in the following way. You see, if a person has passed through the Portal of Death he feels himself at first to be in certain conditions which in their outward impression upon him resemble sleep, although inwardly they are quite different. Outwardly man is as though asleep while these conditions last. As soon as the thought begins to live, when it begins to stir and grow, the outer man is really as though he were asleep. He need not be lying down, he may be sitting, but he is as though asleep. Outwardly it is impossible to distinguish this state from sleep, but inwardly it is absolutely different. Not until one passes back into the normal condition of life does one realize: 'I have not been asleep but I have been within the life of thought in just the same way as I am now awake in the physical world and looking with my eyes at what is around me.' But one also knows: 'Now that I am awake, I think, I form thoughts, I connect them; but shortly before, when I was in that other state, the thoughts formed themselves. The one approached the other, explained the other, separated from the other; and what one usually does oneself in thinking was there done by itself.' But one knows that whereas in physical life one is an ego, adding one thought to another, in that other state one swims, as it were, in one thought and then over to another. One is united with the thoughts; then one is within a third and then swims away from it. One has the feeling that space simply no longer exists.

No longer is it the way it is in physical space, where if one had gone to a certain point and looked back and then went on further, and if one wished to return to the first point, then one would have to travel along the road again; one would have to make the journey both ways. That is not the case in that other state. Space is different there; one springs through space, so to speak. At one moment we are in one place, the next we are far away. We do not pass through space. The laws of space have ceased. We now actually live and weave within the thoughts themselves. We know that the ego is not dead, it is weaving in the web of thoughts. But although we are living within the thoughts, we cannot immediately be their master; the thoughts form themselves and we are drawn along with them. We do not ourselves swim in the stream of thoughts but the thoughts take us on their shoulders, as it were, and carry us along. This state must also cease. And it ceases when we pass through the Portal of the Elements. Then the whole process becomes subject to our will, then we can follow a definite line of thought with intention. We then live in the whole life of thought with our will. This is again a moment of tremendous significance. For this reason I have even referred to it exoterically in public lectures by saying that the second stage is reached by identifying ourselves with our destiny. Thereby we acquire the power to be within the weaving thoughts with our own will.

At first, when one has passed through the Portal of Death, one is in the spiritual world which does as it likes with one. One learns to act for oneself in the spiritual world by identifying oneself with one's destiny. This can only be achieved by degrees. Thoughts then acquire being which is identical with our own. The deeds of our being enter the spiritual world. But in order to achieve this in the right way one must pass through the second portal. When, with the power acquired from identifying oneself with destiny, one begins to weave in the thoughts in such a way that they do not carry one along as in a dream-picture, but one is able to eliminate a thought and call up another – to manipulate them at will – when this begins one experiences what may be called the 'passing through the portal'. And then the power of will we are now using shows itself as a simply fearful monster. This has been known for thousands of years in mysticism as the encounter with the 'lion'. One must go through this encounter with the lion. In the life of feelings this gives rise to a dreadful fear, a fear of what is taking place in the world of thought, of this living union with it, and this fear must be overcome, just as the loneliness of the Portal of Death must be overcome. This fear can in the most manifold ways simulate other feelings that are not fear; but it is, in reality, fear of what one approaches. And what now occurs is that one finds the possibility of mastering this wild beast, this 'lion' who meets us. In Imagination it actually appears as if it were opening wide its enormous jaws, wishing to devour us. The power of will which we want to use in the spiritual world threatens to devour us. One is incessantly overcome by the feeling: 'You are obliged to will, but you must do something, you must seize something.' Yet concerning all these elements of will which one contains, one has the feeling: 'If you seize it, it devours you, eradicates you from the world.' This is the experience of being devoured by the lion. So – and one can speak of this in pictures – rather than surrendering to the fear that the elements of will in the spiritual world will seize, devour, and strangle us, one must swing oneself to the back of the lion, grasp these elements of will, and make use of them for action. That is what must be done when this happens.

You can now understand the essentials. If one has first passed through the Gate of Death, one is outside the body, and can only use the forces of will outside. One must insert oneself into the cosmic harmony. The forces that must be used outside the body are also within us, only they rule unconsciously. The forces that circulate our blood and make our hearts beat come from the spirituality into which we plunge when we immerse ourselves in the element of will. We have these forces within us. If, therefore, a person is taken possession of by the element of will without having gone through the prescribed esoteric path, without having passed through the Gate of Death, those forces seize him which otherwise circulate in his blood and beat in his heart; and then he does not use the forces that are outside his body but those that are within him. This would be 'grey magic'. It would cause a person to seize the spiritual world with the forces with which one is not permitted to seize the spiritual world. What matters is that one sees the lion, that this monster is actually before one and that one knows: this is what it looks like, this is how the forces of will desire to lay hold of one; they must be mastered from outside the body. If one does not approach the second portal or actually behold the lion, one remains always in danger of wanting to rule the world out of human egotism. That is why the true path of knowledge leads us first of all from within the physical body and physical existence and only then to approach the conditions that are to be arrived at with the essences which are outside.

Opposing this there is the inclination of most people to enter the spiritual world by a more comfortable way than through true meditation. Thus it is possible, for example, to avoid the Gate of Death, and, if the inner predisposition is favourable, to approach the second portal. One can reach this through giving oneself up to a particular image, an especially fervent image which speaks about dissolving oneself in the Universal All and the like, recommended in good faith by certain pseudo-mystics. By this means the exertions of thinking are stupefied and the emotions are stimulated. The emotions are whipped into fiery enthusiasm. By this means one can, to begin with, certainly be admitted to the second portal and be given over to the forces of will, but one does not master the lion; one is devoured by the lion and the lion does with one what it likes. This means that fundamentally occult things are taking place, but in essence they are egoistic. That is why it is constantly necessary – although one might say there is also a risk of this from the point of view of true esotericism today – not to censure that which one might say is only a mystical feeling and experience which is lashed into a fury. This appeal to what stimulates a man inwardly, whipping him out of his physical body but leaving him still connected with the forces of the blood and the heart, the physical forces of the blood and the heart, does undoubtedly bring about a kind of perception of the spiritual world which may also have much good in it; but it causes him to grope about insecurely in the spiritual world, and renders him incapable of distinguishing between egotism and altruism. This brings one directly, if one must stress this, to a difficult point, for with respect to real meditation and everything related to it, modern minds have for the most part fallen asleep. They do not like to exert their thinking as strongly as is necessary, if they are to identify themselves with the thinking. They far prefer to be told to give themselves in loving surrender to the Cosmic Spirit, or the like, where the emotions are whipped up and thinking is evaded. People are led in this way to spiritual perceptions, but without full consciousness of them, and then they are not able to distinguish whether the things they experience spring from egotism or not. Certainly enthusiasm in feeling and perception must run parallel to selfless meditation, but thought must also run parallel to it. Thinking must not be eliminated. Certain mystics, however, try to suppress thought altogether, and to surrender themselves wholly to the glow of frenzied emotion.

Here too there is a difficult point, for this method is useful; those who stimulate their emotions go forward much more quickly. They enter the spiritual world and have all kinds of experiences – and that is what most people desire. The question with most people is not whether they are entering the spiritual world in the right way but only whether they are entering it at all. The uncertainty that arises here is that if we have not first passed through the Gate of Death but go directly to the Gate of the Elements, we are there prevented by Lucifer from really perceiving the lion; so that before we become aware of it, it devours us. The difficulty is that we are no longer able to distinguish between what is related to us and what is outside in the world. We learn to know spiritual beings, elemental spirits. One can learn to recognize a rich and extensive spiritual world, without having passed through the Gate of Death, but these are spiritual beings who for the most part have the task of maintaining the human blood circulation and the work of the human heart. Such beings are always around us in the spiritual, in the elemental world. They are spirits whose life-element is in the air, in the encircling warmth and also in the light; they also have their life-element in the Music of the Spheres, which is no longer physically perceptible. These spiritual beings weave and lace through everything that is living. Of course, then, we enter this world. And the thing becomes alluring because the most wonderful spiritual discoveries can be made in this world. If a person – who has not passed through the Gate of Death but has gone directly to the Portal of the Lion without seeing the lion – perceives an elementary spirit whose task is to maintain the activity of the heart, this elementary spirit, who also maintains the heart-activity of other people, may under certain circumstances bring information about other human beings, even about people of the past, or indeed prophetic tidings of the future. The experience may be accompanied with great success, yet it is not the right path because it does not make us free in our mobility in the spiritual world.

The third portal that one must pass through is the Portal of the Sun. And there we must, when we reach this portal, undergo yet another experience. While we are at the Portal of Death, we perceive a winged Angel's head; while we are at the Portal of the Elements, we perceive a lion; at the Portal of the

Sun, we must perceive a dragon, a fierce dragon. And this fierce dragon we must truly perceive. But now Lucifer and Ahriman together try to make it imperceptible to our spiritual vision. If we do perceive it, however, we realize that in reality this fierce dragon has most fundamentally to do with ourselves, for he is woven out of those instincts and sensations which are related to what in ordinary life we call our 'lowest nature'. This dragon comprises all the forces, for instance, that we use – if you will forgive the prosaic expression – for digestion and many other things. What provides us with the forces of digestion, and many other functions bound up with the lowest part of our nature, appears to us in the form of a dragon. We must contemplate him when he coils out of us. He is far from beautiful and it is therefore easy for Lucifer and Ahriman so to influence our subconscious life of soul that unconsciously we do not want to see this dragon. Into the dragon are also woven all our absurdities, all our vanities, our pride and self-seeking, as well as our basest instincts.

If we do not contemplate the dragon at the Portal of the Sun – and it is called the Portal of the Sun because in the sun-forces live those forces from which the dragon is woven, and it is the sun-forces that enable us to digest and to carry out other organic processes (this occurs really through living together with the sun) – if we do not contemplate the dragon at the Portal of the Sun, he devours us and we become one with him in the spiritual world. We are then no longer distinct from the dragon, we actually are the dragon which we have experienced in the spiritual world. This dragon may have very significant and, in a sense, grand experiences, experiences more fascinating than those which come at the Portal of Death or beyond it. The experiences one has at the Portal of Death are, to begin with, colourless, shadowlike and intimate – so light and intimate that they may easily escape us, and we are not in the least inclined to be attentive enough to hold them fast. We must always exert ourselves to allow what easily comes to life in the thoughts to expand. It expands ultimately into a world, but long and energetic striving and work is necessary before this world appears as reality permeated with colour, sound and life. For we must let these colourless and soundless forms take on life from infinity. If one discovers, for example, the simplest air or water spirit through what we may now call 'head clairvoyance' (by which is meant the clairvoyance that arises from animation of thinking), this air or water spirit is at first something that flits away so lightly and fleetingly over the horizon of the spiritual world that it does not interest us at all. And if it is to have colour or sound, this must draw near it from the whole sphere of the cosmos. This happens, however, only after long inner effort. This occurs only through waiting until one is blessed. For just suppose – speaking pictorially – that you have one of these air spirits; if it is to approach in colour, the colour must stream into it from a mighty part of the cosmos. One must have the power to make the colours shine in. This power, however, can only be acquired, can only be won, by devotion. The radiating forces must pour in from without through devotion. But if we are one with the dragon we shall be inclined, when we see an air or water spirit, to ray out the forces which are within us, and precisely those which are in the organs usually called the 'lower' organs. This is much easier. The head is in itself a perfect organ but in the astral body and etheric body of the head there is not much colour because the colours are expended in forming, for example, the brain and especially the skull. When we approach the threshold of the spiritual world and in 'head clairvoyance' draw the astral and etheric bodies out of the physical body, there is not much colour in them. The colours have been expended to shape the perfected organ, the brain. When, however, in 'belly clairvoyance' [*'Bauchellsehen'*] we draw the astral body and etheric body out of the organs of stomach, liver, gall-bladder, and so forth, the colours have not yet been as expended in building up perfected organs. These organs are only on the way to perfection. What comes from the astral body and etheric body of the stomach is beautifully coloured; it gleams and glitters in all possible radiant colours; and if the etheric and astral bodies are drawn out of these organs, the forms seen are imbued with the most wonderful colours and sounds. So it could happen that someone may see wonderful things and sketch a picture with gorgeous colouring. This is certainly interesting, as it is also interesting for the anatomist to examine the spleen, liver or intestines, and from the standpoint of science this is also indispensable. But when it is examined by someone very experienced, what appears in these beautifully coloured pictures is that which underlies the process of digestion two hours after eating.

There is certainly no objection to investigating these things. The anatomist must necessarily do so and the time will come when science will gain a great deal by knowing what the etheric body does when the stomach digests food. But we must be totally clear about this: if we do not connect this with our dragon, if we do not consciously approach the Portal of the Sun, if we are not aware that we summon into the dragon what is contained in the etheric and astral body of the belly, we then radiate it forth into picture-clairvoyance – and then we receive a truly wonderful world. The most beautiful and easiest of attainments does not at first come from the higher forces, from 'head clairvoyance', but from 'belly clairvoyance'. It is most important to know this. From the point of view of the cosmos there is nothing vulgar in an absolute sense, but only in a relative sense. In order to produce what is necessary for the process of digestion in man the cosmos has to work with forces of colossal significance. What matters is that we do not succumb to errors or illusions but know what the things are. When we know that something which looks very wonderful is nothing other than the process of digestion, this is extremely important. But if we believe that some celestial world is being revealed by such a picture, then we are falling into error. An intelligent person will have no objection to the cultivation of science based on such knowledge, but only to things being put in a false light. This is what we are concerned with. Thus it can happen, for instance, that someone will always at a certain moment draw out the etheric and astral bodies directly through an occurrence within the digestive processes, at a certain stage of digestion. Such a person may be a natural clairvoyant. One must only know what we are concerned with.

Through 'head clairvoyance', where all the colours of the etheric and astral bodies are used for the production of the wonderful structure of the brain, it will be difficult for a person to fill what is colourless and soundless with colours and sounds. But with 'belly clairvoyance' it will be comparatively easy to see the most wonderful things in the world. In this kind of clairvoyance, of course, also lie forces which a person must learn to use. The forces used in digestion are involved in a process of transformation and we experience them in the right way when we learn more and more to cultivate the identification with destiny. And this is also the ground from which we learn: that which at first appeared as a flying Angel's head we must trace again to the other element that we have dealt with, so that we do not trace only the forces which serve digestion but also those of a higher kind, those which lie within the sphere of our karma, our destiny. If we identify ourselves with it, we succeed in bearing forth the spiritual entities we see around us, which now have the inclination towards colours and sounds flowing in from cosmic space. The spiritual world then naturally becomes concrete and full of stability, truly so concrete that we fare there as well as we fare in the physical world.

One great difficulty at the Portal of Death is that we really have the feeling – and we must overcome it – 'I am essentially losing myself'. But if one has stretched oneself and has identified oneself with the life of thought, one may at the same time have the consciousness, 'I lose myself but I find myself again'. That is an experience that one has. One loses oneself on entering the spiritual world, but one knows that one will find oneself again. One must make the transition: to reach the abyss, to lose oneself in it, but with trust that one shall find oneself again there. This is an experience that one must go through; all that I have described are inner experiences that one must go through. And one must come to know that what takes place in the soul is important. It is just as if we were obliged to see something; if one is shown the way by a friend, it is easier than if one thinks it out for oneself. But one can attain all that has been described if one submits oneself to constant inner work and inner self-control through meditation, as you will find described in the book *Knowledge of the Higher Worlds: How is it Achieved?* and in the second part of *Occult Science: An Outline*.

It is of very great importance that we should learn to pass through these alien experiences beyond the threshold of the spiritual world. If, as is natural to the human being in his naked need, one is prone to imagine the spiritual world merely as a continuation, a duplication of the physical world, if one expects everything in the spiritual world to look just the same as in the physical world, then one cannot enter. One must really go through what one experiences as a reversal of everything experienced in the physical world. Here in the physical world one is accustomed, for example, to open one's eyes and see light, to receive impressions through the light. If one were to expect, in the spiritual world, that one could open a spiritual eye to receive impressions through the light, then one could not enter, for one's expectations would be false. Something like a fog would be woven around the spiritual senses, concealing the spiritual world as a mass of fog conceals a mountain. In the spiritual world, for instance, one cannot see objects illuminated by light; on the contrary, one must be very clear that one streams with the light oneself into the spiritual world. In the physical world, if a ray of light falls upon an object, one sees it; but in the spiritual world one is oneself within the ray of light and it is in this way that one touches the object. One knows oneself to be shimmering with the ray of light, in the spiritual world; one knows oneself to be within the streaming light. This knowledge can give an indication towards acquiring concepts capable of helping us onward in the spiritual world. It is, for instance, extremely useful to picture to ourselves: how would it be, if we were now within the sun? Because we are not within the sun we see objects illuminated by the sun's rays, by the refracted rays of the sun. But one must imagine oneself to be within the sun's rays and thus touching the objects. This 'touching' is an experience in the spiritual world; indeed, experience there consists in knowing that one is alive within that world. One knows that one is alive in the weaving of thoughts. As soon as this condition begins, that one knows one is conscious in the weaving of thoughts, then comes an immediate awareness of self-knowledge in the luminous streaming light. For thought is of the light. Thought weaves in the light. But one can experience this only when one is really immersed in the light, if one is within this weaving of thoughts.

The human being has now reached a stage where he must acquire such concepts as these, so that he may not pass through the Gate of Death into the spiritual world and find himself in completely strange worlds. The 'capital' given to man by the Gods at the primal beginning of the Earth has gradually been consumed. Human beings no longer bear with them through the Gate of Death the remains of an ancient heritage. They must now gradually acquire concepts in the physical world which, when they proceed through the Gate of Death, will serve after crossing to make visible to them the tempting, seductive, dangerous beings confronting one there. The fact that spiritual science must be communicated to humanity, must take shelter in humanity at the present time, is connected with these great cosmic relations. And one can observe already in our time, in our destiny-laden time [World War I], that crossings are really being created. Human beings are now passing through the Gate of Death in the prime of youth; in obedience to the great demands of destiny, they have, in a sense, consciously allowed death to approach them in the days of their youth. I do not mean now so much the moment before death on the battlefield, for instance. In those cases there may be a great deal of enthusiasm and so forth, so that the experience of death is not so saturated with as clear an attention as one would like to believe. But when the death has actually occurred, it leaves behind a still unspent etheric body, upon which the dead one can look, so that he now beholds this phenomenon, this fact of death, with much greater clarity than would be possible for him if it occurred as the result of illness or old age.

Death on the battlefield is more intense, an event which works more powerfully in our time than a death occurring in other ways. It therefore works upon the soul which has passed through the Gate of Death as an enlightenment. Death is terrible, or at least may be terrible for the human being so long as he remains in the body. But when he has passed through the Gate of Death and looks back at death, death is then the most beautiful of all experiences possible in the human cosmos. For between death and a new birth this looking back to the entrance to the spiritual world through death is the most wonderful, the most beautiful, the most glorious event possible. Although we hardly remember anything of the physical circumstances of our birth – no person remembers his physical birth with the ordinary, undeveloped faculties – nevertheless the phenomenon of death is ever-present to the soul that has passed through the Gate of Death, from the moment of the sudden emergence of consciousness onwards. It is always present, yet it stands there as the most beautiful presence, as the 'awakener'. Within the spiritual world, death is the most wonderful instructor, an instructor who can prove to the receptive soul that there is a spiritual world, because through its very being it destroys the physical, and from this destruction allows the spiritual to emerge. This resurrection of the spiritual, with the complete stripping off of the physical, is an event ever-present between death and a new birth. It is a sustaining, wonderful event, and the soul gradually grows in his under-standing of it, grows in a totally unique way if it is to a certain extent 'self-selected' – not, of course, in the sense of a person seeking his own death but by having voluntarily considered it. If he has of his own free will allowed death to come to him, this moment gains immensely in lucidity. And a person who has not hitherto thought much about death or has concerned himself little with the spiritual world may in our time receive in his death a wonderful instructor. This is a fact of great significance, precisely in this war, regarding the connection of the physical with the spiritual world. I have already stressed this in many lectures about this difficult time; but what can be done through mere teaching, through words, does not suffice. Yet great enlightenment is in store for mankind of the future because there have been so many deaths. They work upon the dead, and the dead, in their turn, set to work on the future cultural development of humanity.

I am able to communicate to you directly certain words which came from one who in our day passed through the Gate of Death in his early years, who has, I would like to say, come through. These words are, precisely for that reason, rather startling, because they testify to the fact that the dead one – who experienced death with the particular clarity one feels on the battlefield – is finding now in these alien experiences after death how he works himself away from earthly conceptions into spiritual conceptions. I will communicate these words here. They are, if I may so characterize them, intercepted by someone who wanted to bring that which the dying soldier would if he were allowed to return:

Within the streaming
Light I feel
The life force.

Death has waked
Me from sleep,
From spirit sleep.

I shall live on
And do, out of myself,
What the power of light
Radiates into me.

Im leuchtenden,
Da fühle ich
Die Lebenskraft.
Der Tod hat mich
Vom Schlaf erweckt,
Vom geistesschlaf.

Ich werde sein
Und aus mir tun,
Was Leuchtekraft
In mir erstrahlt.

This was to a certain extent what the suffering soul had learned from looking back to his death, the learning he had experienced. It was as though his being were filled with what must be learned from the sight of death, and he wished to give this information, to reveal it.

Within the streaming Light I feel the life force.

Therefore he feels that he is more alive to grasping the spiritual world than he was before death. He feels death as an awakener, an instructor:

Death has waked me from sleep, from spirit sleep.

And now he feels that he will be a doer in the spiritual world:

I shall live on, and do, out of myself ...

but he feels that this action is that of the forces of light within him, and he feels the light working within him:

I shall live on
And do, out of myself,
What the power of light
Radiates into me.

One can see everywhere, can rightly see, that what one can

come to perceive in the spiritual world can again and again deliver the most pure confirmation of what can become universally familiar through the form of knowledge called Imagination. This is what we should so like to see resuscitated, rightly resuscitated, through our spiritual-scientific movement; that we have not to do with just a naked knowledge of the spiritual world, but that this knowledge becomes so alive in us that we adopt another way of feeling with the world, of experiencing with the world, so that the idea of spiritual science begins to live in us. It is this inward enlivening of the thoughts of spiritual science which, as I have repeatedly said, will be fundamentally demanded of us, so that it can be our contribution to the evolution of the world. This must be done in order that the thoughts born of spiritual science, which soar into the spiritual world as light forces, may unite with the radiant cosmos, in order that the cosmos may unite with that which those who have passed through the Gate of Death in our fateful times wish to incorporate into the spiritual movement of culture. Then will begin what is implied in these words with which we will conclude our lecture:

From the courage of the fighters,
From the blood on fields of strife,
From the suffering of the forsaken,
From the people's sacrifice
There shall blossom fruit of spirit –
If souls, conscious of the spirit,
Turn their sense to the spirit realm.

X. Beyond the Sphere of Scientific Knowledge[35]

Vienna, 1 June 1922

THIS CONGRESS has been announced as a congress on the philosophy of life, and no doubt you will take it as such. Anyone who wishes to talk about philosophical questions today, however, cannot ignore natural science, and in particular the philosophical consequences that natural science has brought with it. Indeed, for centuries – since the fifteenth or sixteenth century, we may say – science has increasingly come to dominate human thinking in the civilized world.

Now it would take a great many words to survey the triumphs of science in the field of human knowledge, and the transformation of our whole life brought about by the achievements of scientific research. And it would be merely a repetition of what you all know already. Philosophically speaking, what is interesting about science is something quite different. I mean the function it long ago assumed of educating the civilized world. And it is precisely in discussing this educational role in the development of modern man that we come up against two paradoxes, as I should like to call them. Let me begin with these paradoxes.

The first thing that has followed from the scientific method of research is a transformation of human thinking. Any impartial observer of earlier philosophical trends must conclude that, because of the conditions which then determined man's development, thinking inevitably added something subjective to what was given by experiment and the observation of nature. We need only recall those now outmoded branches of knowledge, astrology and alchemy, to perceive how nature was approached in former times – how human thinking as a matter of course added to what was there something that it wished to express, or at any rate did not suppress.

In the face of the scientific attitude of recent times, this has ceased. Today, we are virtually obliged simply to accept the data given us by observation and experiment, and to work them up into natural laws, as they are called. Admittedly, to do so we make *use* of thought; but we make use of it only as a means of arranging phenomena so that through their own existence they manifest to us their inner connection, their conformity to law. And we make it our duty not to add any of our own thought to our observation of the world. We see this, indeed, as an ideal of the scientific attitude – and rightly so.

Under these conditions, what has become of human thinking? It has actually become the servant, the mere tool of research. Thought as such has really nothing to contribute when it comes to investigating the conformity to law of external phenomena.

Here, then, is one of my paradoxes: that thought as a human experience is excluded from the relationship that man enters into with the world. It has become a purely formal aid for comprehending realities. Within science, it is no longer something self-manifesting.

The significance of this for man's inner life is extraordinarily great. It means that we must look upon thinking as something which must retire in wisdom and modesty when we are contemplating the outside world, and which represents a kind of private current within the life of the soul.

And it is precisely when we now ask ourselves how, in turn, can *science* approach *thinking* that we come up against the paradox, and find ourselves saying: if thinking has to confine itself to the working-up of natural processes and can intervene only formally, in clarification, combination and organization, it cannot also fall within the natural processes themselves. It thus becomes paradoxical to raise the question (which is certainly justified from the scientific point of view): how can we, from the standpoint of scientific law, understand thinking as a manifestation of the human organism? And to this, if we stand impartially and seriously within the life of science, we can only reply today: to the extent that thinking has had to withdraw from the natural processes, contemplation of them can go on trying to encompass thinking, but it cannot succeed. Since it is methodologically excluded, thinking is also really excluded from the natural processes. It is condemned to be a mere semblance, not a reality.

Not many people today, I believe, are fully conscious of the force of this paradox; yet in the depths of their subconscious there exists in countless numbers of people today an *awareness* of it. Only as thinking beings can we regard ourselves as human; it is in thinking that we find our human dignity – and yet this, which really makes us into human beings, accompanies us through the world as something whose reality we cannot at present acknowledge, as a semblance. In pointing to what is noblest in our human nature, we feel ourselves to be in an area of non-reality.

This is something that burdens the soul of anyone who has become seriously involved with the research methods both of the inorganic sciences and of biology and who wishes to draw the consequences of these *methods*, rather than of any individual results, for a philosophy of life.

Here, we may say, is something that can lead to bitter doubts in the human soul. Doubts arise first in the intellect, it is true; but they flow down into the feelings. Anyone who is able to look at human nature more deeply and without prejudice – in the way I shall be demonstrating in detail in the lectures that follow – knows how the state of the spirit, if it endures long enough, exerts an influence right down to the physical state of the person, and how from this physical state, or disposition, the mood of life wells up in turn. Whether the doubt is driven down into our feelings or not determines whether we stride courageously through life, so that we can stand upright ourselves and have a healthy influence among our fellow human beings, or whether we wander through life disgruntled and downcast – useless to ourselves and useless to our fellow human beings. I do not say – and the lectures which follow will show that I do not need to say – that what I have just been discussing must always lead to doubt; but it can easily do so, unless science is extended in the directions I shall be describing.

The splendid achievements of science *vis-à-vis* the outside world make extraordinary demands on man's soul if, as from the philosophical standpoint here expounded he certainly must do, he adopts a positive attitude to science. They demand that he should be capable of meeting doubt with something stronger and more powerful than would otherwise be needed.

Whilst in this respect science would appear to lead to something negative for the life of the soul, yet – and this brings me to my second paradox – on the other hand it has resulted in something extremely positive. Here, I express once more a paradox that struck me particularly when, more than 20 years ago now, I worked out my *Philosophy of Spiritual Activity* and attempted, whilst maintaining a truly scientific outlook on life, to fathom the nature of human freedom.

For, with its conformity to law, science does easily lead, in theory, to a denial of human freedom. In this respect, however, science develops theories that are just the opposite of its practical effect. When we go further and further into the semblance nature of thinking and, by actually pursuing the scientific *attitude* – not scientific *theories* – arrive at a right inward experience of that nature, then we conclude: if it is only a semblance and not a reality, then the process of thought does not, like a natural force, have a compelling effect. I may thus compare it – and this is more than a mere comparison – to a combination of mirror-images. Images before me cannot compel me. Existent *forces* can compel me, whether they are thought of as existing outside me or inside me; *images* cannot compel me. If, therefore, I am able to conceive my moral impulses within that pure thinking which science itself fosters in us by its methods, if I can so shape moral impulses within me that my attitude to their shaping is that to which science educates me, then in these moral impulses conceived by pure thinking I have *not* compelling forces but forces and semblances that I myself am free to accept or not. That is to say: however much science, from its very premises, is bound, and with some justification, to deny freedom, yet in educating him to semblance thinking it educates the person of our culture to freedom.

These are the two poles, the one relating to the life of thought and the other to the life of the will, with which the human soul is confronted by present-day scientific opinions. In distinguishing them, however, we indicate at the same time how the scientific view of life points beyond itself. It must take up some attitude towards human thinking; yet it excludes that thinking. By so doing, it suggests a method of research that can be fully justified in the eyes of science and yet lead to a comprehensible experience of thinking. It suggests, on the other hand, that because it cannot itself arrive theoretically at freedom, the scientific attitude must be extended into a different region, precisely in order to attain the sphere of freedom.

What I am presenting as a necessity deriving from science itself – an extension into a region that science, at least as understood today, cannot reach – is attempted by the philosophy of life I am here advocating. Today, of course, since it stands at the beginning of its development, it can achieve this extension only imperfectly. Yet the attempt must be made, because more and more people in the civilized world today are being affected by the problems of thinking and freedom that I have described. It is no longer possible for us today to believe that only those in some way involved with science are faced with demands and questions and riddles of this kind. Even the remotest villages, to which no scientific results of any consequence penetrate, are nevertheless brought by their education to the kind of thinking that science demands; and this brings with it, though quite unconsciously as yet, uncertainty about human freedom. It is therefore not only scientific questions that are involved here, but quite clearly general human ones.

What it comes to is this: taking our stand on the ground of scientific education, can we penetrate further along the path of knowledge than does present-day science?

The attempt to do so can be made, and made in such a way that the methods used can be justified to the strictest scientist, and made by paths that have been laid down in complete accordance with the scientific attitude and with scientific conscientiousness. I should like now to go on to speak of these paths.

Yet, although many souls already unconsciously long for it, the present-day path of knowledge is still not easy to explain conceptually. In order that we may be able to understand one another this evening, therefore, I should like to introduce, simply as aids to understanding, descriptions of older paths that mankind has followed in order to arrive at knowledge lying beyond the ordinary region science deals with today.

Much of what, it is believed today, should just remain an article of faith and is accepted as ancient and honourable tradition leads the psychologically perceptive observer of history back into age-old epochs of humanity. There, it turns out that these matters of faith were sought after, as matters of knowledge suited to their time, by certain individuals through the cultivation of their own souls and the development of hidden spiritual powers, and that they thus genuinely constituted matters of knowledge. People today no longer realize how much of what has emerged historically in man's development was once actually discovered – but discovered by earlier paths of knowledge.

When I describe these paths, I do so, of course, with the aid of methods I shall outline later; so that in many cases those who form their picture of the earlier epochs of mankind only from outward historical documents, and not from spiritual documents, may take exception to my description. Anyone who examines impartially even the outward historical documents, and who then compares them with what I shall have to say, will nevertheless find no real contradiction. And secondly, I want to emphasize that I am not describing these older paths of knowledge in order to advocate them today. They suited earlier epochs, and nowadays can even be harmful to man if, under a misapprehension, he applies them to himself. It is simply so that we shall understand each other about present-day ways of knowledge that I shall choose two earlier ways, describe them, and thus make clear the paths man has to walk today, if he wishes to go beyond the sphere of scientific knowledge as it is now understood.

As I have said, I could select others from the wealth of earlier ways of knowledge; but I am selecting only two. First, then, we have a way which in its pure form was followed by individuals in ancient times in the East – the way of yoga.

Yoga has passed through many phases, and the aspect to which I shall attach the greatest value today is precisely one that has come down to later epochs in a thoroughly decadent and harmful state. What I shall be describing, the historian will thus be forced, when considering later epochs, to present as something actually harmful to mankind. But in successive epochs human nature has experienced the most varied developments. Something quite different suited human nature in ancient epochs and in later ones. What could, in earlier times, be a genuine means of cognition was later perhaps used only to titillate man's itch for power over his fellow human beings. This was certainly not true of the earliest periods, the ones whose practice of yoga I am describing.

What did it comprise, the way of yoga, which was followed in very ancient times in the Orient by individuals who were scholars, to use the modern term, in the higher sphere? It comprised among other things a particular kind of breathing exercise. (I am singling out this one from the wealth of exercises that the yoga pupil or the yoga scholar, the yogi, had to undertake.) When nowadays we examine our breathing, we find that it is a process which for the most part operates unconsciously in the healthy human organism. There must be something abnormal about the person who is aware of his

breathing. The more naturally the process of breathing functions, the better it is for ordinary consciousness and for
ordinary life. For the duration of his exercises, however, when
he wished to develop cognitive powers that are merely dormant in ordinary consciousness, the yogi transformed the
process of respiration. He did so by employing a length of time
for inhaling, for holding the breath and for exhaling, different
from that used in ordinary, natural breathing. He did this so
as to make conscious the process of respiration. Ordinary
respiration does not become conscious. The transformed
respiratory rhythm, with its timing determined by human
volition, is entirely conscious. But what is the result? Well, we
have only to express ourselves in physiological terms to realize
what the yogi achieved by making conscious his respiration.
When we breathe in, the respiratory impulse enters our
organism; but it also goes via the spinal cord into the brain.
There, the rhythm of the respiratory current combines with
those processes that are the physical carriers of mental activity, the nerve and sense processes. Actually, in our ordinary
life, we never have nerve and sense processes alone; they are
always permeated by our respiratory rhythm. A connection,
interaction, harmonization of the nerve and sense processes
and of respiration always occurs when we allow our minds to
function. By transmitting his altered respiratory rhythm into
the nerve and sense process in a fully conscious way, the yogi
also made a conscious connection between the respiratory
rhythm and the thought rhythm, logical rhythm or rather
logical combination and analysis of thoughts. In this way he
altered his whole mental activity. In what direction did he
alter it? Precisely because his breathing became fully conscious his thoughts permeated his organism in the same way
as did the respiratory current itself. We could say that the yogi
set his thoughts moving on the respiratory currents and, in the
inner rhythm of his being, experienced the union of thought
and breath. In this way, the yoga scholar raised himself above
the mass of his fellow human beings and was able to proclaim

to them knowledge they could not gain for themselves.

In order to understand what was really happening here, we must look for a moment at the particular way in which knowledge earlier affected the ordinary, popular consciousness of the masses.

Nowadays, when we look out at the world we attach the greatest value to seeing pure colours; to hearing pure sounds when we hear sounds, and similarly to obtaining a certain purity in the other perceptions – such purity, that is, as the sensory process can afford. This was not true for the consciousness of people in older civilizations. Not that, as a certain brand of scholarship often mistakenly believes, people in earlier times projected all sorts of imaginings on to nature; the imagination was not all that unusually active. Because of man's constitution at that time, however, it was quite natural for older civilizations not to see only pure colours, pure sounds, pure qualities in the other senses, but at the same time to perceive in all of them something spiritual. Thus, in sun and moon, in stars, in wind and weather, in spring and stream, in the creatures of nature's various realms, they saw something spiritual where we today see pure colours and hear pure sounds, the connection between which we only later seek to understand with the aid of purified thinking. And there was a further consequence of this for earlier humanity: that no such strong and inwardly fortified self-consciousness as we have today existed then. Besides perceiving something spiritual in everything about him, man perceived himself as a part of this whole environment; he did not separate himself from it as an independent self. To draw an analogy, I might say: if my hand were conscious, what would it think about itself? It would conclude that it was not an independent entity, but made sense only within my organism. In some such way as this, earlier man was unable to regard himself as an independent entity but felt himself rather a part of nature's whole, which in turn he had to see as permeated by the spiritual.

The yogi raised himself above this view, which implied the

dependence of the human self. By uniting his thought process with the process of respiration that fills all man's inner substance, he arrived at a comprehension of the human self, the human I. The awareness of personal individuality, implanted in us today by our inherited qualities and, if we are adults, by our education, had in those earlier times to be attained, indirectly, through exercises. The consequence was that the yogi obtained from the experience of self something quite different from what we do. It is one thing to accept something as a natural experience, as the sense of self is for us, and quite another to attain to it by the paths that were followed in early eastern civilization. *They* lived with what moves and swells and acts in the universe; whereas today, when we experience all this from a certain elevation, we no longer know anything of the universe directly. The human self, therefore, the true nature of the human soul manifested itself to the yogi through his exercise. And we may say: since what could be discovered in this way passed over as revelation into the general cultural consciousness, it became the subject-matter of the most important spiritual products from those ancient times.

Once again, let me mention one of many. Here we have an illumination from the ancient Orient, the magnificent song *Bhagavad Gita*. In the *Gita* we have the experience of self-awareness; it describes wonderfully, out of the deepest human lyricism, how, when by experiencing he recognizes it and by recognizing he experiences it, this self leads man to a sympathy with all things, and how it manifests to him his own humanity and his relationship with a higher world, with a spiritual and supersensible world. In ever new and marvellous notes, the *Gita* depicts this awareness of the self in its devotion to the universal. To the impartial observer of history, who can immerse himself in these earlier times, it is clear that the splendid notes of the *Gita* have arisen from what could be experienced through these exercises in cognition.

This way of attaining knowledge was the appropriate one

for an earlier epoch of civilization in the Orient. At that time, it was generally accepted that one had to retire into solitude and a hermit's life if one sought connection with supersensible worlds. And anyone who carried out such exercises did condemn himself to solitude and the life of the hermit; for they bring a person into a certain state of sensibility and make him over-sensitive towards the robust external world. He must retire from life. In earlier times it was just such solitary figures who were trusted by their fellow human beings. What they had to say was accepted as knowledge. Nowadays, this no longer suits our civilization. People today rightly demand that anyone they are to trust as a source of knowledge should stand in the midst of life, that he should be able to hold his own with the robustness of life, with human labour and human activity as the demands of the time shape them. Human beings of today just do not feel themselves linked, as the people of earlier epochs did, to anyone who has to withdraw from life.

If you reflect carefully on this, you will conclude: present-day ways of knowledge must be different. We shall be speaking of these in a little while. But before doing so, and again simply by way of explanation and not with any idea of recommending it, I want to describe the principles underlying a way that was also appropriate to earlier times – the way of asceticism.

The way of asceticism involved subduing and damping down bodily processes and needs, so that the human body no longer functioned in its normal robust fashion. Bodily functions were also subdued by putting the external physical organism into painful situations. All this gave to those who followed this ascetic path certain human experiences which did indeed bring knowledge. I do not, of course, mean that it is right to inhibit the healthy human organism in which we are born into this life on earth, where our aim is to enable this organism to be effective in ordinary life. The healthy organism is unquestionably the appropriate one for external sensuous nature, which is after all the basis of human life between birth and death. Yet it remains true that the early ascetics, who had damped down this organism, did in fact gain pure experience of their spirituality, and knew their souls to inhabit a spiritual world. What makes our physical and sensuous organism suited for the life between birth and death is precisely the fact that, as the ascetics' experiences were able to show, it hides from us the spiritual world. It was, quite simply, the experience of the early ascetics that by damping down the bodily functions one could consciously enter the spiritual worlds. That again is no way for the present. Anyone who inhibits his body in this way makes himself unfit for life among his fellow human beings, and makes himself unfit *vis-à-vis* himself as well. Life today demands people who do not withdraw, who maintain their health and indeed restore it if it is impaired, but not people who withdraw from life. Such people could inspire no confidence, in view of the attitude of our age. Although the path of asceticism certainly did lead to knowledge in earlier times, it cannot be a path for today.

Yet what both the way of yoga and the ascetic way yielded in knowledge of the sensible world is preserved in ancient and, I would say, sacred traditions, and is accepted by mankind today as satisfying certain needs of the soul. However, people are not interested to know that the articles of faith thus accepted were in fact discovered by a genuine way of knowledge, if one no longer suited to our age.

Today's way of knowledge must be entirely different. We have seen how the one way, yoga, tried to arrive at thinking indirectly, through breathing, in order to experience this thinking in a way in which it is not perceived in ordinary life. For the reason already given, we cannot make this detour via breathing. We must therefore try to achieve a transformation of thinking by other means, so that through this transformed thinking we can reach knowledge that will be a kind of extension of natural knowledge. If we understand ourselves correctly, therefore, we shall start today not by manipulating thinking indirectly via breathing but by manipulating it directly and by doing certain exercises through which we make thinking more forceful and energetic than it is in ordinary consciousness.

In ordinary consciousness we indulge in rather passive thinking, which adheres to the course of external events. To follow a new supersensible way of knowledge, we place certain readily comprehended concepts at the centre of our consciousness. We remain within the thought itself. I am aware that many people believe that what I am now going to describe is present already in later forms of yoga, for example in that of Patanjali. But as practised today, it certainly does not form a part of eastern spirit-training – for even if a person carried out the yoga exercises nowadays they would have a different effect, because of the change in the human organism, from the effect they had on the people of earlier epochs.

Today, then, we go straight to thinking, by cultivating meditation, by concentrating on certain subjects of thought over a long period of time. We perform, in the realm of the soul, something comparable to building up a muscle. If we use a muscle over and over again in continuous exertion, whatever the goal and purpose, the muscle must develop. We can do the same with thinking. Instead of always submitting, in our thinking, to the course of external events, we bring into the centre of our consciousness, with a great effort of will, clear-cut concepts which we have formed ourselves or have been given by someone expert in the field, and in which no associations can persist of which we are not conscious; we shut out all other consciousness, and concentrate only on this one subject. In the words Goethe uses in *Faust*, I might say: yes, it is easy – that is, it appears so – yet the easy is difficult. One person takes weeks, another months, to achieve it. When consciousness does learn to rest and rest continually upon the same content in such a way that the content itself becomes a matter of complete indifference, and we devote all our attention and all our inward experience to the building up and spiritual energization of mental activity, then at last we achieve the opposite process to what the yogi went through. That is, we tear our thinking away from the process of respiration.

Today, this still seems to people something absurd, something fantastic. Yet just as the yogi pushed his thinking into his body, to link it with the rhythm of his breath and in this way experience his own self, his inner spirituality, so too we release thinking from the remnant of respiration that survives unconsciously in all our ordinary thinking. You will find the systematic exercises described in greater detail in my book *Knowledge of Higher Worlds*, or in *Occult Science*, or again in other books of mine. By these means, one gradually succeeds not only in separating the thought sequence from the respiration process, but also in making it quite free of corporeality. Only then does one see what a great service the so-called materialistic, or rather mechanistic, outlook on life has rendered to mankind. It has made us aware that ordinary thinking is founded on bodily processes. From this can stem the incentive to seek a kind of thinking no longer founded on bodily processes. But this can only be found by building up ordinary thinking in the way described. By doing so, we arrive at a thinking set free from the body, a thinking that consists of purely psychic processes. In this way, we come to know what once had a semblance nature in us – as images only to begin with, but images that show us life independent of our corporeality.

This is the first step towards a way of knowledge suited to modern man. It brings us, however, to an experience that is hidden from ordinary consciousness. Just as the Indian yogi linked himself in his thinking with the internal rhythm of respiration, and so also with his spiritual self which lives in the respiratory rhythm, just as he moved inwards, so we go outwards. By tearing our logical thinking away from the organism to which it is actually connected, we penetrate with it into the external rhythm of the world, and discover for the first time that such a rhythm exists. Just as the yogi made conscious the inner rhythm of his body, so we become conscious of an external world rhythm. If I may express myself metaphorically: in ordinary consciousness, what we do is to combine our thoughts logically and thus make use of thinking to know the external sensuous world. Now, however, we allow thinking to enter a kind of musical region, but one that is undoubtedly a region of knowledge. We perceive a spiritual rhythm underlying all things; we penetrate into the world by beginning to perceive it in the spirit. From abstract, dead thinking, from mere semblance thinking, our thinking becomes a vitalized thinking. This is the significant transition that can be made from abstract and merely logical thinking to a vital thinking which we clearly feel is capable of shaping a reality, just as we recognize our process of growth as a living reality.

With this vital thinking, however, we can now penetrate deeper into nature than with ordinary thinking. In what way? Let me illustrate this from present-day life, although the example is a much-disputed one. Nowadays, we may direct our abstract mental activity, by observation and experiment, onto a higher animal, for instance. With this thinking, we create for ourselves an internal image of how the organs of the animal are arranged, the skeleton, musculature, etc., and how the vital processes flow into one another. We make a mental image of the animal. Then, with the same thinking, we pass to man, and once again make a mental image of him – the configuration of his skeleton, his musculature, the interaction of his vital processes, etc. We can then make an external comparison between the two images obtained. If we tend towards a Darwinian approach, we shall regard man as being descended from animals through an actual physical process; if we are more spiritually and idealistically inclined, we imagine the relationship differently. We will not go into that now. The important point is that there is something we cannot do: because our thinking is dead and abstract, we are not in a position – once we have formed a mental image of the animal – *out of the inner life of thinking itself* to pass over from that into the image of man. Instead, we have first to extract our ideas, or mental images, from the sensory realities, and then to compare these ideas with one another. When, on the other hand, we have advanced to vital thinking, we do indeed form a mental image still, but now it is a *living* mental image, of the skeleton, the musculature, and the interaction of vital processes in the animal. Because our thought has now become a vital one, we can pursue it inwardly as a living structure and pass over *in the thought itself* to the image of man. I might say: the thought of the animal grows into the thought of the human being. How this works I can only suggest by means of an example.

Faced with the needle of a magnet, we know that there is only one position in which it remains at rest, and that is when its axis coincides with the North-South direction of the earth's magnetism. This direction is exceptional; to all other directions the needle is indifferent. Everything in this example becomes for vital thinking an experience about total space. For vital thinking, space is no longer an aimless juxtaposition, as it is for dead and abstract thinking. Space is internally differentiated, and we learn the significance of the fact that in animals the spine is essentially horizontal. Where this is not the case, we can demonstrate from a more profound conformity to law that the abnormality is particularly significant; but essentially an animal's spine lies in the horizontal plane – we may say, parallel to the surface of the earth. Now it is not immaterial whether the spinal cord runs in this direction or in the vertical direction to which man raises himself in the course of his life. In vital thinking, accordingly, we come to know that, if we wanted to set upright the line of the animal, that is to orientate it differently in the universe, we should have to transform all its other organs. Thought becomes vital simply through the rotation of 90 degrees from the vertical to the horizontal orientation. We pass over in this way, by an inward impulse, from the animal to the human shape.

Thereby, we enter into the rhythm of natural process and so reach the spiritual foundation of nature. We attain, in our vital thought, something with which we can penetrate into the growth and progress of the external world. We reach once more the secrets of existence, from which we departed in the course of human development with the unfolding of ego-consciousness, the feeling of self.

Now you can all raise a weighty objection here. You can say, for example: there have indeed been individuals with this kind of thinking, ostensibly vital; but the present time, with its insistence on serious research, has rightly turned away from 'vital thinking' as it was expounded, for instance, by the philosopher Schelling or the natural philosopher Oken. I myself agree entirely with those who raise this kind of objection; there is something quite fantastic, something that leaves reality behind and breathes no actuality, about the way in which mental images gained from external processes and substances are inwardly vitalized by Oken and Schelling and then applied to other natural facts and creatures, in order to see 'in the manner of nature'. So long as our vital thinking does not pass on to a mode of knowledge other than this we cannot, even with its aid, reach any assurance of reality. Only by adding exercises of will to the exercises of thought do we secure in vital thoughts a guarantee of spiritual reality.

Exercises of the will can be characterized as follows.

Let us be quite honest with ourselves. In ordinary life, if we think back 10 or 20 years, we have to conclude: in the actual content of the life of our soul, we have in many ways become different people; but we have done so by submitting more or less passively, as children, to heredity, environment and education, and in later life to life itself. Anyone who wishes to attain knowledge of spiritual reality must take in hand, if I may use this somewhat coarse expression, by an inner education and discipline of the will, what is usually experienced rather passively. Here again you will find the relevant exercises, which are intimate exercises of the soul, described in the books I have named. Today, I can only indicate briefly what is involved.

At present, we have certain habits that perhaps we did not have 10 years ago, since life has only recently imposed them on us. Similarly, we can decide to adopt these or those qualities of character. The best thing is to assume qualities of character for whose shaping you have to work on yourself for years on end, so that you must direct attention over and over again to that strengthening and fortifying of the will which is connected with such self-discipline. If you take in hand the development of your will like this, so that you in part make of yourself what the world would otherwise make of you as a person, then the vital thoughts into which you have found your way by meditation and concentration take on a quite special aspect for your experience. That is, increasingly they become painful experiences, inward experiences through suffering, of the things of the spirit. And in the last analysis nobody can attain to higher knowledge who has not passed through these experiences of suffering and pain. We must pass through and conquer these experiences, so that we incorporate and go beyond them, gaining an attitude of indifference to them once more.

What is going on here can be represented as follows. Take the human eye (what I am saying here could be expounded scientifically in every detail, but I have time only for a general outline): as light and colours affect it, changes occur in its physical interior. Earlier mankind undoubtedly perceived these as suffering and mild pain; and if we were not so robust and did not remain indifferent to them because of our make-up, we could not help also experiencing the changes in eye and ear as mild pain. All sensory perception is ultimately grounded on pain and suffering.

In thus permeating the entire life of our soul painfully and in suffering with vital thought, we do not permeate the body with pain and suffering as does the ascetic; we keep it healthy to suit the demands of ordinary life, but we inwardly and intimately experience pain and sorrow in the soul. Anyone who has gone some way towards higher knowledge will always tell you: the pleasure and joy that life has brought me I gratefully accept from fate, but I owe my knowledge to my pain and suffering.

In this way, life itself prepares the seeker after knowledge for the fact that part of the path he travels involves the conquest of suffering and pain. For if we overcome this suffering and pain, we make our entire psychic being into a 'sense-organ', or rather a spirit-organ, just as through our ordinary senses we look into and listen to the physical world. I do not need to discuss epistemological considerations today. I am naturally familiar with the objection that the external mode of knowledge must first also be investigated – but that does not concern us today. What I want to say is simply this: that, in the same sense in which in ordinary life we find the external physical world authenticated by our sensory perceptions, we find, after the soul's suffering has been conquered, the spiritual world authenticated by the soul-organ or spirit-organ which as a complete spiritual being we have become.[9]

Let us call this way of looking 'modern exact clairvoyance', by contrast with all earlier nebulous clairvoyant arts, which belong to the past. With it, we can also penetrate into the eternal substance of man. We can penetrate with exactitude into the meaning of human immortality. But consideration of this must be reserved for tomorrow's lecture, where I shall be speaking about the special relationship of this philosophy of life to the problems of man's psyche. Today, I wished to show how, in contrast to earlier ways of knowledge, man can attain a modern supersensible way of knowledge. The yogi sought to move *into* the human substance and reach the self; we seek to move *out* to the rhythm of the world. The ancient ascetic depressed the body in order to express spiritual experience and allow it to exist independently. The modern way of knowledge does not incline to asceticism; it avoids all arts of castigation and addresses itself intimately to the very life of the soul. Both the modern ways, therefore, place man entirely inside life, whereas the ways of asceticism and yoga drew people away from life.

I have tried today to describe to you a way that can be

followed by developing powers of knowledge, now sleeping in the soul, in a more spiritual sense than they were formerly developed.

By doing this, however (I should like to suggest in conclusion), we also reach deeper into the essence of nature. The philosophy of life of which I speak stands in no sort of opposition to the science of today. On the contrary, it takes precisely the genuine mood of enquiry which is there in scientific research and, through its exercises, develops this as a separate human faculty.

Science today seeks exactness and feels particularly satisfied if it can achieve it by the application of mathematics to natural processes. Why is this? It is because the perceptions with which external nature provides us, through the senses, for observation and experiment are wholly outside us. We permeate them with something we develop solely in our innermost human entity – with mathematical knowledge. And Kant's saying is often quoted and even more often practised by scientific thinkers: in all true knowledge there is only so much science as there is mathematics. This is exaggerated if we are thinking of ordinary mathematics. And yet, when we apply these to lifeless natural phenomena, and nowadays even regard it as an ideal, for instance, to be able to count the chromosomes in the blastoderm, we reveal how satisfied we are if we can permeate with mathematics what otherwise stands outside us. Why? Because mathematics is experienced inside us with immediate certainty: we often have to represent this experience to ourselves by means of diagrams, but the diagrams are not essential to the certainty, the truth. Things mathematical are seen and discovered within us, and what we find within us we connect with what we see outside. In this way we feel satisfied.

Anyone who perceives this process of cognition in its entirety must conclude: things can satisfy man as knowledge and lead to a science only if they rest on something he can really experience and observe through his inner powers. With the aid of mathematics, we can penetrate into the facts and structures of the inanimate world; but we cannot move more than a little way at most, and that somewhat primitively, into the organic world. We need a way of looking as exact as that of mathematics with which to penetrate into the higher processes of the outside world. Even one of the outstanding representatives of the school of Haeckel has expressly admitted that we must advance to an entirely different type of research and observation if we wish to move up from the inorganic into the organic realm of nature For the inorganic, we have mathematics, geometry; for the organic, the living, we have nothing as yet that corresponds to a triangle, a circle or an ellipse. By vital thinking we shall achieve them: not with the ordinary mathematics of numbers and figures, but with a higher mathesis, a qualitative approach working creatively, one which – and here I must say something which many people will find abominable – which touches the realm of the aesthetic.

By penetrating with mathematics of this kind into worlds that we cannot otherwise penetrate, we extend the scientific attitude upwards into the biological sphere. And we may be sure that eventually the epoch will come when people will say: earlier times rightly emphasized that the amount of science extracted from inorganic nature is proportional to the amount of quantitative mathematics, in the broadest sense, that can be applied to it; the amount of science extracted from the vital processes is proportional to the extent to which we can probe them with a living thought structure and an exact clairvoyance.

People will not believe how close this modern kind of clairvoyance is, in reality, to the mathematical outlook. Eventually, when it is realized how, from the spirit of modern knowledge of nature, knowledge of spirit can be gained, this spiritual science will be found to be justified precisely from the standpoint of our modern knowledge of nature. It has no wish to run counter to the important and imposing results of natural science. It seeks to attempt something different: we can look with our external senses at the physical form of someone standing before us – his gestures, his play of feature, the individual expression of his eyes – and yet perceive merely externals, unless we look through all this to something spiritual in him, by which alone the whole human being stands before us. In the same way, unless we travel the ways of the spirit, we look with science only at the external physiognomy of the world, its gestures and its mask. Only when we penetrate beyond the outward physiognomy that natural phenomena present to us, beyond the mask and gestures, into the spiritual region of the world, do we recognize something to which we are ourselves related, something of the eternal in the world.

That is the aim of the spiritual science whose methods I have sought to describe to you today by way of introduction. It does not wish to oppose triumphant modern science but to accept it fully in its importance and substance, just as we accept fully the external man. But just as we look through the external man at the soul so it seeks to penetrate through natural laws, not in a lay and dilettante fashion but with a serious approach, to the spiritual element underlying the world. And so this spiritual science seeks not to create any kind of opposition to natural science but to be its soul and spirit.

XI. Anthroposophy and Psychology

Vienna, 2 June 1922

WHEN THE riddles of existence touch the human soul, they become not only great problems in life, but life itself. They become the happiness or sorrow of man's existence. And not a passing happiness or sorrow only, but one he must carry for a time through life, so that by this experience of happiness or sorrow he becomes fit or unfit for life.

Now, man's attitude to his own soul is such that the most important questions about it and about its spiritual essence do not arise from any actual doubts he has regarding the spiritual element within him. It is precisely because he is certain of his spiritual substance and because he cannot help seeing in it his human dignity and his true significance as a man that the question of the fate of his soul becomes for him a tremendous riddle. To deny the mind in man himself does not, of course, occur to even the most rigid materialist. He acknowledges the mental as such, regarding it as a result of physical, material processes. Yet anyone who, with no such theory but simply from his deepest emotional needs, queries the fate of this soul of his will find himself confronted by a plethora of phenomena and experiences. And these become riddles to him just because he is fully conscious of the mental or spiritual life, and must accordingly ask: is this spiritual life a passing breath, rising from physical existence and returning with it once more into the generality of natural phenomena, or is it connected with a spiritual world within which it has eternal significance?

Of the many experiences in the realm of the psyche which present the riddles of the soul to our 'mind's eye', I will select only two.

There are, it may be objected, very few people on whom such experiences obtrude so much that they become even conscious, let alone theoretical, problems. But that is not the point. The point is that these experiences take hold of the subconscious or unconscious, establish themselves there, and flow up into consciousness only as a general temper or distemper of the soul, making us courageous and vigorous in life or making us dejected, so that at no point can we properly come to grips with life. As I have said, I want to pick out only two of these experiences.

The first appears before the 'mind's eye' every evening when we fall asleep, when the mental and psychic experiences that have floated up and down during the day sink down into the unconscious as if extinguished. Now when he looks at this experience or, as is most often the case, when the unconscious awareness of it affects his soul, man is overcome by a sense of the powerlessness of his mental life in face of the outside world. And just because man sees in this life his most valuable and dignified quality and cannot deny that he is in the true sense of the word a spiritual being, he is assaulted from within by this sensation of powerlessness and has to ponder the question: does the general process of nature overtake mental experiences when man passes through the Gate of Death, just as it always does at the onset of sleep? The first experience, if I may so put it, is a sense of the powerlessness of mental life.

The second experience is in a way a direct opposite of the first. We perceive it distinctly or indistinctly, consciously or unconsciously, when on waking, perhaps after passing through a fantastically chaotic dream world not attuned to reality, our spirit descends into our bodily existence. At such times we feel it informing our senses, feel too that our psychic experience is being permeated by the interplay between the outside world and our senses, which are of course physical and physiological. We feel the spiritual element descending further into our body; we inform our organs of will with it and become alert and self-possessed, able to make use of our body, our organism. On reflection, however, we cannot help realizing: anatomy and physiology make a valiant attempt to penetrate and analyse the bodily functions from without; yet looking from within, we ourselves, by means of ordinary consciousness, do not know anything about the interrelationship between our spiritual element and our bodily functions. A glance at the simplest bodily function controlled by the will, the lifting of an arm or movement of a hand, tells us: first there exists in us the thought or concept of this arm-lifting or hand-movement. How this thought or concept flows down into our organism, however, how it informs our muscles, and how finally there comes about what again we know only through observation – what actually goes on inside remains hidden from ordinary consciousness. So, too, in that wonderful mechanism that physics and physiology show us, the human eye or some other sense-organ, there remains hidden the spiritual element that informs this wonderful mechanism.

We are thus faced with problems both by the powerlessness of our mental life and by the darkness into which we feel our spirit descending when it flows down into our own body. We are forced to conclude (most people certainly do not do so consciously, but it affects them as the temper of their soul): this spiritual element in its relationship with the organism is unknown to us just when it is creative; it is unknown to us at the very point in physical life where it manifests its outgoing function.

What every naïve individual thus experiences extends, in a different form, to psychology itself. It would need a great many words to explain scientifically how these enigmas creep into the subject; but we can put it, rather superficially perhaps, as follows.

On the one hand, psychology looks at the mind and asks: what is the relation between this and the physical, the external and corporeal? In looking at the physical, on the other hand, and at what physical science has to say about it, some people – and in this respect psychology has a long history – believe that we must regard the mental as the really effective cause of the physical; others believe that we must regard the physical as the really empowering element, and the mental only as a kind of effect of it. The unsatisfactory nature of both views has been perceived by recent psychologists. They have therefore set up the curious theory of psycho-physical parallelism, according to which one cannot say that the body affects the mind or the mind the body, but only: corporeal processes are parallel to mental ones, and mental processes to bodily ones; one can only say what mental processes accompany the corporeal or what corporeal ones the mental.

Psychology itself, moreover, is conscious of this powerlessness of the mind! If we attempt to examine the mind, even as it presents itself to the psychologist, with ordinary consciousness, we find that it has something passive about it, so that we cannot see how it can penetrate dynamically the life of the body. Anyone who looks at the psychic characteristics of thinking and feeling (volition is impenetrable, so that for psychology much the same is true of will as of thinking and feeling) – anyone who looks at thinking and feeling with the tools of psychology finds them powerless, and cannot locate anything that would really be capable of effectively activating the physical. It is then that the psychologist experiences his sense of the powerlessness of mental life in the eyes of ordinary consciousness. The most varied attempts have certainly been made to overcome this feeling. But the disputes of philosophers and the changing philosophies that have succeeded one another provide the impartial observer of humanity with factual evidence of the impossibility for ordinary consciousness of approaching the mind's experience. Everywhere there obtrudes a sense of the powerlessness of the mind as it is perceived by ordinary consciousness.

With regard to this particular point, a series of works have appeared here in Vienna which represent milestones in the development of philosophy. Although I cannot associate myself in any way with their content, I believe that, from the standpoint of ordinary consciousness, these books are extraordinarily significant. They include Richard Wahle's *The Whole of Philosophy and its End*, which is designed to show that ordinary conscious-ness is incapable of reaching any significant conclusion about mental life, and that what philosophical investigation is here attempting ought to be handed over to theology, physiology, aesthetics and social science. And Richard Wahle went on to work out these ideas still more clearly in his *Mechanism of Mental Life*. We may say: here for once, ordinary consciousness is revealed as basically incapable of saying anything about the problems of mental life. The ego, the psyche, everything that earlier psychology brought to light – all these collapse in the face of the self-criticism of ordinary consciousness.

In recent years, however, psychology has, understandably and indeed of necessity, not attempted to deal directly with the things of the mind – in face of which, as we have seen, ordinary consciousness is powerless – but has sought to discover something about what are usually called mental phenomena indirectly, via the physical phenomena that spring from them. In this way, experimental psychology has come into being. This is a necessary product of our present attitude to life and methods of research. And anyone taking the philosophical standpoint that I do will never for one moment deny that experimental psychology is completely justified, though he may not perhaps agree entirely with this or that detail of its methods and results.

It is here that the other enigma of the soul comes in. However much we learn about what can be experienced by the human body in experimental psychology, the fact re-mains: everything that appears to be discovered in this way about purely psychic functions is, strictly speaking, only indirect knowledge, acquired via the body. It all belongs to a sphere which, at man's death, is given over to the general process of nature, so that through it can be learnt nothing about the soul, whose fate in the world is of such paramount concern to man. Thus we may say: for psychology, also, the great riddle of the soul reappears.

This point, too, has been made by a modern psychologist

who for many years lived and worked here in Vienna, and who
will never be forgotten by those who sat at his feet here, as I
did. In the first volume of his unfinished work on psychology,
he asks: what can any psychology ever achieve by establishing
– whether experimentally or non-experimentally, I might add
– how concepts combine and separate, how attention operates, how memory develops in life, etc.? – if, precisely because
of the scientific character of this psychology, with its emula-
tion of natural science, we must renounce all claim to
understand the fate of the human soul once the body crum-
bles into its elements? This was said not by some eccentric or
other but by that rigorous thinker Franz Brentano, who made
psychology his central concern in life and who sought to apply
to his work the strict scientific method of modern times. Yet
he it was who presented the riddle of the soul to his contem-
poraries in the way I have just outlined, as something
scientifically unavoidable.

From all this the impartial observer today must draw a
conclusion. It is that, in the study of man, scientific methods
will take us only to the point they have now reached, but that
we cannot deal with the soul by means of ordinary consciousness – entirely adequate as this is for science and for ordinary
life. And so, since for scientific reasons this fact must be
apparent to the impartial observer today, I speak to you from
the standpoint of a philosophy of life that concludes: it is
impossible, with the soul-powers that manifest themselves to
ordinary consciousness and operate in ordinary life and
ordinary science, to investigate the life of the soul. There must
be developed other powers that to ordinary consciousness are
more or less sleeping or, let us say, latent in the soul.

To adopt the right attitude to such a conception of life, we
need something which, if I may say so, is found only rarely in
people today. I would call it intellectual modesty. There must
come a moment in life when we say to ourselves: when I was a
little child, I developed a mental life that was so dim and dreamy
that it has been forgotten like a dream; only gradually did there

arise from this dreamlike mentality of the child something that enables me to orientate myself in life, to bring my thoughts, my impulses and my decisions into step with the world, and to become a capable being. Out of the vagueness and lack of differentiation of the child's mental life, interwoven with the body, has emerged that experience which derives from our inherited qualities, as these develop with the growth of the body, and which derives also from our customary education.

Anyone looking back, with intellectual modesty, on his development during his life on earth will not be above saying to himself at a certain point: why shouldn't this continue? The soul-powers which are the most important to me today, and by which I orientate myself in life and become a capable being, were dormant during my existence as a child. Why shouldn't there be dormant in my soul other powers that I can develop from it?

We cannot help reaching this conclusion, which springs from intellectual modesty. I call it intellectual modesty because people are inclined to say: the form of consciousness I have once attained as an adult is that of the normal person; any impulse in the life of the soul to be different from this so-called normal consciousness is eccentric or hallucinatory or visionary or something similar. The philosophical standpoint from which I speak definitely starts from a healthy psyche and attempts on this basis to develop powers dormant in the soul, cognitive powers, which then become clairvoyant powers in the sense in which I spoke yesterday of exact clairvoyance. What the soul has to undertake I indicated yesterday. I mentioned my books *Knowledge of Higher Worlds, Occult Science, Riddles of the Soul* and so on. There you will find details of those exercises which, starting from a healthy soul-life, lead upward to the development of the soul, which thus in fact attains a kind of spiritual vision with which it can see into a spiritual world, just as with the ordinary sense-organs it can perceive the physical and sensuous world. In each of these books there is a first part, which is accepted as something that can be definitely useful to man even by many opponents of the philosophy of life I am advocating. It shows that by certain exercises of an intellectual, emotional and moral kind man can produce in himself a state of soul and body that can be regarded as wholly healthy. They also enable him to be on his inner guard against anything which, deriving from an unhealthy life of the soul, leads to mediumism, hallucinations and visions. For everything brought about in this way is unacceptable to a true psychology. Visions arise not from the sphere of the soul, but because morbid structures exist in the organism; the same is true of mediumism. None of these have anything to do with sound psychology and sound psychic development, and indeed from the point of view of this sound psychology all must be condemned. Opponents today, however, find fantastic and harmful the exercises which follow these preparatory ones, and which are designed to draw from the soul those powers of thinking, feeling and volition which, once they are trained, introduce man into a spiritual world in such a way that he learns to orientate himself in it and can enter it at will.

I have already suggested how, as modern man, we manage by certain mental exercises to remove thinking from its ordinary state of passive surrender to the phenomena of the outside world, and to what appear inwardly as memories but are also connected with the outside world. We transcend this kind of thinking by carrying out exercises in meditation seriously, patiently and energetically, and by repeating them over and over again. Depending on predisposition, it may take one person years, another not so long; but each can note, as he arrives at the crucial point, how his thinking, from what I have previously called dead and abstract thinking, becomes inwardly vital thinking in tune with the rhythm of the world. A balanced view of the world and of life thus strives not to conjure up visions or hallucinations from the soul but to experience the life of thoughts and concepts with an intensity that we otherwise experience only through the outward senses.

You need only compare the vitality of our experience of the

colours we perceive through the eye, and the sounds we hear through the ear, with the pallor of our experience of thought in ordinary consciousness. By energizing our mental life in the way I suggested yesterday, we can gradually give the mere life of thought and concept the same intensive quality as the life of the senses. Man today, seeking to know the spiritual, does not therefore, if he is a reasonable being, seek hallucinations and visions. He strives quite calmly to achieve the ideal of the life of the senses, with its intensity and plasticity, in his mental activity. And if you devote yourselves as students of the spirit to meditations such as I have described, you need not be in any way dependent on the unconscious or subconscious. You can refer to the exercises, they are all directed at what I am trying to describe – and you will find that everything that is carried out by way of exercises in the life of the soul is done as consciously, as reasonably, as precisely we may say, as are operations in mathematics or geometry.

To sum up: we are concerned here not with the old nebulous clairvoyance, but with a clairvoyance brought about by fully conscious and balanced experiences and exercises of the soul. The self-possession at each step is such that we can compare what a person experiences and makes of himself here with what we otherwise experience in the case of a geometrical problem. If not, the exercises have no value.

A conceptual life of this kind is energized, is independent of breathing, is set free of the body, is a spiritual function only; and in it, as we know by direct perception, thinking is carried out not by the body but in the purely spiritual sphere. Only when modern man attains this kind of conceptual life does he feel his thinking, in contrast to abstract thinking, as something vital and not as something dead. Our sensation when we experience the transition from ordinary abstract thinking to vital thinking is exactly as if we found a dead organism suddenly come to life. And although this vital thinking is a spiritual process, it is not so linear, not so superficial as ordinary abstract thinking. It is full and pictorial. And this picture-quality is what counts.

Now, however, a very great deal depends on our carrying over the balanced attitude, required during the actual exercises, to the moment when this vitalized or pictorial thinking appears in us. If at this moment we surrender ourselves to the images we have struggled to achieve, believing we find in them realities of a spiritual kind, then we are not students of the spirit but simply fantasy-mongers. This is something we must certainly not become, for it could not provide us with a firmly based philosophy of life for modern man. Only when we say to ourselves: we have attained one component of spiritual life, but it is a semblance component; it merely tells us something about powers that operate within ourselves, about what we ourselves can do through our own human nature; only when we really say to ourselves, this pictorial knowledge cannot give us any information about any kind of outside world, not even about what we are in the outside world; only if we perceive *ourselves* in this semblance-making and know *ourselves* as a power living within it – only then do we have the right attitude to this experience and feel ourselves as spiritual beings outside the body, and yet feel ourselves within the inner imaginative quality of our being.

Only by having the courage to continue the exercises to the next stage do we attain true spiritual perception. This next stage not only involves developing the capacity to focus our consciousness upon certain concepts that are readily comprehended – as we comprehend geometrical concepts, which we know to contain no unconscious element – so as to increase our strength of soul; it must also, and more particularly, involve being able calmly and at will to banish these concepts from our consciousness. This is, in some circumstances, a difficult task! In ordinary life, forgetting is not particularly difficult, as our ordinary consciousness is only too well aware. But when one has just struggled, although without driving oneself into auto-suggestion – which cannot occur if we are self-possessed – to focus one's consciousness upon certain concepts, then unusual strength is required to banish them from consciousness again. However, one must develop this greater strength gradually; and just as at first we concentrated all our attention and inner strength of soul, so that we might dwell upon such a concept in a state of meditation, so now we must dispel these concepts, and all other concepts, calmly and voluntarily from consciousness. And there must be able to enter, from our will, what one might call 'empty consciousness'. What 'empty consciousness' (if only for a few moments) implies, can be judged by reflecting on what happens to ordinary consciousness when it has to forgo both sense-impressions and recollections – when for some reason or other man is deprived of external impressions and even memories: he falls asleep; that is, consciousness is suppressed and dimmed. The opposite of this is what must happen: completely controlled, conscious wakefulness, despite the fact that the will has swept consciousness completely clear.

If we thus first strengthen the soul and then empty it, yet keep it conscious, there will appear before it, as colour to the eye and sounds to the ear, a spiritual environment. We can look into the spiritual world. And so we may say: to the spiritual investigation here intended, it is perfectly under-standable that ordinary consciousness cannot reach the spirit and the soul, and indeed that it turns out, as Richard Wahle found for instance, that ordinary consciousness ought not to speak of an 'I' at all! For in this sphere, ordinary experience can only indicate and label with words a dark element which is immersed in and contrasted with the clear light, and which will never emerge until we have developed powers that are usually lacking. It is a sober recognition of the limits of ordinary consciousness, tied to the body, that impels us to develop in ourselves those powers that alone are capable of really discovering the soul and the spirit.

There is another point to consider, however, if you seek to arrive by this path at a sound and not a morbid psychology. Taking the mediumistic, visionary and hallucinatory as mor-bid, the fact is that anyone who falls into this kind of morbid psychic activity is entirely absorbed into it. For the duration of his sickness of soul, at least, he becomes one with this activity. Quite the reverse with the exercises I have been proposing here. Anyone who explores the soul with their aid does, it is true, leave behind his physical body with its capacity for ordinary thinking and ordinary orientation in life. He steps out of this body and learns to see imaginatively, free of body; he develops a visual thinking. Yet not for a moment is he completely subsumed in this higher man, if I may so call it without arrogance. He always remains capable of regaining his body and acting just as calmly as before; there always stands beside this more highly developed man that ordinary man with his healthy common sense who is a sober critic of everything to which in his vision this higher being attains.

By developing plastic, vital thinking and then creating an empty consciousness, we reach a view of our own psychic nature, one that embraces in a single image all we have encountered in this life since we entered it. Our past life does not stand before the soul as is usual in the memory, with isolated reminiscences emerging, independently or after some exertion. Instead, all at once our life is surveyed like a mighty tableau, not in space but in time. All at once, with a single glance of the soul, we survey our life; but we see it as it informs our growth and the energies of our physical body. We see ourselves as we have been here on this earth as thinking, feeling, willing beings, but in such a way that thinking, feeling and willing now densify and at the same time take their places organically within the human substance. We can see into our spiritual life in its direct association with the physical. We cease trying to establish by philosophical speculation how the soul affects the body. In seeing the soul, we also see how at every moment our physical life on earth has been informed by what the tableau shows us.

The next step must now be to strengthen the energized concepts that we have introduced into ourselves by removing them from our consciousness. We do this by continually repeating the exercises, just as we strengthen muscles by repeated exercise. And by continuing with these energized concepts, we also manage to eliminate from our consciousness this whole newly achieved tableau of the life of the soul from birth to the present. This requires more effort than the simple elimination of images, but one does eventually achieve it. We succeed in removing from consciousness what in our earthly existence we call our inner life, so that now our consciousness is empty not only of current impressions but also of all that we experience within as if in a second and finer body (which yet informs our growth and our memory), a finer being, an ethereal being as it were, and now, for the first time, a supersensible being. And when we do so, our consciousness, which though fully awake is now empty and yet has attained a greater inward power, will be able to see further in the spiritual world. It will now be able to look at the nature of its own soul before this descended from spiritual worlds to an earthly existence. Now, what we call the eternity of the human soul is taken out of the sphere of mere philosophical speculation and actually beheld. We learn to look at the purely spiritual that we were in a spiritual world, before we descended to clothe ourselves, through conception, foetal life and birth, in a physical earthly body.

Although attained by a method as exact as mathematical concepts, this may seem fantastic to many people today. Still more paradoxical may appear what remains to be said, not only about the soul when it still had a spiritual existence but also about the concrete nature of this experience. These things can only be suggested in this lecture; more will be said in subsequent lectures. The suggestions can perhaps be explained in the following terms.

Let us first ask ourselves: what do we actually see when, in ordinary life, as beings who recognize, understand and perceive, we enter into a relationship with our natural environment? We actually see only the external world. This is clear from what I mentioned at the beginning today. We actually see only the outside world, the cosmos. What takes place within us we see, too, but only by making it into something external through physiology and anatomy. Imposing as these sciences may be, we see what is within only by first externalizing it and then investigating it exactly as we are accustomed to do with external processes. Yet it remains dark down there in the region into which we descend, where we feel our spiritual element flowing into our body. In the last analysis, we see in ordinary life only what is outside ourselves; by direct observation we cannot look directly into man and see how the spiritual informs the bodily organs. Anyone, however, who can examine life impartially from the spiritual viewpoint I have established will conclude: noble and great is external appearance and the laws we discover in the external world of the stars and of the sun, which sends us light and warmth; noble and great is our experience when we either simply look – and we are complete people when we do so look – or when we investigate scientifically the laws by which the sun sends us light and warmth and conjures forth the green of plants; noble and mighty is all this – but if we could look into the structure of the human heart, its inner law would be even nobler and greater than what we perceive outside!

Man can sense this with his ordinary consciousness. But the science that rests on exact clairvoyance can raise it to the status of true research. It can say: the changes in the atmosphere appear to us to be far-reaching, and there exists an ideal of science which, here too, will discover greater and more potent laws; but greater still is what is present and goes on in the structure and functions of the human lung! It is not a question of size. Man is a microcosm in face of the macrocosm. But as Schiller said: 'In space, my friend, dwells not the sublime.' He means the highest form of the sublime. This highest form can be experienced only in the human organism itself.

Between birth and death it is not investigated by man with his ordinary consciousness. Exactly the opposite is true, however, of our existence before we unite with the body – our spiritual existence, in a spiritual environment. In this life on earth, the inner world is dark and the outside world of the cosmos bright and full of sound; in the purely spiritual life before our earthly embodiment, the outer cosmic world is dark, and our world is then the inner world of man. We see this inner world! And truly, it seems to us no smaller and no less majestic than does the cosmos when we see it with our physical eyes during our earthly existence. As if it were our 'outside world', we come to understand the law of our spiritual inner world, and we prepare ourselves, in the spiritual realm, for dealing later with our bodily functions, with what we are between birth and death. For what we are between birth and death extends before us like a world, before we descend into this physical existence on earth.

This is not speculation. It is direct perception arising from exact clairvoyance. It is something which, starting from this exact clairvoyance, leads us some way into the connection between the eternal element in man and the life on earth – that eternal element which remains hidden from us between birth and death, and of which we see the first gleams when we are able to perceive it in the still unembodied state. And with this we explore a part of human eternity itself. We do not even have a word in our modern languages for this part of human eternity. We rightly speak of immortality; but we ought also to speak of 'unbornness'. For this now confronts us as a direct experience.

This is one aspect of exact clairvoyance, one aspect of human eternity, of the great riddle of the human soul, and thus of the supreme problem of psychology in general. The other aspect arises from those other exercises, which I yesterday termed exercises of the will, through which we so take in hand our will that we learn to make use of it independently of the body. I explained that these exercises induce us to overcome pain and suffering within the soul, in order to make it into a 'sense-organ' (to speak loosely) or a spiritual organ (to speak exactly) of vision, so that we not only look at the

spiritual but see its authentic shape. And when we learn to
experience in this way outside our body, not only with our
thoughts but with our will itself – that is, with our entire
human substance – there appears before the soul the image of
death, in such a way that we now know the nature of
experience without the body, both in thinking and in willing
and in what lies between, feeling. In a creative and imaginative way we learn to live without the body. And in doing so we
gain an image of our passage through the gate of death; we
learn how in reality, too, we can do without the body and how,
passing through the gate of death, we enter once more that
spiritual sphere from which we descended into this bodily
existence. What is eternal and immortal in us becomes not
only philosophical certainty but direct perception. By training the will, we disclose for the soul's contemplation the other
side of eternity – immortality – just as unbornness is disclosed
by the training of thought.

When the soul becomes a spiritual organ in this way,
however, it is as if, at a lower level, a person born blind had
been operated on. What for those endowed with sight is a
world of colours, the blind person has hitherto been accustomed to perceive by touch alone. Now, after the operation,
he sees something quite new The world in which he previously lived has changed. So too, anyone whose 'mind's eye'
is opened in the way I have described finds that his environment is changed. How far it is changed I wish to bring out
today in only one respect.

Even with our *unopened* 'mind's eye' we can see in life how,
for example, a person takes his childish steps, then grows up
and reaches a fateful moment in his life: he meets someone,
and their souls link up so that the two people combine their
fates and move on through life together. (As I said before, I
want to single out just one event.) In ordinary consciousness
we are drawn to regard what happens in life as a sum of chance
occurrences; to regard it, too, as more or less chance that we
are brought at last to this fateful meeting with the other

person. Only a few individuals, like Goethe's friend Knebel, gain an inner wisdom of experience simply in growing older. He once put this to Goethe in the following words: if at an advanced age one looks back on the course of one's steps in life, one finds that these steps seem to reveal a systematic arrangement, so that everything appears to have been present in embryo and to have developed in such a way that one was led by a kind of inner necessity to what we now see to have been a fateful event. Human existence as seen with the 'mind's eye' unveiled is as different from the life observed by the unopened eyes as the world of colour is from the merely tactile one of the blind person.

Looking at the child's soul life and the interplay of sympathy and antipathy, we see how it develops from these first steps; how then, welling up out of his innermost being, the man himself, out of his innermost longings, directs his steps and brings himself to the fateful moment. This is sober observation of life. When we look at life in this way, however, we see it rather as we see the life of an old person. We should not say that an old person's life simply exists 'in its own right'. By logical processes we know how to refer it to its infant beginnings; its very idiosyncrasies *make* us so refer it. What simple logic does for the old person's life is done for human life in general by exact clairvoyance, by true vision. If we are really to look at life as it develops from the innermost longings of the soul, we must follow it back. And when we do so, we come to *earlier* lives on earth, in which were prepared the longings that appear in the *present* and lead to *our* activities.

I have not been able to do more today than suggest that what leads to this comprehensive contemplation of life is not a tissue of fantasy, but an exact method. It is a contemplation which, by means of an advanced psychology, penetrates to the eternal in human nature. And on this foundation there now arises something that is a certainty, something that wells up out of the knowledge appropriate to us as modern people today and forms a basis for true inner piety and true inner religious life.

Anyone with an insight (and I may say that I am using the word 'insight' in its literal sense) into the way the individual soul struggles free of the body, in order to enter a spiritual realm, will have a different way of looking at our social life too. Armed with this new attitude, he can see how friendships, relationships of love, and other associations are formed; how soul finds its way to soul, moving outside the family and other social groups; how physical proximity may be a means to the community of souls, the sympathy and togetherness of souls. He now knows that, just as the body falls away from the individual soul, so the physical element and all earthly events fall away from the friendships and from the relationships of love; and he sees how the soul-relationship that has come into being between people continues into a spiritual world, where it can also be spiritually experienced.

On a foundation of knowledge, not of faith, we can now say: as they stride through the Gate of Death, human beings find themselves once more together. And just as the body, which impedes our sight of the spirit, disappears in the spiritual world, so too in that world every impediment to friendship and love now disappears. Human beings are closer together there than in the flesh. A mode of knowledge that may still appear abstract in relation to true psychology culminates in this religious feeling and vision. Yet the philosophy of life I am here presenting does not seek to infringe religious faith. This philosophy can be tolerant; it can recognize fully the value of every individual religious faith, and even exercise it in process; but at the same time, as a nurse to this religious life, it provides an epistemological basis for this religious life too.

I have sought today to say something basic about the relationship to psychology of a spiritually appropriate modern view of life. I know, better than many an opponent perhaps, the objections that can be raised to the beginnings of such a philosophy. But I believe I also know that, albeit entirely unconsciously, the longing for such a psychology is present today in countless souls. It therefore needs to be said over and over again: just as one does not need to be a painter to feel the beauty of a picture, so too one does not need to be a spiritual scientist oneself – although one *can* become one up to a point – to be able to test whether what I am saying here is true. Just as one can feel the beauty of a picture without being a painter oneself, so with ordinary common sense one can perceive what the spiritual scientist says about the soul. That one *can* see it, I think I have established all the more firmly in recognizing how souls thirst for a more profound approach to psychology and to the great riddles of existence in relation to the soul. The aim of a modern view of life such as has been outlined here today does in fact represent the desire of countless people, though they are not ordinarily aware of it; it forms the pain, the sorrow, the privation, the wish of countless people – of all those who are serious about what we must regard as constructive forces in face of the many forces of decline present in our age.

Anyone today who wishes to advocate a philosophy for the times must realize that he has to speak, think and will in harmony with what the souls in our serious age, if in many cases unconsciously, strive for. And I believe – if I may close on this note – that just such a philosophy as I have adumbrated does hold something of what countless souls strive for today, something of what they need as spiritual content and vital spiritual activity for the present and for the immediate future.

XII. Sense-free Perception[36]

Vienna, 26th September 1923

ANYONE WHO speaks today about supersensible worlds lays himself open at once to the quite understandable criticism that he is violating one of the most important demands of the age. This is the demand that the most important questions of existence be seriously discussed from a scientific point of view only in such a way that science recognizes its own limitations, having clear insight into the fact that it must restrict itself to the physical world of earthly existence and would undoubtedly become a degenerate fantasy if it were to go beyond these limits. Now, precisely the type of spiritual scientific perception about which I spoke at the last Vienna Congress of the Anthroposophical Movement (and shall speak again today), lays claim not only to being free from hostility towards scientific thinking and the scientific sense of responsibility of our times, but also to working in complete harmony with the most conscientious scientific demands of those very persons who stand on the ground of the most rigorous natural science. It is possible, however, to speak from various points of view regarding the scientific demands of the times which are imposed on us by the theoretical and practical results in the evolution of humanity, which have emerged in such a splendid way in the course of the last three or four centuries, but especially during the nineteenth century. Therefore, I shall speak today about supersensible knowledge in so far as it tends to fulfil precisely this demand.

We can observe the magnificent contribution which scientific research has brought us even up to the most recent time – the magnificent contribution in the findings about relationships throughout the external world. But it is possible to speak in a different sense regarding the achievements which have come about precisely in connection with this current of human evolution. For instance, we may call attention to the fact that, through the conscientious, earnest observation of the laws and facts of the external world of the senses, as is supplied by natural science, very special human capacities have been developed, and that just such observation and experimentation have thrown a light also upon human capacities themselves. But I should like to say that many persons holding positions deserving the greatest respect in the sphere of scientific research are willing to give very little attention to this light which has been reflected upon man himself through his own researches.

If we only give a little thought to what this light has illuminated, we see that human thinking, through the very fact that it has been able to investigate both narrow and vast relationships, the microscopic and the telescopic, has gained immeasurably in itself, has gained in the capacity of discrimination, has gained in power of penetration, to associate the things in the world so that their secrets are unveiled, and to determine the laws underlying cosmic relationships, and so forth. We see, as this thinking develops, that a standard is set for this thinking, and it is set precisely for the most earnest of those who take up this research: the demand that this thinking must develop as selflessly as possible in the observation of external nature and in experimentation in the laboratory, in the clinic, etc. And the human being has achieved tremendous power in this respect. He has succeeded in setting up more and more rules whose character prevents anything of the nature of inner wishes of the heart, of opinions, perhaps even of fantasies regarding one's own being such as arise in the course of thinking, from being carried over into what he is to establish by means of the microscope and the telescope, the measuring rule and the scales, regarding the relationships of life and existence.

Under these influences a type of thinking has gradually

developed about which one must say that it has worked out its passive role with a certain inner diligence. Thinking in connection with observation, with experiment, has nowadays become completely abstract – so abstract that it does not trust itself to conjure anything of the nature of knowledge or of truth from its own inner being.

It is this gradually developed characteristic of thinking which demands before everything else – and above all it seems – the rejection of all that the human being is in himself by reason of his inner nature. For what he himself is must be set forth in activity; this can really never exist wholly apart from the impulse of his will. Thus we have arrived at the point – and we have rightly reached this point in the field of external research – of actually rejecting the activity of thinking, although we became aware in this activity of what we ourselves mean as human beings in the universe, in the totality of cosmic relationships. In a certain sense, the human being has eliminated himself in connection with his research; he prohibits his own inner activity. We shall see immediately that what is rightly prohibited in connection with this external research must be especially cultivated in relationship to man's own self if he wishes to gain enlightenment about the spiritual, about the supersensible element of his own being.

But a second element in the nature of man has been obliged to manifest its particular side in modern research, a side which is alien to humanity even though friendly to the world: that is, the human life of sentiment, the human life of feeling. In modern research, human feeling is not permitted to participate; the human being must remain cold and matter-of-fact. Yet one might ask whether it were possible to acquire within this human feeling forces useful in gaining knowledge of the world. One can say, on the one hand, that inner human caprice plays a role in feelings, in human subjectivity, and that feeling is the source of fantasy. On the other hand, one can reply that human feeling can certainly play no distinct role as it exists chiefly in everyday and in scientific life. Yet, if we recall – as science itself must describe it to us – that the human senses have not always, in the course of human evolution, been such as they are today, but have developed from a relatively imperfect stage up to their present state, if we recall that they certainly did not express themselves in earlier periods as objectively about things as they do today, an inkling may then dawn in us that there may exist, even within the life of subjective feeling, something that might evolve just as did the human senses themselves, and which might be led from an experience of man's own being over to a comprehension of cosmic relationships in a higher sense. Precisely as we observe the withdrawal of human feeling in connection with contemporary research must the question be raised: could not some higher sense unfold within feeling itself, if feeling were particularly developed?

But we find eminently clear in a third element in the being of man how we are impelled from an altogether praiseworthy scientific view to something different: this is the will aspect of the life of the soul. Whoever is at home in scientific thinking knows how impossible it is for such thinking to grasp the relationships of the world other than through causal necessity. We link in the most rigid manner phenomena existing side by side in space; we link in the strictest sense phenomena occurring one after another in time. That is, we relate cause and effect according to their inflexible laws. Whoever speaks not as a dilettante but as one thoroughly at home in science knows what a tremendous power is exerted by the mere consideration of the realms of scientific fact in this manner. He knows how he is captivated by this idea of a universal causality and how he cannot do otherwise than to subject everything that he confronts in his thinking to this idea of causality.

But there is human will, this human will which says to us in every moment of our waking life of day: 'What you undertake in a certain sense by reason of yourself, by reason of your will, is not causally determined in the same sense that applies to any sort of external phenomena of nature.' For this reason, even a person who simply feels in a natural way about himself, who looks into himself in observation free from preconception, can scarcely do otherwise than also to ascribe to himself, on the basis of immediate experience, freedom of will. But when he turns his glance to scientific thinking, he cannot admit this freedom of will. This is one of the conflicts into which we are brought by the condition of the present age. In the course of our lectures we shall learn much more about the conflicts. But for one who is able to feel this conflict in its full intensity, who can feel it through and through – because he must be honest on the one side concerning scientific research, and on the other side concerning his self-observation – the conflict is something utterly confounding, so confounding that it may drive him to doubt whether there is anywhere in life a firm basis from which one may search for truth.

We must deal with such conflicts from the right human perspective. We must be able to say to ourselves that research drives us to the point where we are actually unable to admit what we are every day aware of: that something else must somehow exist which offers another approach to the world than that which is offered to us in irrefutable manner in the external order of nature. Through the very fact that we are so forcibly driven into such conflicts by the order of nature itself, it becomes for human beings of the present time a necessity to admit the impossibility of speaking about the supersensible worlds as they have been spoken about until a relatively recent time. We need go back only to the first half of the nineteenth century to discover individuals who, by reason of a consciousness in harmony with the period, were thoroughly serious in their scientific work, and yet who called attention to the supersensible aspect of human life, to that aspect which opens up to the human being a view of the Divine, of his own immortality; and in this connection they always called attention to what we may at present designate as the 'night aspects' of human life. People deserving of the very highest regard have called attention to that wonderful but very problematical world into which the human being is transferred every night:

to the dream world. They have called attention to many mysterious relationships which exist between this chaotic picture-world of dreams and the world of actuality. They have called attention to the fact that the inner nature of the human organization, especially in illness, reflects itself in the fantastic pictures of dreams, and how healthy human life enters into the chaotic experiences of dreams in the forms of signs and symbols. They pointed out that much which cannot be surveyed by the human being with his waking senses finds its place in the half-awake state of the soul, and out of such matters conclusions were drawn. These matters border upon the subject that many people still study today, the 'subconscious' states of the life of the human soul, which manifest themselves in a similar way.

But everything which appears before the human being in this form, which could still give a certain satisfaction to an earlier humanity, is no longer valid for us. It is no longer valid for us because our way of looking into external nature has become something different. Here we have to look back to the times when there existed still only a mystically coloured astrology. Man then looked into the world of the senses in such a way that his perception was far removed from the exactness which we demand of science today. Because he did not demand of himself in his sense life that complete clarity which we possess today, he could discover in a mystical, half-conscious state something from which he could draw inferences. This we cannot do today. Just as little as we are able to derive today, from what natural science gives us directly, anything other than questions regarding the true nature of man, just so little can we afford to remain at a standstill at the point reached by natural science and expect to satisfy our supersensible needs in a manner similar to that of earlier times.

That form of supersensible knowledge of which I shall speak here has an insight into this demand of our times. It observes what has become of thinking, feeling and willing in man precisely through natural science, and it asks, on the other side, whether it may be possible by reason of the very achievements of contemporary humanity in thinking, feeling and willing to penetrate further into the supersensible realm with the same clarity which holds sway in the scientific realm. This cannot be achieved by means of inferential reasoning, by means of logic; for natural science justly points out its limitations with reference to its own nature. But something else can occur: the inner human capacities may evolve further, beyond the point at which they stand when we are in the realm of ordinary scientific research, so that we now apply to the development of our own spiritual capacities the same exactness which we are accustomed to applying to research in the laboratory and the clinic. I shall discuss this first in connection with thinking itself.

Thinking, which has become more and more conscious of its passive role in connection with external research, and is not willing to disavow this, is capable of energizing itself inwardly to activity. It may energize itself in such a way that, although not exact in the sense in which we apply this term to measure and weight in external research, it is exact in relationship to its own development in the sense in which the external scientist, the mathematician, for example, is accustomed to follow with full consciousness every step in his research. But this occurs when that mode of supersensible cognition of which I am here speaking replaces the ancient vague meditation, the ancient indistinct immersion of oneself in thinking, with a truly exact development of this thinking. It is possible here to indicate only the general principles of what I have said regarding such an exact development of thinking in *Occult Science: An Outline, Knowledge of the Higher Words: How is it Achieved?* and other books. The human being should really compel himself, for the length of time which is necessary for him – and this is determined by the varying innate capacities of people – to exchange the role of passive surrender to the external world, which he otherwise rightly assumes in his thinking, for that different role: that of introducing into this thinking his whole inner activity of soul. This he should do by taking into his mind day by day, even though at times only for a brief period, some particular thought – the content of which is not the important matter – and, while withdrawing his inner nature from the external world, directing all the powers of his soul in inner concentration upon this thought. By means of this process something comes about in the development of those capacities of soul that may be compared with the results which follow when any particular muscles of the human body – for instance, the muscles of the arms – are to be developed. The muscles are made stronger, more powerful through use, through exercise. Thus, likewise, do the capacities of the soul become inwardly stronger, more powerful by being directed upon a definite thought. This exercise must be arranged so that we proceed in a really exact way, so that we survey every step taken in our thinking just as a mathematician surveys his operations when he undertakes to solve a geometrical or arithmetical problem. This can be done in the greatest variety of ways. When I say that something should be selected for this content of concentration that one finds in any sort of book – even some worthless old volume that we know quite certainly we have never previously seen – this may seem trivial. The important point is not the content of truth in the thing, but the fact that we survey such a thought content completely. This cannot be done if we take a thought content out of our own memory; for so much is associated with such a thought in the most indeterminate way, so much plays a role in the subconscious or the unconscious, and it is not possible to be exact if one concentrates upon such a thing. What one fixes, therefore, in the very centre of one's consciousness, is something entirely new, something that one confronts only with respect to its actual content, which is not associated with any experience of the soul. What matters is the concentration of the forces of the soul and the strengthening which results from this. Likewise, if one goes to a person who has made some progress in this field and requests him to provide one with such a thought content, it is good not to entertain a prejudice against this. The content is in that case entirely new to the person concerned, and he can survey it. Many persons fear that they may become dependent in this way upon someone else who provides them with such a content. But this is not the case; in reality, they become less dependent than if they take such a thought content out of their own memories and experiences, in which case it is bound up with all sorts of subconscious experiences. Moreover, it is good for a person who has had some practice in scientific work to use the findings of scientific research as material for concentration; these prove to be, indeed, the most fruitful of all for this purpose.

If this is continued for a relatively long time, even for years, perhaps – and this must be accompanied by patience and endurance, as it requires a few weeks or months in some cases before success is achieved, and in some cases years – it is possible to arrive at a point where this method for the inner moulding of one's thoughts can be applied as exactly as the physicist or the chemist applies the methods of measuring and weighing for the purpose of discovering the secrets of nature. What one has then learned is applied to the further development of one's own thinking. At a certain moment, then, the person has a significant inner experience: he feels himself to be involved not only in picture-thinking, which depicts the external events and facts and which is true to reality in inverse proportion to the force it possesses in itself, in proportion as it is a mere picture; but one arrives now at the point of adding to this kind of thinking the inner experience of a thinking in which one lives, a thinking filled with inner power. This is a significant experience. Thinking thus becomes, as it were, something which one begins to experience just as one experiences the power of one's own muscles when one grasps an object or strikes against something. A reality such as one experiences otherwise only in connection with the process of breathing or the activity of a muscle – this inner activity now enters into thinking. And since one has investigated precisely every step upon this way, so one experiences oneself in full clarity and presence of mind in this strengthened, active thinking. If the objection is raised, let us say, that knowledge can result only from observation and logic, this is no real objection; for what we now experience is experienced with complete inner clarity, and yet in such a way that this thinking becomes at the same time a kind of 'touching with the soul.' In the process of forming a thought, it is as if we were extending a feeler – not, in this case, as the snail extends a feeler into the physical world, but as if a feeler were extended into a spiritual world that is as yet present only for our feelings if we have developed to this stage, but which we are justified in expecting. For one has the feeling: 'Your thinking has been transformed into a spiritual touching; if this can become more and more the case, you may expect that this thinking will come into contact with what constitutes a spiritual reality, just as your finger here in the physical world comes into contact with what is physically real.'

Only when one has lived for a time in this inwardly strengthened thinking does complete self-knowledge become possible. For we know then that the soul element has become, by means of this concentration, an experiential reality.

It is possible then for the person concerned to go forward in his exercises and to arrive at the point where he can, in turn, eliminate this soul content, put it away; he can, in a certain sense, render his consciousness void of what he himself has brought into this consciousness, this thought content upon which he has concentrated, and which has enabled him to possess a real thinking constituting a sense of touch for the soul. It is rather easy in ordinary life to acquire an empty consciousness; we need only fall asleep. But it requires an intense application of force, after we have become accustomed to concentrating upon a definite thought content, to put away such a content of thought in connection with this very strengthened thinking, thinking which has become a reality. Yet we succeed in putting aside this content of thinking in exactly the same way in which we acquired at first the powerful force needed for concentration. When we have succeeded in this, something appears before the soul which has been possible previously only in the form of pictures of episodes in one's memory: the whole inner life of the person appears in a new way before the eyes of his soul, as he has passed through this life in his earthly existence since birth, or since the earliest point of time to which one's memory can return, at which point one entered consciously into this earthly existence. Ordinarily, the only thing we know in regard to this earthly existence is that which we can call up in memory; we have pictures of our experiences. But what is now experienced by means of this strengthened thinking is not of the same kind. It appears as if in a tremendous tableau so that we do not recollect merely in a dim picture what we passed through ten years ago, for instance, but we have the inner experience that in spirit we are retracing the course of time. If someone carries out such an exercise in his fiftieth year, let us say, and arrives at the result indicated, what then happens is that time permits him to go back as if along a 'time-path' all the way, for instance, to the experiences of his thirty-fifth year. We travel back through time. We do not have only a dim memory of what we passed through fifteen years earlier, but we feel ourselves to be in the midst of this in its living reality, as if in an experience of the present moment. We travel through time; space loses its significance, and time affords us a mighty tableau of memory. This becomes a precise picture of man's life, such as appears, even according to scientific thinkers, when anyone is exposed to great terror, a severe shock – at the moment of drowning, for instance – when for some moments he is confronted by something of his entire earthly life in pictures appearing before his soul – to which he looks back later with a certain shuddering fascination. In other words, what appears before the soul in such cases as through a natural convulsion now actually appears before the soul at the moment indicated, when the entire earthly life confronts one as in a mighty tableau of the spirit, only in a time order. Only now does one know oneself; only now does one possess real self-observation.

It is quite possible to differentiate this picture of man's inner being from that which constitutes a mere 'memory' picture. It is clear in the memory picture that we have something in which persons, natural occurrences or works of art come upon us as if from without; in this memory picture what we have is the manner in which the world comes into contact with us. In the supersensible memory tableau which appears before a person, what confronts him is, rather, that which has proceeded from himself. If, for instance, at a certain definite point of time in his life he began a friendship with a beloved personality, the mere memory picture shows how this person came to him at a certain point of time, spoke to him, what he owes to the person, and so on. But in this life tableau what confronts him is the manner in which he himself longed for this person, and how he ultimately took every step in such a way that he was inevitably led to that being whom he recognized as being in harmony with himself.

That which has taken place through the unfolding of the forces of the soul comes to meet one with exact clarity in this life tableau. Many people do not like this precise clarity, because it brings them to enlightenment regarding much that they would prefer to see in a different light from the light of truth. But one must endure the fact that one is able to look upon one's own inner being in utter freedom from preconceptions, even if this being of oneself meets the searching eye with reproach. This state of cognition I have called imaginative knowledge, or Imagination.

But one can progress beyond this stage. In what we come to know through this memory tableau, we are confronted by those forces which have really formed us as human beings. One knows now: 'Within you those forces evolve which mould the substances of your physical body. Within you, especially during childhood, those forces have evolved which, approximately up to the seventh year, have plastically modelled the nerve masses of the brain, which did not yet exist in well-ordered form after your birth.' We then cease at last to ascribe what works formatively upon the human being to those forces which inhere in material substances. We cease to do this when we have this memory tableau before us, when we see how into all the forces of nutrition and of breathing and into the whole circulation of the blood-stream the contents of this memory tableau – which are forces in themselves, forces without which no single wave of the blood circulates and no single process of breathing occurs. We now learn to understand that man himself in his inner being consists of spirit and soul.

What now dawns upon one can best be described by a comparison. Imagine that you have walked for a certain distance over ground which has been softened by rain, and that you have noticed all the way tracks or ruts made by human feet or wagon wheels. Now suppose that a being came from the moon and saw this condition of the ground, but saw no human being. He would probably conclude that there must be all sorts of forces underneath the earth which have thrust up these traces and given this form to the surface of the ground. Such a being might seek within the earth for the forces which have produced the tracks. But one who sees through the matter knows that the condition was not caused by the earth but by human feet or the wheels of a wagon.

Now, anyone who possesses a view of things such as I have just described does not at all look, for this reason, with less reverence, for example, upon the convolutions of the human brain. Yet, just as he knows that those tracks on the surface of the earth do not derive from forces within the earth, he now knows that these convolutions of the brain do not derive from forces within the substance of the brain but that the spiritual-psychic entity of man is there, which he himself has now beheld, and that it works in such a way that our brain has these convolutions. This is the essential thing – to be driven to this view, so that we arrive at a conception of our own spirit-soul nature, so that the eye of the soul is really directed to the soul-spiritual element and to its manifestations in the external life.

But it is possible to progress still further. After we strengthen our inner being through concentrating upon a definite thought content and after we then empty our consciousness so that, instead of the images we ourselves have formed the content of our life appears before us, now we can put this memory tableau out of our consciousness, just as we previously eliminated a single concept, so that our consciousness is empty of this. We can now learn to apply this powerful force to efface from our consciousness that which we have come to know through a heightened self-observation as a spirit-soul being. In doing this, we efface nothing less than the inner being of our own soul life. We learned first in concentration to efface what is external, and we then learned to direct the gaze of our soul to our own spirit-soul entity, and this completely occupied the whole tableau of memory. If we now succeed in effacing this memory tableau itself, there comes about what I wish to designate as the truly empty consciousness. We have previously lived in the memory tableau or in what we ourselves have set up before our minds, but now something entirely different appears. That which lived within us we have now suppressed, and we confront the world with an empty consciousness. This signifies something extraordinary in the experience of the soul. Fundamentally speaking, I can describe at first only by means of a comparison what now appears to the soul, when the content of our own soul is effaced by means of the powerful inner force we apply. We need only think of the fact that, when the impressions of the external senses gradually die away, when there is a cessation of seeing, hearing, perhaps even of a distinct sense of touch, we sink into a state closely resembling the state of sleep. Now, however, when we efface the content of our own souls, we come to an empty state of consciousness, although this is not a state of sleep. We reach what I might call the state of being merely awake – that is, of being awake with an empty consciousness.

We may, perhaps, conceive this empty consciousness in the

following way. Imagine a modern city with all its noise and din. We may withdraw from the city, and everything becomes more and more quiet around us; but we finally arrive, perhaps deep within a forest. Here we find the absolute opposite of the noises of the city. We live in complete inner stillness, in hushed peace. If, now, I undertake to describe what follows, I must resort to a trivial comparison. We must raise the question whether this peace, this stillness, can be changed still further into something else. We may designate this stillness as the zero point in our perception of the external world. If we possess a certain amount of property and we subtract from this property, it is diminished. As we take away still more, it is further diminished and we finally arrive at zero and have nothing left. Can we then proceed still further? It may, perhaps, be undesirable to most persons, but the fact is that many do this; they decrease their possessions further by incurring debt. One then has less than zero, and one can still diminish what one has. In precisely the same way, we may at least imagine that the stillness, which is like the zero point of being awake, may be pushed beyond this zero into a sort of negative state. A super-stillness, a super-peace may augment the quietness. This is what is experienced by one who blots out his own soul content; he enters into a state of quietness of soul which lies below the zero point. An inner stillness of soul in the most intensified degree comes about during the state of wakefulness.

This cannot be attained without being accompanied by something else. This can be attained only when we feel that a certain state, linked with the picture images of our own self, passes over into another state. One who senses, who contemplates the first stage of the supersensible within himself, is in a certain state of well-being, that well-being and inner blissfulness to which the various religious creeds refer when they call attention to the supersensible and at the same time remind the human being that the supersensible brings to him the experience of a certain blissfulness in his inner being. Indeed, up to the point where one excluded one's own inner self, there was a certain sense of well-being, an intensified feeling of blissfulness. At that moment, however, when the stillness of soul comes about, this inner well-being is replaced completely by inner pain, inner deprivation, such as we have never known before – the sense that one is separated from all to which one is united in the earthly life, far removed not only from the feeling of one's own body but from the feeling of one's own experiences since birth. And this means a deprivation which increases to a frightful pain of soul. Many shrink back from this stage; they cannot find the courage to make the crossing from a certain lower clairvoyance, after eliminating their own content of soul, to the state of consciousness where resides that inner stillness. But if we pass into this stage in full consciousness, there begins to enter, in place of Imagination, that which I have called, in the books previously mentioned, Inspiration – I trust you will not take offence at these terms – the experience of a real spiritual world. After one has previously eliminated the world of the senses and established an empty consciousness, accompanied by inexpressible pain of soul, then the outer spiritual world comes to meet us. In the state of Inspiration we become aware of the fact that the human being is surrounded by a spiritual world just as the sense world exists for his outer senses.

And the first thing, in turn, that we behold in this spiritual world is our own pre-earthly existence. Just as we are otherwise conscious of earthly experiences by means of our ordinary memory, so does a cosmic memory now dawn for us: we look back into pre-earthly experiences, beholding what we were as spirit-soul beings in a purely spiritual world before we descended through birth to this earthly existence, when as spiritual beings we participated in the moulding of our own bodies. So do we look back upon the spiritual, the eternal, in the nature of man, to that which reveals itself to us as the pre-earthly existence, which we now know is not dependent upon the birth and death of the physical body, for it is that which existed before birth and before conception which made a human being out of this physical body derived from matter and heredity. Now for the first time one reaches a true concept also of physical heredity, since one sees what supersensible forces play into this – forces which we acquire out of a purely spiritual world, with which we now feel united just as we feel united with the physical world in the earthly life. Moreover, we now become aware that, in spite of the great advances registered in the evolution of humanity, much has been lost which belonged inherently to more ancient instinctive conceptions that we can no longer make use of today. The instinctive supersensible vision of humanity of earlier ages was confronted by this pre-earthly life as well as human immortality, regarding which we shall speak a little later. For eternity was conceived in ancient times in such a way that one grasped both its aspects. We speak nowadays of the immortality of the human soul – indeed, our language itself possesses only this word – but people once spoke, and the more ancient languages continue to show such words, of unborn-ness (*Ungeborenheit*) as the other aspect of the eternity of the human soul. Now, however, the times have somewhat changed. People are interested in the question of what becomes of the human soul after death, because this is something still to come; but as to the other question, what existed before birth, before conception, there is less interest because that has 'passed', and yet we are here. But a true knowledge of human immortality can arise only when we consider eternity in both its aspects: that of immortality and that of unborn-ness.

But, for the very purpose of maintaining a connection with the latter, and especially in an exact clairvoyance, still a third thing is necessary. We sense ourselves truly as human beings when we no longer permit our feelings to be completely absorbed within the earthly life. For that which we now come to know as our pre-earthly life penetrates into us in pictures and is added to what we previously sensed as our humanity, making us for the first time completely human. Our feelings are then, as it were, shot through with inner light, and we know that we have now developed our feeling into a sense-organ for the spiritual. But we must go further and must be able to make our will element into an organ of knowledge for the spiritual.

For this purpose, something must begin to play a role in human knowledge which, very rightly, is not otherwise considered as a means of knowledge by those who desire to be taken seriously in the realm of cognition. We first become aware that this is a means of knowledge when we enter the supersensible realms. This is the force of love. However, we must begin to develop this force of love in a higher sense than that in which nature has bestowed love upon us, with all its significance for the life of nature and of man. The first steps in the unfolding of a higher love in the life of man, which I must describe, may seem paradoxical.

When you try, with full discretion for each step, to perceive the world in another consciousness than one usually feels, then you come to the higher love. Suppose you undertake in the evening, before you go to sleep, to bring your day's life into your consciousness so that you begin with the last occurrence of the evening, visualizing it as precisely as possible, then visualizing in the same way the next preceding, then the third from the last, thus moving backward to the morning in this survey of the life of the day; this is a process in which much more importance attaches to the inner energy expended than to the question whether one visualizes each individual occurrence more or less precisely. What is important is this reversal of the order of visualization. Ordinarily we view events in such a way that we first consider the earlier and then the subsequent in a consecutive chain. Through such an exercise as I have just described to you, we reverse the whole life; we think and feel in a direction opposite to the course of the day. We can practise this on the experiences of our day, as I have suggested, and this requires only a few minutes. But we can do this also in a different way. Undertake to visualize the course of a drama in such a way that you begin with the fifth act and picture it advancing forwards through the fourth, third, towards the beginning. Or we may place before ourselves a melody in the reverse succession of tones. If we pass through more and more such inner experiences of the soul in this way, we shall discover that the inner experience is freed from the external course of nature, and that we actually become more and more self-directing. But, even though we become in this way more and more individualized and achieve an ever-increasing power of self-direction, we learn also to give attention to the external life in more complete consciousness. For only now do we become aware that the more powerfully we develop through practice this fully conscious absorption in another being the higher becomes the degree of our selflessness, and the greater must our love become in compensation. In this way we feel how this experience of not living in oneself but living in another being this passing over from one's own being to another, becomes more and more powerful. We then reach the stage where, to Imagination and Inspiration, which we have already developed, we can now add the true intuitive ascending into another being: we arrive at Intuition, so that we no longer experience only ourselves, but also learn – in complete individualism yet also in complete selflessness – to experience the other being.

Here love becomes something which gradually makes it possible for us to look back even further than into the pre-earthly spiritual life. As we learn in our present life to look back upon contemporary events, we learn through such an elevation of love to look back upon former earth lives, and to recognize the entire life of a human being as a succession of earthly lives. The fact that these lives once had a beginning and must likewise have an end will be touched upon in another lecture.[37] But we learn to know the human life as a succession of lives on earth, between which there always intervene purely spiritual lives, coming between a death and the next birth. For this elevated form of love, lifted to the spiritual sphere and transformed into a force of knowledge, teaches us also the true significance of death. When we have

SENSE-FREE PERCEPTION 237

advanced so far, as I have explained in connection with Imagination and Inspiration, as to render these intensified inner forces capable of spiritual love, we actually learn in immediate exact clairvoyance to know that inner experience which we describe by saying that one experiences oneself spiritually, without a body, outside the body. This passing outside the body becomes in this way, if I may thus express it, actually a matter of objective experience for the soul. If one has experienced this spiritual existence one time outside the body, clairvoyantly perceived, I should like to say, then one knows the significance of the event of laying aside the physical body in death, of passing through the Portal of Death to a new, spiritual life. We thus learn, at the third stage of exact clairvoyance, the significance of death, and thus also the significance of immortality, for man.

I have wished to make it transparently clear through the manner of my explanation that the mode of supersensible cognition about which I am speaking seeks to bring into the very cognitional capacities of the human being something which works effectually, step by step, as it is thus introduced. The natural scientist applies this exactness to the external experiment, to the external observation; he wishes to see the objects in such juxtaposition that they reveal their secrets with exactitude in the process of measuring, enumerating, weighing. The spiritual scientist, about whom I am here speaking, employs this exactness to the evolution of the forces of his own soul. That which he uncovers in himself, through which the spiritual world and human immortality step before his soul, is made in a precise manner, to use an expression of Goethe's. With every step thus taken by the spiritual scientist, in order that the spiritual world may at last lie unfolded before the eyes of the soul, he feels obliged to be as conscientious in regard to his perception as a mathematician must be with every step he takes. For just as the mathematician must see clearly into everything that he writes on the paper, so must the spiritual scientist see with absolute precision into everything that he makes out of his powers of cognition. He then knows that he has formed an 'eye of the soul' out of the soul itself through the same inner necessity with which nature has formed the corporeal eye out of bodily substance.[9] And he knows that he can speak of spiritual worlds with the same justification with which he speaks of a physical-sensible world in relationship to the physical eye. In this sense the spiritual research with which we are here concerned satisfies the demands of our age imposed upon us by the magnificent achievements of natural science – which spiritual science in no way opposes but, rather, seeks to supplement.

I am well aware that everyone who undertakes to represent anything before the world, no matter what his motive may be, attributes a certain importance to himself by describing this as a 'demand of the times'. I have no such purpose; on the contrary, I should like to show that the demands of the times already exist, and the very endeavour of spiritual science at every step it takes is to satisfy these demands of the times. We may say, then, that the spiritual scientist whom it is our purpose to discuss here does not propose to be a person who views nature like a dilettante or amateur. On the contrary, he proposes to advance in true harmony with natural science and with the same genuine conscientiousness. He desires truly exact clairvoyance for the description of a spiritual world. But it is clear to him at the same time that, when we undertake to investigate a human corpse in a laboratory for the purpose of explaining the life which has disappeared from it, or when we look out into cosmic space with a telescope, we then develop capacities which tend to adapt themselves at first solely to the microscope or telescope, but which possess an inner life and which misrepresent themselves in their form. If we dissect a human corpse, we know that it was not nature that directly made the human being into this bodily form, but that the human soul, which has now withdrawn from it, made it. We interpret the human soul from what we have here as its physical product, and one would be irrational to assume that this moulding of the human physical forces and forms had not arisen out of what preceded the present state of this human being. But from all that we hold back, as we meanwhile investigate dead nature with the forces from which one rightly withdraws one's inner activity, from the very act of holding back is created the ability to develop further the human soul forces. Just as the seed of the plant lies out of sight under the earth when we have laid it in the soil, and yet will become a plant, so do we plant a seed in the soul in the very action of conscientious scientific research. He who is a serious scientist in this sense has within himself the germ of imaginative, inspired and intuitive knowledge. He needs only to develop the germ. He will then know that just as natural science is a demand of the times so likewise is supersensible research. What I mean to say is that everyone who speaks in the spirit of natural science speaks also in the spirit of supersensible research, only without knowing this. And that which constitutes an unconscious longing in the innermost depths of many persons today is the impulse of supersensible research to unfold out of its germ.

To those very persons, therefore, who oppose this spiritual research from a supposedly scientific standpoint, one would like to say, not with any bad intention, that this brings to mind an utterance in Goethe's *Faust* all too well known, but which would be applied in a different sense:

The little man would not sense the Devil
Even if he held him by the throat.

I do not care to go into that now. But what lies in this saying confronts us with a certain twist in that demand of the times: that those who speak rightly today about nature are really giving expression, though unconsciously, to the spirit. One would like to say that there are many who do not wish to notice the 'spirit' when it speaks, although they are constantly giving expression to the spirit in their own words!

The seed of supersensible perception is really far more widespread today than is supposed, but it must be developed. The fact that it must be developed is really a lesson we may learn from the seriousness of the times in reference to external experiences. We may add in conclusion that the elements of a fearful catastrophe really speak to the whole of humanity today through various indications in the outside world, and that it is possible to realize that tasks at which humanity in the immediate future will have to work with the greatest intensity will struggle to birth out of this great seriousness of the times. This external seriousness with which the world confronts us today, especially the world of humanity, indicates the necessity of an inner seriousness. And it is about this inner seriousness in the guidance of the human heart and mind towards man's own spiritual powers, which constitute the powers of his essential being, that I have wished to speak to you today. For, if it is true that man must apply his most powerful external forces in meeting the serious events awaiting him over the whole world, he will need likewise a powerful inner courage. But such forces and such courage can come into existence only if the human being is able to feel and also to will himself in full consciousness in his innermost being, not merely theoretically conceiving himself but practically knowing himself. This is possible for him only when he comes to know that this being of his emerges from the source from which it truly comes, from the source of the spirit; only when in ever-increasing measure, not only theoretically but practically, he learns to know in actual experience that man is spirit, and can find his true satisfaction only in the spirit; that his highest powers and his highest courage can come to him only out of the spirit, out of the supersensible.

Sources of the lectures by Rudolf Steiner

'The Path of Knowledge and its Stages: The Rosicrucian Spiritual Path', 20 October 1906, is included in *Esoteric Development* (GA96), published by Anthroposophic Press, 1982.

'Three Paths of Practice', 2 September 1906, 'Oriental and Christian Teaching', 3 September 1906, and 'Rosicrucian Training and Mysteries of the Earth', 4 September 1906, are included in *At the Gates of Spiritual Science* (GA95), published by Rudolf Steiner Press, 1986.

'The Ancient Yoga Civilization and the Michael Civilization of the Future', 30 November 1919, is included in *The Mission of the Archangel Michael* (GA194) published by Anthroposophic Press, 1961.

'The Way of Inner Development', 7 December 1905, is included in *Esoteric Development* (GA54), published by Anthroposophic Press, 1982.

'Practical Training in Thought', 18 January 1909, is published by Anthroposophic Press, 1966 (GA108).

'Occult Science and Occult Development', 1 May 1913, is included in *Occult Science and Occult Development* (GA152), published by Rudolf Steiner Press, 1966.

'The Three Decisions on the Path of Imaginative Cognition', 2 March 1915, is included in *The Destinies of Individuals and Nations* (GA157), published by Rudolf Steiner Press, 1987.

'Beyond the Sphere of Scientific Knowledge', 1 June 1922, and 'Anthroposophy and Psychology', 2 June 1922, are included in *The Tension Between East and West* (GA83), published by Anthroposophic Press, 1983.

'Sense-free Perception', 26 September 1923, is included in *Esoteric Development* (GA84), published by Anthroposophic Press, 1982.

Notes

GA = *Gesamtausgabe*, the collected edition of Rudolf Steiner's works in the original German (published by Rudolf Steiner Verlag, Dornach, Switzerland).
RSP = Rudolf Steiner Press, UK
AP = Anthroposophic Press, USA

1. The lecture of 20.10.1906 is taken from the volume *Esoteric Development*, AP, 1982.
2. In contrast to the widely attended public lectures in the Architects' House in Berlin and the descriptions of the path of knowledge in the periodical *Luzifer* (later incorporated into *Gnosis*), which provided the foundation for the book *Knowledge of the Higher Worlds: How is it Achieved?*, RSP, 1993 (also available as *How to Know Higher Worlds*, AP, 1994). This lecture was given to 'members' of the Theosophical Society who were well acquainted with the basic concepts of spiritual science.
3. In this context one may compare *The Chymical Wedding of Christian Rosenkreutz* by Johann Valentin Andreae; *Fama Fraternitatis*, translated into modern German by Walter Weber; and three essays on *The Chymical Wedding of Christian Rosenkreutz* by Rudolf Steiner (1917/18) (included in *A Christian Rosenkreutz Anthology*, edited by Paul M. Allen, Rudolf Steiner Publications, New York, 1981).
4. The Theosophical Society, founded in 1875 by H. P. Blavatsky and Colonel Henry Olcott, made occult knowledge accessible to wider circles of people than had previously been the case. In 1902 Rudolf Steiner was requested to take over the leadership of its German section. Initially he used terminology which was current in that Society. After separating from it and founding the Anthroposophical Society, he sought to find appropriate German terms for describing supersensible realities. (See Rudolf Steiner, *The Anthroposophic Movement*, eight lectures 1923, GA258, RSP, 1993). As is already evident in the paragraph after next, he also strove from the beginning to clarify the specifically Central European path of knowledge.
5. This categorization of types is dealt with more extensively in

the lectures 1/2.10.1922 in this volume, as well as in Rudolf Steiner's complete lecture cycle *The Tension Between East and West*, ten lectures, Vienna 1922, GA83, AP, 1983.

6. Those referred to as 'Masters' are the founders and inspirers of particular spiritual streams and cultural epochs, such as Zarathustra, Hermes, Moses, Abraham etc. See Rudolf Steiner, *Turning Points in Spiritual History*, GA60, Rudolf Steiner Publishing Company, 1934.

7. The basic 'teachings' of spiritual science here referred to are described at length in the works of Rudolf Steiner. *Theosophy*, (GA9, AP, 1994) for instance, provides thoughts on attaining knowledge of higher worlds and deals with the themes of reincarnation and karma. *Occult Science: An Outline* (GA13, RSP, 1969) provides insights into world evolution, human races and culture, and, like *Knowledge of the Higher Worlds: How is it Achieved?* (GA10, RSP, 1969), describes the path of inner development, and the unfolding of the 'lotus flowers'. The deciphering of the Akashic Record and the difficulties and dangers attendant upon it are described by Rudolf Steiner in *Theosophy of the Rosicrucian* (GA99, RSP, 1966).

8. *Truth and Science* (GA3, Mercury Press, New York, 1993) and *The Philosophy of Spiritual Activity* (GA4, RSP, 1992).

9. Just as the visible world is accessible to the senses, so the astral or soul-world and the Spiritland or Devachan can be perceived by soul or spiritual organs of perception, which must first be developed. Behind and within the visible, physical world experienced through our senses are the worlds, also called 'planes', from which this world of appearances originates, and these are accessible to spiritual organs of perception. The plane closest to our ordinary experience is the one we are connected to through our own world of feelings; this has many different inner regions and is termed 'soul-' or 'astral world'. Beyond it lies the lower and higher Spiritland or Devachan (see the relevant chapters in *Theosophy*). Just as one can attain higher levels of consciousness in thinking than in dreams, so for the differentiated perception of soul- and spirit-worlds one requires the appropriate supersensible organs of perception, which are described as lotus flowers (chakras) and depicted symbolically as swastikas, wheels and rosettes. (See the descriptions in the lectures of 2.9.1906 and

1.5.1913 in this volume.) The terms life-, formative-forces or
etheric body refer to the wise, life-sustaining forces inherent
within an organism; astral or soul body refers to the inner self-
contained supersensible feeling life. By Akashic Record is understood the spiritual sphere which retains a memory of everything
having a soul-spiritual origin or correlation (see the lecture of
1.5.1913 in this volume).

10. Preceding stages in the evolution of the earth are termed:
Moon, Sun and Saturn. Within these planetary conditions
evolution occurs in stages which are called 'life conditions'
(also life rounds or realms), which themselves are further
differentiated into 'form conditions' ('globes') and into still
smaller periods, termed 'root races' and 'races'. The root-
races are whole historical epochs, the races their smaller
divisions. For instance, Lemuria, Atlantis and post-Atlantis
are root-races. The post-Atlantean root-race is subdivided
into the following races or historical epochs: Indian, Ancient
Persian, Egyptian and Babylonian, Greek and Roman, and
our present age. (See *Occult Science* [planetary conditions],
Cosmic Memory, Rudolf Steiner Publications, New York,
1959, [root races] and *Genesis: Secrets of the Bible Story of
Creation*, GA122, RSP, 1982 [life- and form conditions].)

11. See 'Secret Symbols of the Rosicrucians' in *A Christian
Rosenkreutz Anthology* (see note 3).

12. Lecture of 19.10.1906, GA96 (not translated).

13. Kamaloka is a time of soul-purification after death (see *Occult
Science*, the chapter on 'sleep and death').

14. The three following lectures of 2,3 and 4.9.1906 are taken
from the volume *At the Gates of Spiritual Science*, GA95,
RSP, 1986. One should remember that these lectures are
an integral part of a complete sequence or cycle of 14
lectures which Rudolf Steiner gave to the members. They
form a conclusion to descriptions which had concerned
themselves with the essence of the human being, higher
worlds, earth evolution and ancient cultures. There are no
titles or headings in the original – these have been added to
indicate the content of each lecture.

15. According to the ancient classical work *The Yoga-sutras of
Patanjali*.

16. From the essay by the English theosophist Mabel Collins *Light on the Path.*

17. The last part of this lecture (pages 139–49) has been left out; it deals with the geological structure of the earth in connection with stages of self-development.

18. To make clear how the various paths of self-development had to change since that great and significant event of world history, the death and resurrection of Christ, a much later description by Rudolf Steiner (of 30.11.1919) has been included in this volume. It is taken from the lecture cycle *The Mission of the Archangel Michael,* GA194, AP, 1961.

19. The idea of threefoldness was first presented by Rudolf Steiner in 1917 in his book *Von Seelenrätseln,* GA21, in the 6th appendix (on the physical and spiritual functions of the human being). This concept has far-reaching significance for education, medicine and sociology. In this context see also *Towards Social Renewal,* GA23, RSP, 1977, and *The Renewal of the Social Organism,* GA24, AP/RSP, 1985.

20. Gustav Theodor Fechner, 1801–87. See Rudolf Steiner *Riddles of Philosophy,* GA18, AP, 1973. Also *Gefährdung und Heilung der Sinne,* by Norbert Glas, 2nd edition, Stuttgart 1976; *Vom Geist der Sinne,* by Ernst Lehrs, Frankfurt 1973; *Die zwölf Sinne des Menschen,* by Hans Erhard Lauer, 2nd edition, Schaffhausen 1978.

21. There exists a lecture with the same title given by Rudolf Steiner on this theme on 25.10.1906, GA55, in *Supersensible Knowledge,* AP, 1987.

22. This lecture of 7.12.1905 comes from a public introduction to spiritual science (Berlin, Architects' House) and is taken from the volume *Esoteric Development,* AP, 1982.

23. Subba Rao (Row) 1856–90, lawyer in Madras, occultist and friend of H. P. Blavatsky. There appeared a posthumous volume of his entitled *Esoteric Writings.*

24. This lecture was continued on 19.4.1906, GA54 (not translated). We did not include the continuation since it covers the same ground as the other lectures printed here.

25. This lecture (for members) of 18.1.1909 is taken from the volume *Practical Training in Thought,* GA108, AP, 1966. The lecture *Overcoming Nervousness* (GA143, AP, 1969, 11.1.1912)

is thematically related in some respects and contains relevant exercises.

26. Sir Rowland Hill (1795–1879) introduced in 1837 the idea of the postage stamp to simplify the postal system. He was later made minister for postal services.

27. This report is mentioned by R. Hagen in *Die erste deutsche Eisenbahn*, 1885, page 45. Its existence is nowadays disputed.

28. Nagler, 1770–1846.

29. The lecture (for members) of 1.5.1913 is taken from the volume *Occult Science and Occult Development: Christ at the Time of the Mystery of Golgotha*, GA152, RSP, 1983.

30. Lucifer and Ahriman – the expressions originate in biblical and Iranian-Persian descriptions – are spiritual beings working in polarity to each other: by falling under the influence of one or other of these beings, the human soul is either one-sidedly inspired to raptures of enthusiasm or drawn down into a cold, superficial and analytical frame of mind. They are powers of temptation and seduction whose untimely influence is evil; nevertheless they also enable us to develop individual freedom (see *Occult Science*).

31. See *Occult Science*, GA13, and *Genesis: Secrets of the Bible Story of Creation*, GA122, RSP, 1982.

32. Lecture of 2.5.1913, GA152, (see note 29).

33. The lecture (for members) given in Berlin on 2.3.1915 is taken from the volume *Destinies of Individuals and of Nations*, GA157, RSP, 1987.

34. Lecture of 22.2.1915, GA157 (as above).

35. The lectures of 1 and 2.6.1922 are the beginning of a lecture cycle given at the great public congress of the Anthroposophical Society in Vienna, which was published under the title *The Tension Between East and West*, GA83, AP, 1983. The theme referred to here is continued in the subsequent lectures.

36. The lecture of 26.9.1923 is included in the volume *Esoteric Development*, AP, 1982.

37. Ibid.

Rudolf Steiner
Nature Spirits
Selected Lectures

Based on knowledge attained through his highly-trained clairvoyance, Rudolf Steiner contends that folk traditions regarding nature spirits are based on spiritual reality. He describes how people possessed a natural spiritual vision in ancient times, enabling them to commune with nature spirits. These entities—which are also referred to as elemental beings—became immortalised as fairies and gnomes in myth, legend and children's stories.

Today, says Steiner, the instinctive understanding that humanity once had for these elemental beings should be transformed into clear scientific knowledge. He even asserts that humanity will not be able to reconnect with the spiritual world if it cannot develop a new relationship to the elementals. The nature spirits themselves want to be of great assistance to us, acting as 'emissaries of higher divine spiritual beings'.

ISBN 1 855840 18 9; 208pp; £11.95

Rudolf Steiner
Evil
Selected Lectures

Despite the fact that evil is an omnipresent theme of our age,
it remains one of the most problematic. Public references to it
are continually made, but to what extent has society truly
begun to understand its riddle?

In this selection of insightful lectures Rudolf Steiner
addresses the subject of evil from the results of his spiritual
research, offering an original and complex picture. He
describes evil as a phenomenon which arises when a thing
appears outside its true context, enabling something which is
initially 'good' to become harmful. He speaks of the effect of
particular spiritual beings—principally Lucifer and
Ahriman—who work as polar forces, laying hindrances in our
path. Yet, paradoxically, confronting and coming to terms
with such difficulties ultimately furthers our development.
Thus Steiner speaks of evil as a necessary phenomenon in
human evolution, allowing for the possibility of freedom.

ISBN 1 855840 46 4; 224pp; £11.95

Rudolf Steiner
Life Beyond Death
Selected Lectures

Although western humanity has conquered the outer world
with the aid of technology and science, death remains an
unsolved and largely unexplored mystery. Rudolf Steiner, an
exceptional seer, was able to research spiritually the question
of what happens to human consciousness after the physical
body passes away. In these remarkably matter-of-fact lectures
he affirms that life continues beyond death. Far from being
dissipated, the individual's consciousness awakens to a new
reality, beginning a great journey to the farthest expanses of
the cosmos. Here it embarks on a process of purification and
preparation.

Rudolf Steiner indicates that one of the most important tasks
for our present civilization is the reestablishment of living
connections with those who have died. He gives suggestions
as to how this can be done safely, and describes how the dead
can be of help to those on earth.

ISBN 1 855840 17 0; 256pp; £12.95

Rudolf Steiner
Angels
Selected Lectures

Religious and spiritual writings have always made reference to
beings from the spiritual hierarchies, especially those known
in Christian tradition as Angels. These spirits are the closest
to human beings and act as our invisible guides and
companions. They influence the life of the individual as well
as the evolution of humanity and the cosmos.

From his own clairvoyant vision Rudolf Steiner confirmed the
existence of such spiritual beings, and showed how modern
minds could gain access to their world. As he explains in these
inspiring lectures, it is important for us to understand and
cooperate with the work of the Angels today as this is crucial
for the further development of humanity.

ISBN 1 855840 60 X; 192pp; £10.95